Corporal Punishment
around the World

Recent Titles in
Global Crime and Justice

Corporal Punishment around the World

MATTHEW PATE AND LAURIE A. GOULD

FOREWORD BY GRAEME R. NEWMAN

Global Crime and Justice

Graeme R. Newman, Series Editor

 PRAEGER

AN IMPRINT OF ABC-CLIO, LLC
Santa Barbara, California • Denver, Colorado • Oxford, England

Library of Congress Cataloging-in-Publication Data

Pate, Matthew.
  Corporal punishment around the world / Matthew Pate and Laurie A. Gould.
    p. cm. — (Global crime and justice)
  Includes bibliographical references and index.
  ISBN 978–0–313–39131–6 (hardback) — ISBN 978–0–313–39132–3 (ebook)
1. Corporal punishment. I. Gould, Laurie A. II. Title.
K5103.P38   2012
364.6.'7—dc23   2012017133

ISBN: 978–0–313–39131–6
EISBN: 978–0–313–39132–3

16 15 14 13 12   1 2 3 4 5

This book is also available on the World Wide Web as an eBook.
Visit www.abc-clio.com for details.

Praeger
An Imprint of ABC-CLIO, LLC

ABC-CLIO, LLC
130 Cremona Drive, P.O. Box 1911
Santa Barbara, California 93116-1911

This book is printed on acid-free paper ∞

Manufactured in the United States of America

Contents

Series Foreword

HISTORIES OF CRIMINAL punishment typically dwell on the awful bodily punishments of a few centuries ago—hanging and disemboweling, drawing and quartering, decapitation, cat-o'-nine-tails, branding, cutting off various body parts, and so on. Jeremy Bentham, the great (though unjustifiably vilified) reformer of the eighteenth century had nightmares about the various forms of excruciating punishments illustrated and described in the classic *Lives of the Saints*. And of course, in his own time one could stroll down to the public square and watch someone hanged. No more of that today! We are far too civilized!

Well, not quite. The global revolution in information technology has brought these gory punishments to life, made them accessible to anyone who has access to the Internet, and these days that includes just about everyone on the planet. It takes only a little skill to find actual real-life videos of hangings, tortures, and beheadings on the Internet. So, whether watched or implemented, corporal punishment is a global phenomenon. We are not as distant from its use as we thought. It is not something that exists only in books. It has become, once again, a *public* punishment. Indeed, in the twenty-first century the opportunity to witness corporal punishments, including executions of the most horrific kind on the Internet, surpasses those available to people of the Middle Ages and before. However, the authors also show that corporal punishment has been conditioned by an early and highly effective form of globalization that came well before the revolution in information technology—colonialism.

So *Corporal Punishment* fits our Global Crime and Justice series perfectly. It is global and continues to be applied to offenders for their crimes and to others for their misbehavior. Whether this fits our global idea of justice is another matter. The United Nations opposes the use of corporal punishment (including capital punishment) on offenders, and the U.N. Committee on Rights of the Child has long opposed its use against children in both schools and families. The authors observe that there is also a gap between legislation against corporal punishment and its actual practice.

This book unflinchingly reviews the amount and distribution of corporal punishment in all its forms throughout history and throughout the world today. It provides a global view of corporal punishment, a special form of violent discipline that continues to be widely used against criminals and children. It shows how the use of corporal punishment is unevenly distributed through the world and explains why this is so. The book's particular focus is on corporal punishment, but there is much in this book that applies to or raises questions about the role of punishment in modern society, whether corporal or not.

Graeme R. Newman
Series Editor

Foreword

There is a documentary that I regularly have my students watch as part of a course on social deviance. The movie, *Titicut Follies*, directed by Frederick Wiseman in 1967, pioneered the cinéma vérité technique of documentary movies, an approach that "tells it like it is" without voice over or commentary. It provides a glimpse of the inmates of an institution for the criminally insane, and of those who care for or contain them. Putting aside the overall emotional impact of the movie, there is one scene that never fails to shock my students. It is a scene in which a doctor is force-feeding an inmate who has gone on a hunger strike. This scene is repeated at various points throughout the movie until we see the inmate leaving the institution in a coffin. There are two reasons why it shocks them. First, the dreadful invasion of the inmate's body by a tube forced through his nose and into his stomach is, of course, shocking. It also shocks by the ironies it displays—a doctor "saving" the inmate's life at the same time revealing the callousness by which all inmates in the institutions are contained or "cared for." The second reason is one that occurs not only in this terrible scene but throughout every scene in which the institutional personnel are shown:

They all smoke cigarettes!

The doctor doing the force-feeding has a cigarette dangling from his lips, the ash dropping off and on to the gurney on which the patient lies. The guards smoke, the nurses smoke, the social worker smokes, and the attending psychiatrist smokes throughout the meetings he attends with staff and inmates. When I tell my students that right in our classroom in the 1970s and before, we almost all smoked, students and professors, it is beyond belief.

What has this to do with corporal punishment? We would like to think that corporal punishment has gone the way of cigarettes. Most Western countries have legislated public smoking out of existence—to the extent that to light up a cigarette in the classroom would be something akin to using or displaying gross profanity. We would like to think the same of corporal punishment. To advocate the use of corporal punishment on criminals in America and other Western countries meets with the cry of "barbaric." Its use in schools is thoroughly derided (but still used especially in institutional settings), though its use in families, while derided, is nonetheless practiced by many (as there are, perhaps, many closet smokers).

This book shows that, although corporal punishment has been legislated out of existence in many countries, there are many countries in which it is widespread, indeed embraced publicly both as a criminal punishment and as a way of disciplining children. In a few countries it is unlawful to use corporal punishment by parents on their children, and in some instances it is even unlawful to strike an animal for disciplinary reasons.

Another lesson we learn from *Titicut Follies* is: Where do we draw the line between just plain violence (or violation of the body) and corporal punishment? Do we define force-feeding a fully conscious individual as corporal punishment, or is it simply corporal abuse? Especially, as in this scene the doctor is ostensibly doing it to save the patient's life! Is striking a child for disciplinary reasons child abuse? (Or for that matter, is smoking in the home where there are children, child abuse?) Many of my students called the force-feeding of the inmate torture because of its long, drawn-out procedure. So what is the relationship or distinction between corporal punishment and torture? And, by implication, the distinctions if any between corporal punishment, torture, and "enhanced interrogation? And is capital punishment just an extreme form of corporal punishment? If so, how do we explain its retention in some Western and other countries claiming to be civilized and to therefore thoroughly abhor corporal punishment? In fact, can the death penalty be called punishment at all when techniques of putting to death are intended to be painless? Surely the definition of punishment requires that pain be intentionally administered to the subject (or perhaps the better word is "object").

There are many distinctions to be drawn and the authors do not shy away from them. In early chapters they deal with all these difficulties of definition and set up some ground rules, even if in later chapters circumstances require that they occasionally deviate from them. They are well aware that there is apparent and latent *value* in a definition or distinction. If one is absolutely opposed to corporal punishment in any form, one will call it violence or child abuse, depending on the setting. Many of these distinctions are bound up in the language of punishment itself, whether corporal or not. We are told by both critics and defenders of punishment, especially those philosophers of the eighteenth-century Enlightenment, that all punishment is in itself evil and therefore its use must, in every instance, be morally (and politically) justified. It is therefore very difficult to review and analyze the use of corporal punishment without getting sidetracked into these moral and political arguments. It is important for the reader to realize that this book is not about justifying corporal punishment, nor does it actively take a position for or against it. This dispassionate position is necessary for an even treatment of the facts of corporal punishment around the world and its appearance in many different countries of many different religious, cultural, economic and political backgrounds. Yet the information that Pate and Gould place before their readers will very likely affect their views of the moral and political aspects of corporal punishment. Indeed, it may well affect their views of punishment in general.

In this tour de force of corporal punishment throughout the world—geographically and historically—Pate and Gould masterfully tread where no others have dared. This is the first and only book to chart the course of corporal punishment around the world with such broad strokes, yet with fine detail presented in their revealing case studies of Nigeria, Singapore, Saudi Arabia, Bolivia, and The Bahamas. In these case studies we see the historical, cultural, political, environmental, and religious factors come to life. In the explanatory chapters that follow them we see how monumentally difficult it is to explain why some countries have retained corporal punishments and others discarded them—whether as criminal punishments or as punishments in schools or within families.

What stands out in the authors' thorough review of the social scientific research on corporal punishment distribution throughout the world is one very interesting paradox, at least for me. This is the complicated and differentiated legacy of corporal punishment that colonialism has left depending on the particular countries. In recent history, the major colonial empires of Britain and most of the European powers left their marks on just about every region of the world. These Western countries brought civilization to their colonies. In general, they abolished slavery, established school systems, established a military and police bureaucracy, and with some adaptations imposed the rule of law on top of local informal justice systems. Some of these preexisting justice systems already used corporal punishment or the death penalty; some did not. In some instances the colonial powers intervened in what they thought were overly harsh corporal or capital punishments, and in others they imposed their own especially harsh punishments that reflected the harsh punishments typically applied in their own military. The authors, through their case studies and in their subsequent analysis show the give and take of this colonial process. They also offer a variety of alternative or additional explanations for the unequal distribution of corporal punishment around the world. Many, if not all such explanations appear on the face of it also to apply to other kinds of punishment that are not ostensibly corporal, such as, for example, prison. Pate and Gould have opened up a new field of rich research that one hopes they will continue and that others will be eager to follow.

Graeme R. Newman
Anglesea, February 2012

Acknowledgments

There are a number of individuals without whose support this project would have been impossible. Accordingly, we want to give all due credit to those people who encouraged, supported, cajoled, and tolerated this book into existence.

Chief among those to whom we owe a great debt is Graeme Newman. Graeme had written extensively on this topic long before either of us had ever imagined a career in academics. By the time the first edition of Graeme's seminal treatise, *Just and Painful: A Case for Corporal Punishment of Criminals*, was released, one of us was navigating grade school and the other was a wide-eyed college freshman. As such, we acknowledge that our foray into his domain of mastery is an honored place for a pair of such neophytes. For two long years, Graeme patiently read multiple drafts, offering invaluable insights and support along the way. To simply say "thank you" fails to capture the extent of our gratitude toward and deep admiration of our friend and mentor. Graeme, we are in your debt.

I (Laurie) would like to thank my husband, Vern, for his love, support and sense of humor. Without his day-to-day help and his insistence that I eat a vegetable every now and again, this book would not have been finished. Thank you for always being there for me and for your continued support. I would also like to acknowledge my parents, Frederick and Susanne Gould, whose encouragement has meant the world to me. My mom was my most enthusiastic supporter and I miss her greatly. My dad has been a constant source of inspiration. He instilled in me a love of learning and for that I am truly grateful.

I (Matthew) want my wife, Kathleen, to know how much I appreciate her considerable part in all this. Not only did she consent to my quitting a perfectly good job just so I could run off to graduate school, she let me have custody of the dogs to do it. After four years spent half a continent apart, she again endured my months of cloister while this volume took form. Thank you for your love, tolerance, inspiration, and for being proud of me. I would also like to make a special mention of my parents, Mike and Judy Pate. They knew to surround their loquacious child with a lot of books. In those pages, they gave me the whole world. Also, my grandparents, Buddy and Maxine Bryant, should be acknowledged. My grandfather is the consummate yarn-weaving story-teller and my grandmother is the most voracious reader I know. Thank you for giving me an appreciation of well-chosen words.

Beyond those already mentioned, there is a cavalcade of colleagues, coworkers, cats, dogs, and friends who indulgently allowed us to drone on about "the book." We appreciate your well-feigned enthusiasm for what must have been a very, very long story about a curious topic. We promise to talk about something else now.

Introduction

Portia:	Ay, but I fear you speak upon the rack, Where men enforced do speak anything.
Bassanio:	Promise me life, and I'll confess the truth.
Portia:	Well then, confess and live

—Wm. Shakespeare
The Merchant of Venice
Act III, Scene 2

The term, "corporal punishment," is one of those unique turns of phrase that instantly evokes strong mental images. They run an eerie gamut from a mother's gentle swat to Torquemada's dungeons. Perhaps none are more visceral than the crack of a whip against flesh laid bare. In all likelihood, humans have used pain to manipulate one another for as long as we have existed. Pain is simple. Pain can be created in an instant. The ability to command the pain of another is power. On that occasion when the simple ability to exact brute force ceased to be sufficient reason for one human to bow to the whim of another, justifications for pain were summoned from all corners: divine will; the inherent order of man; tradition; filial piety. . . and many more.

This volume takes up a simple question: What gives a social authority (institution or individual) the right to cause a member of that society to experience physical pain? Closely related, one might also ask: How does the authority administering the pain (or their agent) know what is sufficient to absolve[1] the recipient of whatever wrong that has been done? Clearly, as a species we have evolved many different sets of rules to answer these questions. Using a cross-cultural comparison of corporal punishment practices through history, some tentative answers begin to emerge. Before those answers may be approached, a few definitions are in order.

Chief among these is the term, "corporal punishment," itself. When used in this book, corporal punishment may be taken to mean the infliction of ritualized physical pain or ordeal, the primary object of which is to bind the recipient or observers to the rules, norms, or customs of a larger social institution.

These rules, norms, and customs may take many forms. They may define or assert social, class, family, spiritual or organizational norms, values or expectations. While this definition may seem overly broad to some, corporal punishment as an ordering mechanism is a very board phenomenon. As such, any attempt to circumscribe it must necessarily cast a wide net.

Likewise, there are a few key features within this definition. The first is intentionality. The "pain" inflicted is a direct act, the immediate purpose of which is to induce an undesired state in the subject. The social function of the punishment must be to instill in the subject (or the audience, thereto) that the punishment comes as a consequence of failing to meet some socially derived standard, even if that standard is simply acknowledgment of the power to punish.

The second element of this definition is physicality. One might argue that imprisonment is a form of physical pain in that it reduces the inmate's freedom of movement, association, action, and so on. Certainly, there is a strong physical component to confinement, but the punishment is arguably more psychological and less visceral. Corporal punishment must be acute even if it is delivered in metered fashion.

The third element of corporal punishment is its ritualized delivery. Sometimes the ceremony is very public and obvious. The spectacle of the Inquisitions immediately come to mind. Sometimes the ceremony is private or even solitary, as in the case of certain ascetic religious observances. To be certain, whether public or private, corporal punishment is ritualized behavior. In fact, the ritual of delivery is arguably the place where corporal punishment most often develops its social potency.

To bring this into better focus, Victor Turner's work on rituals as symbolic action provides a useful context. Turner defined ritual as "prescribed formal behavior for occasions not given over to technological routine, having reference to beliefs in mystical beings and powers."[2] For Turner, a symbol is the smallest unit of ritual that still retains the specific properties of ritual behavior. As he termed them, symbols are a "storage unit" filled with a vast amount of information.[3] Objects, activities, words, relationships, events, gestures, or spatial units may all take on the quality of being a symbol.[4]

Turner also notes the close relationship between ritual, religious beliefs, and symbols. As he states, "[Ritual is] a stereotyped sequence of activities involving gestures, words, and objects, performed in a sequestered place, and designed to influence preternatural entities or forces on behalf of the actors' goals and interests."[5]

Rituals are storehouses of socially meaningful symbols through which information is revealed and regarded as authoritative. This is to say that they communicate the crucial values of the community.[6] These values may in turn emanate from a variety of authoritative sources. Turner asserts that their power derives from a reference to the supernatural. Hence, they are invested with transformative potential for human behavior and attitudes. For Turner, the handling of symbols in ritual exposes their powers to act on and change the persons involved in ritual performance. Where Turner is primarily concerned with ritual in a religious context, we may expand this understanding to political, economic, and other social hierarchies or power structures.

For rituals of corporal punishment perhaps no symbolic object is invested with more meaning than the whip. Cloaked in millennia of social meaning, it is both noun and verb. It is the physical embodiment of dominance and submission.

Beyond these definitional strictures, corporal punishment should also be positioned relative to capital punishment. Inherently, the two represent a kind of ultimate control over the subject's body. History richly records countless incidents of corporal punishment that yielded death. If physical torment has death as the express (or acceptable) object, the line becomes clearer. Torture until the subject expires is clearly *de facto* capital punishment.

For the sake of the present discussion, the line of demarcation for corporal punishment rests on overt intent. What is the terminal purpose or goal of the punishment? Is it to render docile the subject's body, such that he may join/rejoin the collective once the punishment has ended; or is it merely a torture-prelude to inevitable death? In short, what is to become of the subject after punishment? Having satisfied this inquiry, the punishment can be properly located as corporal or capital.

A corollary set of questions may also arise with regard to ceremonial pain as part of a sexual act: Do sadomasochistic sex, bondage, domination, and other similar acts qualify as corporal punishment under this definition? In a word, no. As these acts, while nominally punishment are more accurately a pleasure (albeit pleasure derived via participation in a pain ritual), they do not meet the "intent" (sic. goal) dimension of the present definition. Moreover, they serve no intrinsically broad social function beyond the gratification of the immediate participants (or witnesses).

With this as predicate, it can safely be said that few, if any, human institutions are rigidly uniform across cultures and time. Anthropologists coined the term "cultural universal" for the very small subset of social phenomena common to all societies. Even within that tightly circumscribed category, it is better to think of these universal phenomena as a collection of themes and variations. Among the attributes and institutions all cultures exhibit are family groups, funeral rites, symbolic language, tool making, notions of roles, and hierarchy.[7] They also contain socially approved methods for identifying and correcting undesirable behavior.

In an effort to better understand larger questions of the human condition, one must analyze the constituent parts of society and culture. There are many logical places to start such an enterprise. Analysis of kinship networks, spirituality, mechanisms of knowledge transmission, or evolution of organizational structures would each yield valuable insight into the people that produced them. Be that as it may, these phenomena are all predicated on an even more basic process: social stability. This is to say that the social group must be sufficiently stable and ongoing to support lasting institutions of a higher order. To promote said stability, all cultures develop ordering mechanisms to define the limits of appropriate behavior. Here too, however, there exists tremendous variation—not just in what behavior is declared out of bounds, but in how the group responds to the transgressor's unacceptable deed.

In that light, another continuous thread in this cross-cultural history of corporal punishment is an attempt to explore the phenomenon in as value-neutral terms as is possible. While no work of social science could claim to be without bias, the purpose here is not to advocate for any particular position for or against corporal punishment, but rather to show how certain social, economic, political, and cultural circumstances gave rise or sustain corporal punishment practices. This said, it is acknowledged that some acts (both historical and modern) are of such a grotesquely violent nature that a wholly neutral presentation is at best difficult. In such cases, it may be useful for the reader to focus less on the theatrical or wanton aspects of the punishment, deferring instead to an analysis of the social conditions permissive of such an act.

Any punishment is a key component of the social response to unacceptable behavior, however that behavior may be defined: disobedience; disorder; deviance; abnormality; sin; or crime. Punishment does many things, but most of all, it defines the contours of the social order. It asserts a hierarchy and promotes a system of norms and values. In most cases, it also serves the conjoined purposes of correcting the individual being punished as well as instructing others on the consequences of similar acts. In some limited circumstances, punishments may also be used as a means of indoctrinating an outsider into a new social group. A prime example of this is the physical subjugation of conquered people, as part of absorbing them into an unfamiliar political, economic, or social structure (i.e., persons bound into slavery, military conscription, or as colonial subjects).

Because the focus of this volume is corporal punishment around the world, there is an express notion of inconsistent practices. Again, the idea of theme and variation comes to the fore. In their cross-cultural studies of language, Charles Osgood, William May, and Murray Miron identify a critical element of this kind of research, "The essential thing is this: to note differences within any phenomenal [social] domain and to order them in a rigorous fashion, one must have certain similarities in the dimensions of variation."[8]

The organization of this volume reflects this idea of "similarity in variations." To that end, there are five main spheres in which the institution of corporal punishment is discussed. The first of these is a brief history of corporal punishment. The second examines corporal punishment as an element of religious practice. The third explores corporal punishment in the home. The fourth is corporal punishment as a tool of discipline in educational settings. The fifth is corporal punishment as an ordering mechanism in other formal social organizations.

Following these first five areas, the next two chapters explore in detail how a number of modern nations use corporal punishment to achieve certain social ends. For ease of comparison, the first case study chapter focuses on Africa and Asia; and the second on South America and the Caribbean. Immediately following the case studies, Chapter 8, "Explaining Current Global Trends," moves the discussion from a predominantly descriptive presentation of corporal punishment to an exploration of the deeper motivations and social functions that prompt retention of corporal punishment in modern societies.

By way of further preface, a few additional words about each individual chapter are warranted. While none of the included chapters is meant to serve as an exhaustive treatment of corporal punishment within any particular sphere, the unified theme throughout this volume is the ubiquity and persistence of the phenomenon. Most assuredly there are many cultures, historical epochs, and contexts in which corporal punishment figures centrally but are nonetheless omitted here. Their absence is not meant to imply any value judgment other than a desire to provide the most generalizable presentation of the topic.

The concept of generalizability itself yields an appropriate bridge by which to discuss the first chapter, "History of Corporal Punishment." In this chapter, the institution of corporal punishment is revealed to be as old as humankind. It is ubiquitous and likely known to all human civilizations. Moreover, corporal punishment is shown to be a persistent mechanism of order and discipline in many social institutions. Relatively modern authors like George Scott suggest the value of physical pain as a tool to punish was probably among the first things primitive man discovered.[9] As such, an extended discussion of corporal punishment throughout history is necessary to give modern punishment a proper context. Absent a solid, detailed, and direct connection to its historical antecedents, modern corporal punishment practices lose their cultural and social contexts, without which they could appear as only random barbarity or senseless cruelty.

Accordingly, Chapter 1 starts near the dawn of recorded human history. The reader learns that corporal punishment was formally inducted into the constellation of state-sponsored penalties as early as 2000 BC. Virtually all societies of the ancient world employ physical punishments against offenders. In some parts of the world, this custom will persist unbroken into the present. One also sees that corporal punishment finds many applications in several other historical institutions. It has a particularly notable presence in educational settings. Its presence and propriety there have been debated no less than two millennia.

Corporal punishment has an especially dark cast as an element of religious institutions. As an inducement to confession, few acts of human barbarism equal accounts from the Inquisitions of the Catholic Church and the persecutions of countless others in the name of divine will. The place of corporal punishment in religious observance is more fully explored in the following chapter.

As this history depicts, some societies, Imperial Russia, for instance, elevated infliction of pain to a high art. Indeed, tsarist regimes were so dependent on their indigenous flail, the knout, that the weapon became synonymous with keeping social order in the country. Here as in many other parts of the world, one sees corporal punishment not just used to punish criminals or correct wayward children, but as a tool to reassert the stratified class system.

A central point made repeatedly in the chapter concerns the twined interests of many seats of social power. At many points in European history, the interests of secular governments, economic powers, and religious bureaucracy were sufficiently overlapped as to facilitate single, but multipurposed acts of pain. The power to "legitimately" administer pain and death—or have them visited upon your person—reaffirms each participant's place in the social hierarchy.

Chapter 2, "Religion and Corporal Punishment," further elaborates many of the basic themes first elucidated in the preceding discussion of history. This chapter extends those ideas by showing how religious doctrine strongly informs jurisprudence in the modern Islamic world. To be sure, however, the two institutions have often overlapped in Christendom as well.

This chapter also broadens the definition of what constitutes corporal punishment by exploring the ascetic traditions and corporal mortification rituals in a number of world religious systems. While some might argue this overreaches the core parameters of corporal punishment, the reasoning underlying their inclusion holds that physical punishment need not come at the hands of others in order to merit consideration. At a certain level, physical tortures, deliberate suffering, and denial have the same consequences irrespective of their source. To exclude them would obscure millennia of monastic, mendicant, and hermetic practices, all of which preference the divine or spiritual to the material.

The third chapter, "Corporal Punishment in the Home," presents the phenomenon of corporal punishment in the most intimate of social settings, the home. The historical roots of corporal punishment within families are likely as ancient as in any other context. This chapter begins with the observation that the civilizations of antiquity had well-developed ideas about the role of physical discipline in the ordering of a house. While Western society of the modern era most closely associates this discipline with the correction of children, they are hardly the exclusive recipients. Children, along with wives, servants, and slaves might be subject to the physical chastisement of the *pater familias*.

An equally important element of this chapter regards the distinction between firm physical discipline and abuse. Often this line is quite blurry if not nonexistent. The ancient meme of "sparing the rod, spoiling the child" is examined in several cultures. From this analysis one sees a great variety in cultural sensibilities and legal regulation of corporal punishment in the home (particularly with regard to children). In this chapter, the latent effects of corporally punishing children are examined. In this discussion, questions are posed about the possible links between corporal punishment and future aggression, mental and emotional problems, developmental issues, and other possible negative consequences.

The fourth chapter, "Corporal Punishment in Educational Settings," explores discipline in the first social institution outside of the family home that many people experience. This chapter begins with the observation that corporal punishment in educational settings is very similar to corporal punishment in the home. The critical difference being the person charged with administering the discipline. As with the other areas presented in this volume, corporal punishment in educational settings is an ancient phenomenon. Moreover, the propriety of it as an educational tool appears to be an equally ancient subject of debate.

Moving the discussion into the modern era, one sees that a slight majority of the world's nations have banned corporal punishment in schools. Even so, it is often difficult to tell whether the school officials of a given country actually observe whatever ban may be in place. The permissibility of corporal punishment has been a regular topic for courts in many nations. In the United States no uniform federal proscription exists, the courts and Congress deferring instead to more localized sensibilities of individual states. In this context a particularly chilling set of facts emerge with regard to disparities in treatment. In specific, researchers conclude that minority students and students with disabilities are subject to corporal punishment more than other students.

Whatever corporal punishment may be visited on students in the United States, theirs is by no means the most perilous in the world. This chapter provides numerous international examples of outright violence and arguable brutality against school children. While couching it as an understudied topic, this chapter suggests there may be numerous negative consequences for children subject to repeated corporal punishment. These long-term problems may include bullying, violent behavior (school violence in particular), lower academic achievement, and higher dropout rates.

In the fifth chapter, "Corporal Punishment in Institutional Settings," physical discipline is examined as a mechanism to punish offenders and manage correctional populations. Even at this nascent point in the discussion of corporal punishment, one need not belabor the historical ubiquity of the lash as a tool to manage prisoners. As the hoe and digging stick transformed agriculture, so too did the whip as an instrument of justice.

This chapter provides a lengthy discussion of corporal punishment in the justice systems of several nations. Particular emphasis is given to the judicial evolution of corporal punishment in U.S. and British prisons. In this extended consideration of disciplinary policy, one sees proof of the familiar saying, "old habits die hard." Whatever retreat corporal punishment may have made in the United States and Europe, it is alive and well in many other parts of the world. To more fully elucidate current global trends, the specific practices of several nations in the Middle East, Asia Minor, and the Pacific Rim are discussed at length. Even among retentionist nations, one sees a variety in principle and practice.

As a way to foster a more detailed understanding of current global trends, Chapters 6 and 7 present case studies of five countries where corporal punishment is still included as part of their justice system. A delineation based on justice systems is appropriate because inclusion in that aspect of society generally implies the acceptance of corporal punishment in others.

Chapter 6 provides a detailed look at corporal punishment in the countries of Nigeria, Singapore, and Saudi Arabia. The history of Nigeria's support of corporal punishment retention can be traced to three dominant influences. The first of these is the spread of Islam in the early nineteenth century. The second is the legacy of the slave trade. Lastly, related to the slave trade are Nigeria's lingering post-colonial political and economic structures.

Singapore's path to retention is arguably less complex. Their modern sensibilities with regard to corporal punishment derive largely from their time as a British colony. Even in light of the fact that judicial corporal punishment is banned in the modern United Kingdom, several former British colonies have retained the practice. As will be explored in the chapter on corporal punishment history, the British crown continued corporal punishment in its colonial possessions long after it had abandoned them at home.

The Kingdom of Saudi Arabia derives its extensive use of corporal punishment from the orthodox strain of Islam known as Wahabbism. With a legal system based principally on the Qur'an, the Saudi Arabian justice system is estimated to administer more corporal punishment than any other nation in the world. Corporal punishment can take the form of an exaggerated version of *lex talionis* with punishments ranging from a few strokes with a whip to eye gouging.

The seventh chapter is similar in structure to its predecessor in that two more country case studies are presented. Moving from Africa and Asia to the New World, corporal punishment practices in Bolivia and The Bahamas are given detailed consideration. In both these countries one sees evidence of familiar historical influences.

Bolivia, a long-time Spanish colonial possession, presents an interesting case as a modern retentionist country. Corporal punishment is less a part of the "secular" or Eurocentric government than it is among Bolivia's indigenous peoples. Following his election as president, Aymara Indian Evo Morales initiated a campaign promoted as an effort to give indigenous people more self-rule over matters of justice. Subsequently, a system of indigenous justice or "communal justice" was formally recognized in the newly adopted Bolivian Constitution. The ability for indigenous populations to administer their own system of justice has direct bearing on the legitimization of corporal punishment in Bolivia. As will be discussed, this seemingly "inclusive" change arguably contains the seeds of less noble intentions.

The last country to be discussed in detail is The Bahamas. The Bahamas is an especially interesting case among retentionist countries, if only for the fact that the nation had banned corporal punishment only to bring it back a few years later. As in other countries, one sees the influence of a colonial past, but one mixed with a judicial evolution of corporal punishment policy and sensitive to predominant cultural leanings.

The final chapter, "Explaining Current Global Trends," moves the discussion of global corporal punishment from a more historical and descriptive perspective to an analysis of the social forces that variously influence either abolition or retention. This chapter presents a summary of the authors' previously published research on the deeper social implications and consequences of corporal punishment retention. In short, the chapter poses the question: Why do some countries continue to use corporal punishment; and why do others abandon it? While no absolute answers are offered, the analysis suggests a number of possible places to expand research on the topic.

All this said, the topic of corporal punishment is expansive well beyond the pages of this book. Few treatments of a social phenomenon—so ancient, yet enduring—could claim to be all-encompassing. Accordingly, no such claim is made here. Even so, this volume is intended to bridge a gap in the literature of punishment. To that end, this volume rests on the shoulders of punishment scholars such as Michel Foucault, Graeme Newman, Georg Rusche, Otto Kirchheimer, Abby Schrader, and, most recently, Peter Moskos. These researchers, and those of their caliber, have helped to expand our understanding of a highly complex social construct. The authors hope this volume continues along the path they blazed before us.

1 ———————————————————————

History of Corporal Punishment

> Historically, the most terrible things—war, genocide, and slavery—have resulted not from disobedience, but from obedience.
>
> —Howard Zinn

THE HISTORY OF corporal punishment reflects the history of humanity itself. While the complexity of intended responses may have increased, infliction of pain on the body dates past antiquity and into the primordial origins of all that is human. The goal of this chapter is to present the "evolution" of corporal punishment across time and cultures. Any cultural phenomenon as complex and symbolically rich as corporal punishment can be fully understood only through a historical lens. As such, the following narrative locates the irregular path of corporal punishment within several historical societies and their constituent institutions. As part of this journey, a number of themes will be introduced that are taken up again in later sections of this book.

As Richard Van Yelyr observes, "With regard to many of the habits and customs of mankind there is much dispute as to the exact time when they first made their appearance, but as far as whipping is concerned there can be no such dispute or contention. It is old as mankind itself."[1]

As Terrence Miethe and Hong Lu state, "Punishment is a basic fact of human life."[2] Graeme Newman similarly notes, "[Punishment] in its severest forms has been present in all major civilizations."[3] The ubiquity of it throughout human history notwithstanding, punishment predates society. As Graeme Newman explains, "It originated in the natural condition of man. In relation to the physical world as well as the social world."[4]

A number of scholars proffer opinions as to why corporal punishment is both ancient and enduring. Accepting that corporal punishment is the likely antecedent to all other punishments, some such as George Scott suggest it arose out of humanity's intrinsic nature, "Man is cruel. He has always been cruel. He is cruel to everything which he considers inferior to himself. He is cruel both to his fellow men and to animals."[5] Scott likewise employs a theme that many subsequent scholars find resonant: the visceral effect of pain, "The savage discovered for himself the punishing element in pain. It was perhaps one of the first things that savage man did discover."[6]

Notable Moments in Corporal Punishment History

2000 BC: Egyptian tomb-robbers beaten. Earliest documented instance of corporal punishment

Eighth century BC: Old Testament/Torah/Pentateuch book of Deuteronomy

Fourth century BC: Greek statesman, Demosthenes distinguishes between punishments for freemen versus slaves

First century AD: Roman educator, Quintilian, advises against corporal punishment of students

622 AD: Muhammad flees to Medina. Qur'an and the Sunnah gain acceptance in Middle Eastern society and justice

624 AD: Tang Code in China sets a schedule of offenses and punishments

1207 AD: Pope Innocent III issues *Cum ex officii nostril*, defining heresy. This ushers in the era of Inquisitions

1478 AD: Start of the Spanish Inquisition

Fifteenth–Sixteenth centuries AD: Protestant leaders Luther, Calvin, and Knox espouse doctrines of strict physical discipline of children

1530 AD: King Henry VIII passes the *Whipping Act*

1754 AD: Russian *Charter to the Nobility* exempts nobles from corporal punishment

1936 AD: *Brown v. Mississippi*. U.S. Supreme Court holds a defendant's coerced confession violates the Due Process Clause of the Fourteenth Amendment

1952 AD: Last public whipping in the United States

1968 AD: *Jackson v. Bishop*. Corporal punishment formally banned in Arkansas prisons. Signals the end of corporal punishment in U.S. prisons.

Although evaluation of such proclamations is beyond the scope of this study, they suggest corporal punishment has endured because it stimulates something deep within the human psyche: Pain transforms us. Peter Moskos frames the experience of flogging in a way that could explain the transaction at any time in the course of human history, "You're about to get whipped. Mentally, more than physically. It's going to hurt—but it's supposed to. Flogging is . . . intended to cause jolting pain. Once the experience is over, you'll never be the same."[7]

By extension, one might argue that societies, by fiat of having (or perpetuating) corporal punishment, are somehow different than ones that do not. If not that exactly, many scholars, Foucault chief among them, have argued that a movement away from dominantly corporal toward dominantly carceral punishment mechanisms (for criminals) represents a qualitative transformation in the regulative forces of society.[8]

In this chapter, the use of corporal punishment will be examined as an element in the histories of several societies. As is explained, sensibilities about the appropriateness of corporal punishment have ebbed and flowed across time. In few societies does one ever see an uninterrupted march away from corporal punishment.

Apart from having an irregular trajectory, corporal punishment through the ages of humanity is not a monotonic phenomenon. Corporal punishment techniques are as varied as the civilizations that have employed them. In this chapter, several different modalities of corporal punishment will be discussed with a particular emphasis on their location within culture and history. To approach it another way, particular social arrangements and cultural epochs yield differing ideas about the appropriateness of a given method of punishment. To say it simply, a given practice may be perfectly normal and acceptable at one point in time (or place), but be completely rebuked at another. Only by comparing practice across time and place do we start to understand those social arrangements that support particular kinds of punishment. By examining particular corporal punishment laws and practices we may also gain a better insight into the cultural mindset and social order that produced them.

ANTIQUITY

Our understanding of corporal punishment throughout human history is in some ways limited by the extant records of its use. Fortunately, many long-vanished civilizations took pains to document the means by which their concept of justice was demonstrated. An example of this is found in the Twentieth Dynasty of Egypt (1187–1064 BC). Eric Peet reports an excerpt from the trial of a tomb-robber, "The field laborer Pay-Kharu, son of Pesh-nemeh, was brought. He was examined by beating with the stick and his feet and hands were twisted. He was given the oath by the Ruler on pain of mutilation not to speak falsehood."[9] This passage reflects a number of grim truths about criminal trials throughout much of history. The modern presumption of innocence is absent and confession wrought through torture was regarded as sufficient to substantiate guilt. Moreover, even to bear witness held its own perils.

As James Breasted observes, even persons who had merely witnessed a crime (and were otherwise wholly innocent or disconnected from events), might still be beaten as a means to elicit information. He recounts the story of the brothers Nesuamon and Wenpehti, whose father had been accused of tomb robbing. Even though they were children at the time of their father's alleged crime, they were "examined by beating with a rod and Wenpehti, who was merely a weaver, received a bastinado to his feet and hands."[10] Michael Rosen recounts the reflection of an Egyptian school boy to his teacher (ca. 2000 BC), "I grew up beside you, you smote my back, and so your teaching entered my ear."[11] To be certain, however, corporal punishment is hardly relegated to antiquity or the time of the pharos.

Somewhat earlier examples of codified corporal punishment can be found in ancient Babylonia. Writing about the laws of Mesopotamia in the second millennia BC, Elisabeth Tetlow documents the common use of "corporal punishment and many forms of corporal mutilation, the principle of *talion* and vicarious punishment."[12] Tetlow also notes the use of corporal punishment in Sumerian and Assyrian societies.[13]

As above, corporal punishment in the ancient world was hardly the exclusive provenance of criminal justice. Fletcher Swift says of child rearing in ancient Israel, "Generally speaking, the education of the child was marked by severity, corporal punishment being highly commended and freely used."[14]

Not surprisingly, the legal codes of ancient Israel had some parallels in earlier Hittite law (1450–1200 BC). This is mainly seen in comparing the similarities of Hittite law to scriptures in the books of Deuteronomy (ca. seventh century BC) and Leviticus (538–332 BC).[15]

According to Victor Matthews and Don Benjamin, tablets containing Hittite legal codes were unearthed in modern Turkey just prior to the turn of the twentieth century. The Hittite code is notable for its criminal sentences structured to compensate victims for loss, rather than punish offenders for crime. Another aspect of Hittite law relevant for present concerns is the possibility of commutation. Death sentences were regularly commuted to corporal punishment and, in turn, corporal punishment was often commuted to fines.[16]

One also sees evidence of corporal punishment in ancient Greece. In his noted work, *Against Timocrates* (ca. 350 BC), famed Greek orator Demosthenes states, "If, gentlemen of the jury, you will turn over in your minds the question what is the difference between being a slave and being a free man, you will find that the biggest difference is that the body of a slave is made responsible for all his misdeeds, whereas corporal punishment is the last penalty to inflict on a free man."[17]

William Wayte, however, casts a somewhat humorous doubt on the regularity of corporal punishment in ancient Greece:

> A Byzantine writer, who lived when degrading punishments were the rule, could not understand the personal dignity of the old Athenians who, like modern Frenchmen [ca. 1893], could tolerate shooting a soldier, but not flogging him. Plato's enactment of corporal punishment can hardly be accepted as genuine Attic legislation . . . it is impossible to believe it was inflicted on free Athenians.[18]

This said, the bulk of scholarship on the matter does not accord with Wayte's view. Not only do we see repeated reference to corporal punishment in criminal matters, but also as a general corrective for children.[19] Even so, Plato's admonishments on the matter appear somewhat inconsistent. On the one hand, in *The Republic* he states, "Train your children in their studies not by compulsion but by games, and you will be better able to see the natural results."[20] He follows later with a familiar theme, "Because a freeman ought not to be a slave in the acquisition of knowledge of any kind. Bodily exercise, when compulsory, does no harm to the body; but knowledge which is acquired under compulsion obtains no hold on the mind."[21]

These sentiments stand in contrast to *Protagoras*, where Plato says, "And if [the child] obeys, well and good; if not, he is straightened by threats and blows, like a piece of bent or warped wood."[22] In *The Laws* Plato suggests, "[O]f all animals the boy is the most unmanageable . . . he must be bound with many bridles . . . he who comes across him and does not inflict upon him the punishment which he deserves, shall incur the greatest disgrace."[23]

The use of corporal punishment in ancient Rome appears to reflect many earlier Greek practices. A particularly interesting permission of corporal punishment is found in Roman families. A number of scholars have written on the *patria potestas*, the legal authority of the Roman father (sic. *pater familias*) to mete out whatever punishment household members and slaves might be due. Such authority included both capital and corporal punishment.[24] Some have suggested the father's prerogative to flog slaves owed to the same status differentials observed by Demosthenes in Greek society.[25] To this end, Catherine Edwards states, "Liability to corporal punishment was one of the most vivid symbols of distinction between free and slave in ancient Rome."[26] Others have theorized that the authority to whip a slave emanates from the father's authority to whip any other household subordinate.[27]

Richard Sellar provides instructive context for the social implications surrounding the corporal punishment of a free man in Roman society:

> [To] the Romans the anguish [of corporal punishment] was in significant measure social and psychological, the insult to the *dignitas*. The notion of honor and insult are central to much of the legal writing about corporal punishment. Official exemption from beating is explicitly associated with honor by the jurists: "all who are exempted from beating with rods ought to have the same *honoris reuerentium* as decurions [members of a city senate] have."[28]

Saller further explores this concept with reference to Erving Goffman's observation, "The self is in part a ceremonial thing, a sacred object that must be treated with certain ritual care and in turn must be presented in proper light to others."[29] In this respect, Saller argues that corporal punishment intrusively and shamefully pierces the veil of honor for a free man. To support this contention, he relies on the writings of Cato wherein the amenability to being corporally punished is said to encroach on the distinction between free man and slave. All of this builds to what Saller characterizes as, "the special potency of the symbolic act of beating."[30]

This "potency" was not lost on the Roman rhetorician, Marcus Fabius Quintilian (ca. AD 35–100). Quintilian wrote a highly influential treatise on education in which he strongly criticized the use of corporal punishment against students:

> But that boys should suffer corporal punishment, though it be a received custom . . . I by no means approve; first, because it is a disgrace and a punishment for slaves, and in reality (as will be evident if you imagine the age changed) an affront; secondly, because, if a boy's disposition be so abject as not to be amended by reproof, he will be hardened, like the worst of slaves, even to stripes . . . Besides, after you have coerced a boy with stripes, how will you treat him when he becomes a young man, to whom such terror cannot be held out, and by whom more difficult studies

must be pursued? . . . Add to these considerations that many things unpleasant to be mentioned, and likely afterwards to cause shame, often happen to boys while being whipped, under the influence of pain or fear. Such shame enervates and depresses the mind, and makes them shun people's sight and feel a constant uneasiness.[31]

Quintilian's contemporary, Plutarch (AD 46–120), had a unique vantage from which to approach the question of corporal punishment. Plutarch was borne into a wealthy Greek family, but at some point became a Roman citizen. Like Quintilian, Plutarch took a dim view of corporal punishment in educational settings, "It was a happy circumstance in the discipline of those [Athenian] schools that the parent only had the power of corporal punishment; the rod and the ferule were snatched from the petty tyrant; his office alone was to inform the mind; he had no authority to dasterdize the spirit; he had no power to extinguish the generous flame of freedom."[32]

With these examples, we may conclude that the use of corporal punishment was broadly approved in some settings (i.e., the discipline of slaves or punishment of criminals), but perhaps a matter of some debate in others (i.e., education). Beyond the Roman confines of this polemic, the work of thinkers like Quintilian and Plutarch had influence long after their own time. In particular, they proved important in Renaissance Italy.

THE RENAISSANCE

The first evidence of Renaissance educational reforms is seen in the work of Pietro Paolo Vergerio (1340–1420). In fact, it could be argued that his most significant contribution was the "rediscovery" of Quintilian's *Education of an Orator*. His influence is seen in an excerpt from Vergerio's own work, *On the Manners of a Gentleman and on Liberal Studies*, "The master must judge how far he can rely on emulation, rewards, encouragement; how far he must have recourse to sterner measures. Too much leniency is objectionable; so also is too much severity, for we must avoid all that terrifies a boy."[33]

In this passage one sees a call for moderation that is also taken up by a contemporary of Vergerio's, Vittorino da Feltre (1378–1446). William Boyd calls da Feltre, "the first modern schoolmaster."[34] William Woodward's considerable study of da Feltre, prompts a description of him as "quick-tempered" but nonetheless quite controlled.[35] Echoing the approach espoused by Vergerio, Woodward says of da Feltre, "Corporal punishment was seldom resorted to, and then only after deliberation, and as the alternate to expulsion . . . it was a part of [his] purpose to attract rather than to drive, and to respect the dignity and the freedom of his boys."[36]

A final Renaissance Italian that bears mention is Battista Guarino (1374–1460). Guarino exemplifies the moderated approach to educational discipline in this era. In fact, he writes of punishment in a voice nearly identical to that of Quintilian:

> Faults, moreover, imbibed in early years, as Horace reminds us, are by no means easy to eradicate. Next, the master must not be prone to flogging as an inducement to learning. It is an indignity to a free-born youth, and its infliction renders learning itself repulsive, and the dread of it provokes to unworthy evasions on the part of timorous boys. The scholar is thus morally and intellectually injured, the master is deceived, and the discipline altogether fails in its purpose . . . The habitual instrument of the teacher must be kindness, though punishment should be retained as it were in the background as a final resource.[37]

These same themes are continued into the sixteenth century, having taken root in Holland. The Humanist scholar, Desiderius Erasmus Roterodamus, better known as Erasmus (1466–1536), while not a schoolteacher himself, wrote extensively about education and the place of corporal punishment in it.

As with the Italian thinkers above, Erasmus's writings reflect a strong influence by Quintilian. As Erasmus observes, "A poor master, we are prepared to find, relies almost wholly upon fear of punishment as the motive to work. To frighten a whole class is easier than to teach one boy properly; for the latter is, and always must be, a task as serious as it is honorable." In a particularly prescient vein, he extends the thinking beyond the classroom and into the palace, "It is equally true of states: the rule which carries the respect and consent of the citizens demands higher qualities in the Prince than does the tyranny of forces."[38]

Erasmus also succeeds in articulating an important psychological and potentially sadistic dimension of corporal punishment gone awry, "Masters who are conscious of their own incompetence are generally the worst floggers. What else can they do? They cannot teach so they beat. By degrees it becomes a positive pleasure to them to torture, especially when they are self-indulgent men, or slothful or cruel by nature."[39]

In a tone drawn directly from Quintilian, Erasmus also argues that it is ignoble for a person, even children, to suffer the indignity of being beaten. This is especially consequent because he rejects the prevalent Old Testament view that had dominated (and would dominate) European thinking for centuries:

> It is indeed, the mark of the servile nature to be drilled by fear; why then do we suffer children . . . to be treated as slaves, might be? Yet even slaves, who are men like the rest of us, are by wise masters freed from something of their servile state by humane control . . . Is it not meet that Christian peoples cast forth from their midst the whole doctrine of slavery in all its forms?[40]

One also sees the spread of Quintilian's influence into Renaissance France. Michel de Montaigne (1533–1592) expanded Quintilian's thinking in a way that foreshadows the coming Romantic period, "How much more fittingly would their classes be strewn with flowers and leaves than with the bloody stumps of rods! I would have portraits there of Joy and Gladness, and Flora and the Graces, as the philosopher Speusippus had in his school. Where there profit is, let there frolic be also."[41]

Montaigne's disciplinary philosophy emanates chiefly from an understanding that each child will exhibit a different response to a given stimulus; that the emotional and intellectual gravity of particular disciplinary or pedagogical techniques will be experienced uniquely. Accordingly, he strongly admonishes against a monotonic approach to teaching and discipline.[42]

Taken together, Montaigne and Erasmus were among the most influential educators of their time. Moreover, the impact of their writings would be felt for centuries into the future. Evidence of this can be seen in the 1683 writings of Pere Lamy, a member of the Order of the Oratory. As Lamy states, "There are many other ways besides the rod, and to lead pupils back to their duty, a caress, a threat, the hope of a reward, or the fear of humiliation, has greater efficiency than whips."[43]

Jean Baptiste de la Salle (1651–1719) mirrored this perspective with the Institute of Christian Brothers in *The Conduct of Schools*. La Salle writes, "Experience affords sufficient proof, that to perfect those who are committed to our care, we must act in a manner both gentle and firm ... The correction of the pupils is one of the most important things to be done in schools, and one which requires the greatest care."[44] Only in the tumult of the Protestant Reformation were these increasingly common sensibilities subordinated to a more strident discipline.

THE PROTESTANT REFORMATION

The effects of the Protestant Reformation were of inestimable consequence for the course of Western civilization. A prominent theme in early Protestantism was a legalistic recognition of the Bible as the sole and infallible authority for all questions of the human condition. The discipline of children, education, home life, criminal justice, and all other spheres of life were to be resolved through direct scriptural edict.

The Reformation had great consequence for education in particular, because most schools of the era were organized and run by clergy (both Protestant and otherwise). Even when private teachers were engaged, more often than not, they had been trained by the church. One sees this reflected in Martin Luther's (1483–1546) arguably hard-line view of corporal punishment and child-rearing.

Luther's priorities are stated firmly. Salvation of the child's soul is paramount. All other interests, including the physical body are subordinated to this primary consideration. As he observes:

> A false love blinds parents so that they regard the body of their child more than his soul. Hence the wise man says, "He that spareth his rod hateth his son; but he that

loveth him chasteneth him betimes." (Prov. XIII:24) . . . Hence it is highly necessary that all parents regard the soul of their child more than his body, and look upon him as a precious, eternal treasure, which god has entrusted to them for preservation, so that the world, the flesh, and the devil do not destroy him. For at death and in the judgment they will have to render a strict account of their stewardship.[45]

The emphasis on the responsibility of parents to bring their children up properly as demonstrated here is further emphasized. Well-meaning parents would have to meter their sympathies if they truly cared for the child. For Luther there was an ever-present struggle between a parent's well-meaning intentions and that which must be done to secure the child's salvation.

As he states, "Such people as thus fondle and indulge their children must bear the sins of their children as if committed by themselves."[46] Even so, Luther recognizes the possibility for excessive zeal in parental correction, "[S]uch discipline begets in the child's mind which is yet tender, a state of fear and imbecility, and develops a feeling of hate towards the parents, so that it often runs away from home."[47] That said, Luther espoused a grim certainty in the rearing of his own children, "I would rather have a dead than a disobedient son."[48] Although he does not explicitly reference it in the above passage, Luther is obviously guided by Proverbs 23:13–14, "Do not be chary of correcting a child, a stroke of the cane is not likely to kill him. A stroke of the cane and you save him from Sheol."

This kind of zeal is also seen in the later works of John Calvin. Calvin had a particularly narrow tolerance of "heresy." This commitment is seen in instances such as the burning to death of Michael Servetus in Geneva (as well as the fifty-eight other individuals he had executed for similar deviance). As Calvin once said, "When his [God's] glory is to be asserted, humanity must be almost obliterated from our memories."[49]

One also sees evidence of strong influence in leaders like John Knox (ca. 1514–1572). Knox is perhaps best remembered for his part in the overthrow of Roman Catholicism in Scotland and the subsequent rise of Presbyterianism. Much of his success owes to the Scots' development of a well-organized educational system, a system that would also flourish in other parts of the world where Scots would subsequently settle (i.e., North America).

Although Knox says little about pedagogy, one may infer a certain strictness from a combination of extant writings and common practices. Knox states that the purpose of education is "to make the man of God perfect [and to] . . . abolish all contrary Doctrine." These aims were to be achieved through teaching and, if necessary, "punishment."[50]

To that particular mechanism, Will Durant says of Knox, "He rejoiced in the perfect hatred which the Holy Ghost engendereth in the hearts of God's elect against the contemners against his holy statutes."[51]

As an outgrowth of these influences, Farrell documents a notable and enduring symbol of educational discipline in Scotland: the tawse.[52] A tawse was a long, thick leather paddle with a bifurcated end. According to Farrell, it was often used to whip the recipient's bare buttocks.[53] This instrument was a common, if not integral element of the Scottish educational system for centuries. Hendrie, a Scottish school teacher, details the ritual of the tawse:

> Describing his school days in Montrose, 19th century poet Alexander Smart records that when he and his school fellows were to be punished they were ordered to bend over a long wooden bench, to which they were bound so that there was no escape while the master . . . administered what he considered to be the requisite number of strokes of his tawse across their legs and bottoms. At Ayr Grammar School the boys suffered the even greater indignity of being 'horsed,' that is hoisted on the shoulders of two of their classmates, so that their bottoms presented an even better target for the tawse.[54]

Citing a number of British women's periodicals from the nineteenth century, Van Yelyr observes, "Certain children, it is argued, cannot be trained and educated without being made to experience pain, especially those who are sulky, willful, bad tempered, lazy, and have little regard for the truth."[55] Use of the tawes (and all other corporal punishments in educational settings) was finally banned throughout the United Kingdom in 1998.[56] Even so, loopholes in the law remained such that several years passed before the practice was completely abandoned (for additional information see: Chapter 4).

Other Protestant denominations continued in a similar vein. The writings of John Wesley (1703–1791), founder of the Methodist church, exemplify a literal acceptance of Old Testament discipline:

> Break your child's will, in order that it may not perish. Break its will as soon as it can speak plainly—or even before it can speak at all. It should be forced to do as it is told, even if you have to whip it ten times running. Break its will, in order that its soul may live.[57]

This said, there was at least one Protestant leader who denounced such firm methods as a general part of teaching. John Amos Comenius (1592–1670) saw a vast need for reform in educational discipline, "The method used in instructing the young has generally been so severe that schools have been looked on as terrors for boys and shambles for their poor intellects."[58]

He follows this sentiment by saying, "Now no discipline of a severe kind should be exercised in connection with studies or literary exercises, but only where questions of morality are at stake."[59] Even with this clear hesitance about corporal punishment, Comenius ultimately bows to the prevailing sentiments of his time:

> Finally, if some characters are unaffected by gentle methods, recourse must be had to more violent ones . . . Without doubt there are many to whom the proverb 'Beating is the only thing that improves a Phrygian' applies with great force . . . even if such

measures do not produce any great effect on the boy who is punished, they act as a great stimulus to the others by inspiring them with fear.[60]

Where Comenius may be provisionally faulted for ideals not entirely supported by practice, he espouses other techniques that would be whole-cloth rebuked today. Namely, he advocates public humiliation for the slower students. As he states, "It is often of use to laugh at the backward ones."[61]

Retrospectively, then, one may conclude that many of the pedagogical fruits of the Reformation were wrought through active physical discipline. To be sure, however, Protestants have not made this disciplinary journey alone. As described below, the guiding hand of Catholicism has likewise often held a lash.

CATHOLICISM

While the Reformation reasserted an arguable austerity in physical discipline, the purposeful inducement of pain has been a historical feature in the regulative structures of the Catholic church for many centuries. Brian Harrison, a Catholic theologian, addresses an interesting paradox in modern Catholicism, namely the apparent reticence of church officials to directly address the matter of corporal punishment:

> [E]very student of Catholic history and theology knows [corporal punishments and torture] were endorsed for many centuries by the most respected theologians . . . and by the highest ecclesiastical authorities. And yet the issue cannot simply be side-stepped forever. After all, at the very heart of Christianity itself lies the infliction of horrendous pain—the passion and death of the world's Redeemer. The central icon of our faith—the Crucifix—is a terrible instrument of torture.[62]

Even when other elements of the church vigorously embraced all manner of corporal ordeals, Catholic educators appear largely to have eschewed more stringent physical discipline.

In many ways, early Catholicism was the bureaucratic heir to long-standing structures and processes of the Roman Empire.[63] As is more fully discussed in Chapter 2: Religion and Corporal Punishment, the bureaucratic administration of early Catholicism (and indeed Christendom for more than a millennium) was well aligned and often indistinguishable from that of secular authorities.[64] To this end, entwined techniques such as trial by ordeal, torture-evoked confessions, and physical punishments as penance were deeply woven into the social fabric of the Christian world.

As the Apostle Paul told the Roman members of the church, "Let every soul be subject unto the higher powers. For there is no power but of God: the powers that be are ordained of God. Whosoever therefore resisteth the power, resisteth the ordinance of God: and they that resist shall receive to themselves damnation."[65]

Following the themes developed in the preceding sections of this chapter, two spheres of corporal punishment related to Catholicism bear immediate discussion: discipline in church-run schools and the Inquisitions. To the first of these topics, there are numerous examples of Catholic dictum that permit the use of corporal punishment in educational settings, but qualify that permission with a call to moderation.

A passage from the 1599 "Rules for the Professor of Moral Philosophy" in the *Ratio atque Institutio Studiorum Societatis Iesu* issued by the Society of Jesus exemplifies this moderated perspective:

> If an occasion arises when it is not a sufficient remedy for the scandal given to expel from classes, let him bring the matter before the Rector that he may decide what further is fitting to be done. Still as much as is possible the affair must be conducted in a spirit of gentleness, with peace and charity toward all.[66]

This "Plan of Studies" was the authoritative source for regulation not only of subjects taught, but of method to be used throughout Jesuit schools for more than three hundred years. According to R. Ward Holder, the influence of the Jesuits in education would be difficult to overstate. He records the existence of at least 144 Jesuit colleges by the end of the sixteenth century and dubs the order, "the school-masters to the world."[67]

As William McGucken states, "[D]iscipline in the 17th-century Jesuit college was mild. There was, in sharp contrast with the prevailing practice of the day, very little corporal punishment . . . prevention of disorder was better than post factum remedies, and in general they tried to win their students by love rather than by fear."[68]

Renown Catholic educator, Jean Baptiste de la Salle (1651–1719), prescribed similar methods to be used by his teachers of the Institute of Christian Brothers in *The Conduct of Schools*, "[To] perfect those who are committed to our care, we must act in a manner both gentle and firm . . . The correction of the pupils is one of the most important things to be done in schools, and one which requires the greatest care in order that it be timely and beneficial."[69]

Whatever moderation educators could summon was notably absent in the church's sustained and well-remembered efforts to drive out heresy: the Inquisitions. Any balanced discussion of the Inquisitions must necessarily walk a very fine line between sensationalized popular depictions of gory torture (some of which are doubtless accurate) and revisionist accounts of the church describing them as "politically necessary."[70] Wherever the more objective telling might lie, Johnson puts the matter in clearest perspective, "The true test of any religion is how the minority is treated when that religion is in the majority and has the power to persecute."[71]

In what surely ranks among the greatest ironies of early Christendom, members of the early church were subject to persistent and innumerable persecutions. The most sustained of these came at the hands of Roman leaders. A particularly violent example of this was the anti-Christian campaign under the hand of Roman Emperor Diocletian (ca. AD 303), "Racks, scourges, swords, daggers, crosses, poison, and famine, were made use of in various parts to dispatch the Christians; and invention was exhausted to devise tortures against such as had no crime, but thinking differently from the votaries of superstition."[72] Of course this persecution was not limited to Roman authorities. Christians were also cruelly tortured, executed, exiled and generally abused by Persians, Arians, Goths, Vandals, and several other cultures.[73]

Among the more painful lessons of history, Catholic leadership had clearly internalized a deep intolerance for dissension. Augustine (AD 354–430) stands as a perfect case in point. As Elphége Vacandard states, "Heretics and schismatics [Augustine] maintained, were to be regarded as sheep who had gone astray. It is the shepherd's duty to run after them and bring them back into the fold by using, if occasion require it, the whip and the goad."[74]

Michael Gaddis provides a more direct appraisal. He concludes that by the fifth century the church leaders of late antiquity had fully rationalized using force to advance church interests:

> Even those whose conformity was at first merely superficial would eventually, through repetition, take to heart what they professed. This was a fundamentally utilitarian argument: coercion was acceptable because it worked. Practical experience had overcome Augustine's initial worries. Augustine, having reached this useful conclusion, had little trouble convincing himself of its rightness. There was ample scriptural warrant. Christ had compelled Saul to the truth with violence. Sarah had justly chastised her servant Hagar. Moses had punished his disobedient people. The process of correction might be painful, but indulgence was no kindness. Eventually, those saved by severity might come to appreciate the fact. Augustine took great satisfaction in describing how former Donatist congregations, once coerced, now freely thanked God for their deliverance from error—'which thanks they would not now be offering willingly, had they not first, even against their will, been severed from that impious association.' For Augustine, free will and compulsion were not necessarily incompatible.[75]

As Gaddis further suggests, the potent cocktail of moral certainty and rationalized violence often, "reveal[ed] broad commonalities across a range from the individual level of personal relationships to the grand scale of imperial politics."[76] Where the enterprise goes terribly wrong, he argues is in the idea that zealous propagation of God's will could be metered, "The idea of disciplinary violence, exercised for the greater good of its recipients, implied that force and coercion could be carefully measured and precisely calibrated. The reality, of course, was far messier."[77] Even so, efforts to combat heresy prior to the twelfth century never approached the level of torture and execution characteristic of the coming Inquisitions.[78]

Inquisitions began as a series of papal bulls against heresy, in particular Lucius III's *Ad abolendum* of 1184 and Innocent III's *Cum ex officii nostri* of 1207. These defined the crime of heresy, sanctioned church officials to extinguish it, and equated heresy with treason against the state.[79] Nominally, the church sought to persuade repentance rather than coerce it, but the papacy became increasingly aware that more aggressive measures were required. Concomitant to these realizations, the concept of *inquisitio* saw expanded use in canon and civil cases as an aspect of the professionalization of law.

The Inquisitions are generally categorized into four epochs: the Medieval Inquisition (ca. 1184–sixteenth century); the Spanish Inquisition (1478–1834); the Portuguese Inquisition (1536–1821); and the Roman Inquisition (1542–ca. 1860). Formally known as the *Inquisitio Haereticae Pravitatis* (sic. the Inquiry on Heretical Perversity), the Inquisitions of the Catholic church were efforts to detect and drive out persons or ideas counter to church teaching. As Foxe states, the principal focus of inquisitors was, "all that is spoken, or written, against any of the articles of the creed, or the traditions of the Roman Church."[80]

The first of these, the Medieval Inquisition, began in approximately 1184 at the behest of Pope Innocent III. The two major epochs therein were the Episcopal Inquisition (1184–1230s) and the subsequent Papal Inquisition (1230s). The Medieval Inquisition was a response to dissident movements in Europe that the papacy considered apostate or heretical to Christianity. The most notable groups who were subject to these persecutions were the Cathars and Waldensians in France and Italy. While not the most expansive or violent, the Medieval Inquisition established a number of procedures that would become important for later Inquisition periods.

Robin Vose observes an often ignored, but important aspect of the Inquisitions. Apart from the more publicized machinations of inquisitors, the Inquisitions were subject to troubles common among (as well as carrying the influence of) all expansive bureaucratic programs. As she states, "[Inquisitions] were . . . mundane corporate entities, struggling like all such bodies to efficiently make and execute policy while staying more or less within a budget. As they evolved, too, inquisitions developed significant financial roles within local economies as well as political influence at courts both secular and ecclesiastical."[81]

The Inquisitions were in many regards a kind of bureaucratic nexus with authority to dictate matters of the spirit, the purse, and the state. Where they originated as a Papal bull, the Inquisitions were soon buttressed by secular officials. John Vidmar confirms the entwined interests of church, secular, political, and economic interests. As he states, "Abuses were not limited to inquisitors. Politicians could use the Inquisition as a tool to get rid of their enemies. Property was confiscated . . . Occasionally a dead person could be tried for heresy. This was usually done with property in mind."[82] Durant records that secular governments were responsible for covering the expenses associated with the Inquisition, but that they also benefited from any proceeds of it.[83]

A prime example of secular political interests overlapping those of the church is Frederick II. Having been suspected of intent to convert to Islam, Frederick II needed to demonstrate his faithfulness to Rome. As a consequence he declared himself the protector and friend of all the inquisitors, and published the "cruel edicts" commanding unrepentant heretics to be burned and repentant heretics to be imprisoned for life.[84] Similarly, in the statutes of Verona in 1228, the Podestá on taking office, swore to expel all heretics from the city. Even centuries later, such alliances were common.

In 1522, Charles V impaneled a tribunal in the Spanish Netherlands to combat the tide of Protestantism.[85] Likewise, laws were enacted to facilitate the work of inquisitors. According to the *Schwabenspiegel*, or code in force in southern Germany, any ruler who neglected to persecute heresy was to be stripped of all possessions. Furthermore, if the ruler failed to burn those delivered to him as heretics, he was to be punished as a heretic himself.[86]

While an obviously variable model, the process employed by most inquisitors revolved around a somewhat standardized order of business. Inquisitors being largely drawn from mendicant monastic orders, chiefly Dominican and Franciscan monks, traveled town to town to ply their mission.

Far from operating in secret, inquisitors made their coming and purpose well known through public announcements. Sermons were given to proclaim their arrival and to offer those in attendance a limited "period of grace" in which to voluntarily come forward and confess their own (or perhaps more importantly—their neighbors') failings.[87] Those who immediately confessed escaped torture and more severe punishment, but were compelled to denounce any other heretics.

Absent sufficient confessions, the inquisitors, upon having identified individuals of interest, would conduct trials. These trials were highly malleable affairs, both in terms of who was accused and the records kept about the proceedings.[88] Defendants ranged from members of the nobility to peasantry. To be clear, these proceedings were closer to a modern understanding of a tribunal where the inquisitor(s) alone made determinations of guilt or innocence than a jury trial (although a jury of sorts was sometimes impaneled).

The standards of evidence were markedly different than what one might expect today. The accused was compelled to testify. Refusal to do so was tantamount to an admission of guilt. No charges would be read, deferring instead to the accused's own confession. The accused was customarily held in chains, required to furnish their own bedding and pay for the costs associated with the inquiry. If the accused were unable to pay, their property might be seized as compensation.[89] Witnesses of all stripe, character, and motive would be heard. The accused had no right to confront them or necessarily know their identity.

If the accused offered a sufficient confession, they might receive a punishment short of death. Such confessions were often the product of physical torture. As a starting point, individuals might spend years held in chains, alone in a fetid pit of solitary confinement. Should that prove an inadequate inducement, more acute remedies were sought.

Durant suggests more direct torture was used only after a consensus of inquisitors deemed it appropriate. Moreover, he states, "Often torture so decreed was postponed in hopes that the dread of it would induce confession."[90] Durant also provides a most interesting rationale employed by inquisitors in support of torture, "The inquisitors appear to have sincerely believed that torture was a favor to the defendant already accounted guilty, since it might earn him, by confession, a slighter penalty ... [or in the case of a death sentence] priestly absolution."[91]

If the accused failed to satisfy the inquisitors with their confession or professions of faith, they were allowed to solicit advocates for their defense.[92] Paradoxically, coming forth as a witness in support of the accused was a dubious proposition. If one gave testimony in defense of a person later deemed a heretic that same testimony could be used as evidence of one's own guilt. As such, the motivation to speak up in support of the falsely accused was strongly circumscribed by the understandable forces of self-preservation. Association with an accused person was further complicated by established mechanisms to reconcile conflicting accounts of matters at hand.

A given individual's heresy could be proven if the accused was caught in a heretical act. Even so, the stated goal of the inquisitor was to extract a confession, or admission of guilt, after which absolution might be granted. The tactics used to garner these confessions have become the stuff of gory legend.

As a predicate to all other techniques, the accused could be imprisoned for long periods. If imprisonment proved not evocative of confession, other more expedient methods might then be employed. In 1221, Pope Gregory IX issued the *Excommunicamus*, which among other things, expressly permitted the burning of heretics at the stake.[93] In 1252, Pope Innocent IV issued a bull, *Ad Extirpanda*, permitting the use of torture to obtain a confession. Owing to a subsequent papal decree requiring the assistance of civil authorities and commoners, this task often fell to local secular officials, but the inquisitors themselves participated as well.[94]

As above, Inquisitions occurred all across Europe and spread into the New World.[95] Often concurrent, they ran for almost seven centuries. From almost their inception, the Inquisitions were marked by the strident physical coercion visited upon the subjects of their inquiry. That said, any discussion of Inquisition history would be incomplete without particular consideration of the Spanish Inquisition.

While each of the previous Inquisitions was distinguished by their own excesses, the Spanish Inquisition is notable for the unequaled zeal of its agents. The Spanish Inquisition was initiated at the behest of King Ferdinand II and Queen Isabella, with the approval of Pope Sixtus IV. In the late fifteenth century, the Catholic monarchy merged two kingdoms, Aragon and Castile, into a single realm. The religious diversity of the region, owning to large populations of Jews and Muslims, was seen as a substantial threat to the new unified state. As Jean Plaidy observes, "The Catholic sovereigns were determined to have a united country, and they did not believe this ambition could be achieved unless all their subjects accepted one religion. This they were determined to bring about through persuasion, if possible, and if not, by force."[96] One cannot, however, overlook the ethnic and racial dimensions of the Spanish Inquisition. With its particular

focus on Jews and Muslims (as well as their descendants), it becomes retrospectively clear that the proffering of religion was but one among many objectives.[97]
Americo Castro provides an incisive depiction of the anti-Jewish sentiment
prevalent in this era:

> The people who really felt the scruple of purity of blood were the Spanish Jews . . .
> The historical reality becomes intelligible to us only when seen to be possessed of
> both extremes: the exclusivism of Catholic Spain was a reply to the hermeticism of
> the aljamas [Jewish communities] . . . purity of blood was the answer of a society ani-
> mated by anti-Jewish fury to the racial hermeticism of the Jew.[98]

Although the primary groups targeted by the Spanish Inquisition were Jews and
Muslims, they were hardly alone. Heather White documents the fate of five
African slaves who were brought to the Inquisition Tribunal in Cartagena de
Indies, a port city of New Granada (modern Columbia), from the mining town
of Zaragoza in 1620. Fearing the influence of witchcraft in the region, the local
Inquisitor wrote, "these lands are widely infested with male and female witches
and especially the mines of Zaragoza and its surroundings . . . where some two
thousand slaves are living . . . among whom this diabolical sect has spread."[99]

Despite the position of the Spanish Inquisition in the popular imagination, it
remains the locus of considerable debate. Whether one accounts it as William
Battersby does with the proclamation of "politically necessary"[100] or as Terrence
Meithe and Hong Lu do, calling it one of the "most infamous periods of corporal
punishment," the Spanish Inquisition left an indelible mark on world history.[101]
Reflecting the varied qualitative assessments of it, estimations of the death toll
associated with the Spanish Inquisition are wildly disparate. Sources claim the
casualties to be as low as 2,000[102] or as high as 350,000[103] for the roughly 350-
year period. Paul Johnson states that the total number of victims for the Spanish
Inquisition was approximately 341,000, "Of these, 32,000 were killed by burning, 17,659 burned in effigy, and 291,000 given lesser punishments."[104]

As a way to summarize the toll the Inquisition took upon the population of
Spain and its colonies, the words of an inquisitor will suffice. The Queen's secretary, Ferdinand de Pulgar (himself a convert), sent a letter to Archbishop Pedro
Gonzales de Mendoza of Toledo expressing concern over the Inquisition's practice of burning of young *converso* girls, "many of whom had never left their
parent's house." In response to de Pulgar's opposition, a close associate of the
Grand Inquisitor, Tomas de Torquemada, is said to have uttered, "Better a man
to enter heaven with one eye than go to hell with both."[105]

COLONIAL AMERICA AND THE UNITED STATES

Corporal punishment in the United States reflects the constellation of influences
that supported it in other lands. One sees it used against slaves, indentured

persons, criminals, school children, wayward church and family members. One also sees the same underlying motivations: social and political power; religious and cultural hegemony; economic gain; maintenance of stratification; racial and ethnic intolerance.

Owing to customs of the Old World, the use of corporal punishment in early America was facilitated by religious doctrine. Just as the Jews and Muslims were violently oppressed in Spain, the Quakers of New England endured sustained persecution during the seventeenth century.[106] An oft-cited example of this is the punishment of Quaker William Brend. In 1658, Brend, approximately 78-years-old, was taken into custody whereupon he was repeatedly beaten, shackled, and starved. William Sewel presents an account of the terror, "[The] jailer took a pitched rope about an inch thick, and gave him twenty blows over his back and arms, with as much force as he could, so that the rope untwisted . . . he came again with another rope, that was thicker and stronger."[107]

Even in the face of persecution, the Quakers were not absolutely against corporal punishment in all settings. Perhaps the one sphere where Quakers assented to Puritan sensibilities was in the discipline of school children. The Puritans thought children were especially prone to sin and, as such, required firm discipline. Puritan rules for educational settings reflect this.[108] The rules for Freetown School in Dorchester, Massachusetts in 1645 reference an "ordinance of God" authorizing teachers to employ corporal punishment.[109] These rules severely limited a parent's ability to interfere with the teacher's right to discipline children.[110] According to Gertrude Williams, the attitudes reflected in the Freetown rules were so broadly held that even the Quakers, who although more inclined to stress love rather than fear, also sanctioned the use of corporal punishment in their schools.[111]

Standing on the precipice of a new nation a century later, James Madison still worried about the extent of religious persecution in the New World. On January 24, 1774, Madison wrote to his Princeton classmate, William Bradford, expressing dismay at the persecutions of Baptists in northern Virginia. In the letter Madison contrasts the intolerance he witnessed in Virginia with the relatively more ecumenical environment of Bradford's Philadelphia, "That diabolical Hell conceived principle of persecution rages among some and to their eternal Infamy the Clergy can furnish their Quota of Imps for such business. This vexes me the most of any thing whatever."[112]

It would be incomplete to discuss corporal punishment in early America without a consideration of it in regard to slavery and slave-holding. The whip as an inducement to rectitude is embedded in the depths of human history. Indeed, this chapter began with a discussion of ancient Egypt. Collateral to its use in promoting correct behavior, the whip has an equally ancient history as a mechanism to coerce labor. In colonial America, the distinction between an otherwise free man fulfilling a contract of indentured servitude and an outright slave was at best a slight one. Prior to 1700, the Virginia colony enacted a series of laws aimed at the keeping of slaves and servants. Codified in 1660, the first of these establishes a penalty for a white servant running away with a slave:

> Be it enacted that in case any English servant shall run away in company with any Negroes who are incapable of making satisfaction by addition of time . . . the English so running away in company with them shall serve for the time of the said Negroes absence as they are to do for their own by a former act.[113]

The second notable law, enacted eight years later (1668), describes an expansion of possible penalties for having run away:

> Whereas it has been questioned whether servants running away may be punished with corporal punishment by their master or magistrate, since the act already made gives the master satisfaction by prolonging their time by service, it is declared and enacted by this Assembly that moderate corporal punishment inflicted by master or magistrate upon a runaway servant shall not deprive the master of the satisfaction allowed by the law, the one being as necessary to reclaim them from persisting in that idle course as the other is just to repair the damages sustained by the master.[114]

Taken together one sees an element of a pattern long established. Richard Van Yelyr notes a custom in ancient Rome where a sign would be attached to the front of a house, "Slaves who leave this house without special permission will be punished with a hundred lashes."[115]

Of whipping in America, Van Yelyr states that it was the most common method of punishment because it was "the most effective and easily applied."[116] This begs the question as to why corporal punishments were thought by members of societies like that of colonial America to be the most effective. Lawrence Friedman offers an explanation tied to the homogeneity of colonial settlers and their tightly integrated social order, "They punished offenses the way autocratic fathers or mothers punish children; they made heavy use of shame and shaming. The aim was not just to punish, but to teach a lesson so that the sinful sheep would want to get back to the flock."[117] Friedman continues with a comment on the very public nature of the punishments and how that public element putatively enhanced efficacy, "They loved to enlist the community, the bystanders; their scorn, and the sinners' humiliation, were part of the process."[118] In an earlier work, Friedman summarizes colonial society more succinctly, "They were small, inbred and gossipy communities. Public opinion and shame were important elements of punishment."[119]

As Van Yelyr observes, these informal processes of shaming became supplanted by codified punishments. By the end of the colonial era and into early nationhood, whipping was generally approved by state law.[120] While he does not specify where the laws were enacted, Van Yelyr notes that by 1740 many locales had banned certain corporal punishments: namely, "cutting out the tongue, gouging an eye, scalding, burning . . . any cruel punishment other than whipping or beating with a horse-whip, cow-skin, switch or small stick."[121]

To the contrary, Alice Earle provides evidence that such banishments were hardly universal. She notes brandings in Maryland, New Hampshire, and Massachusetts in to the 1770s and ear-cropping in Virginia about the same time.[122] Similar to Earle, Zachary Middleton observes that a number of states passed laws with the nominal purpose of safeguarding white servants (and to a lesser degree black slaves) from the excesses of corporal punishment. He cites a 1717 South Carolina law, "An Act for Better Governing and Regulating White Servants," as evidence that these codes did provide protections to servants, but as per usual, gave distinct advantage to the masters.[123] Friedman also makes an important clarification about colonial punishments. He observes that torture had been strongly limited in written law in many places, but common practices were slow to change. He cites a Massachusetts law (ca. 1672) as an example of slowly shifting sentiments, "[The accused] may be tortured yet not with such Tortures as be Barbarous or inhumane."[124] What exactly constitutes suitably humane or non-barbarous torture is not explained.

That limits began to emerge anywhere in the American colonies presents an interesting paradox. This is particularly apparent in light of the fact that slaves were regarded as property, not persons and as such, amenable to whatever treatment their master deemed appropriate. It is clear, however, that these issues were sufficiently discussed before 1700, if only for the fact of the following Virginia law regarding slave killing:

> Whereas the only law in force for the punishment of refractory servants resisting their master, mistress, or overseer cannot be inflicted upon Negroes, nor the obstinacy of many of them be suppressed by other than violent means, be it enacted and declared this Grand Assembly if any slave resists his master . . . and by the extremity of the correction should chance to die, that his death shall not be accounted a felony, but the master . . . be acquitted from molestation, since it cannot be presumed that premeditated malice . . . should induce any man to destroy his own estate.[125]

One might then contrast this with a later Virginia statute applicable to the theft of hogs. In 1748 Virginia, the first offense of hog-stealing garnered a punishment of twenty-five lashes "well-laid upon the public whipping post." For the second offense, the offender was to be set in the pillory for two hours and have his ears nailed to the device. At the end of two hours, his ears were then to be "slit loose." For the third offense: death. Were the offender a slave, the corporal punishments would "double."[126]

While there were great discrepancies in the relative treatment of slaves and freemen, American correctional institutions (until the mid-twentieth century) appear to have been almost universally horrid for all concerned. Friedman describes a number of county jails as "moral plague spots."[127] As he states, "Prisoners were whipped, starved and tortured . . . all over the country . . . What

went on inside prison walls hardly mattered as long as the walls were impermeable."[128] Van Yelyr, writing in 1941, concurs, "In American and English prisons there is probably a good deal of unauthorized corporal punishment."[129]

Corporal punishment as an element of American criminal justice was
not limited to those who had been sentenced to prison. Rather, as Van Yelyr
observes, the truncheon was often deemed a predicate tool for eliciting confessions, "Court cases . . . have in recent years shown . . . the notorious third-degree
relies, in large part on corporal punishment for securing evidence and admissions
of guilt."[130] From this, one may conclude that prior to reforms sparked by Herbert Hoover's famed Wickersham Commission, the tortures and ordeals of the
Inquisition did not fall as far away or as swiftly as perhaps imagined.

The landmark 1936 case, *Brown v. Mississippi*,[131] represents the first major
ruling on corporal punishment as a means to elicit confession of a criminal act.
In March 1934, Raymond Stuart, a white planter, was murdered. The black
sharecroppers, Arthur Ellington, Ed Brown, and Henry Shields, were arrested.
In an unconscionable act, a group of men including a deputy sheriff went to
Ellington's home and accused him of the crime.

As Chief Justice Hughes's opinion recounts, "[When Ellington refused to
confess, the group] hanged him by a rope to the limb of a tree, and, having let
him down, they hung him again, and when he was let down the second time,
and he still protested his innocence, he was tied to a tree and whipped."[132]
The other defendants received similarly brutal treatment. As Hughes went on to
state, "It is sufficient to say that in pertinent respects the [case] transcript reads
more like pages torn from some medieval account than a record made within
the confines of a modern civilization which aspires to an enlightened constitutional government."[133] Upon review of the case, the Justices unanimously
held that a defendant's coerced confession (in this instance, extracted by extreme
police violence) violates the Due Process Clause of the Fourteenth Amendment
and as such, cannot be entered as evidence.

Just as corporal punishment was an especially enduring practice in criminal
justice, so too did it persist in American education. While just over half of the
states now have laws prohibiting the use of corporal punishment in schools, the
march to that place was a slow one. The first state to ban corporal punishment
was New Jersey (1867).[134] More than a century passed before another state
would enact a similar ban. Massachusetts followed suit in 1971. The debate
surrounding the appropriateness of corporal punishment in schools came to a
head in 1977 with the United States Supreme Court's decision in *Ingraham v.
Wright*.[135] The case revolved around a student who in the course of being
paddled received injuries so great that hospitalization was required. Even in the
face of these injuries, the Court upheld the Constitutionality of corporal punishment as a means of discipline in schools.

In a closely related case, *Baker v. Owen*,[136] the Supreme Court ruled that
school officials had authority over parents in disciplinary issues. This case reaf-
firmed the constitutional authority of school officials to administer corporal

punishment despite parental objections. Taken together, these two cases firmly establish the constitutional authority of schools to administer corporal punishment. Even so, the dominant trend since the late 1970s has been away from its use in academic settings.

What one sees through the course of American history is a move from corporal punishment marked with fits and starts. Its gradual egress from the palette of disciplinary and punishment tools has been the product of judicially evolved policy, changing public tolerances, and greater awareness of excesses. This said, some prominent scholars have argued that corporal punishment, if applied in well-regulated and particular fashion, might still have an ethically valid place in the regulation of human behavior.[137]

Up until this point, the institution of corporal punishment has been discussed primarily as an element of European, North African, and Middle Eastern history. While space does not provide for an exhaustive historical account of corporal punishment in all cultures, any comprehensive historical review must also acknowledge the influence of other traditions, namely those from Russia and China. Formal regulation in these two societies is especially consequent given their vast and enduring influence.

CHINA

Incorporating elements of both Legalist and Confucian ideas about social order and governance, Chinese traditional law encompasses an enormous period of time beginning around the eleventh century BC and extending until the fall of the last Chinese emperor in 1911. As Meithe and Lu observe, Chinese society from the Shang Dynasty (1700–1027 BC) through the Zhou Dynasty (1027–771 BC) were "slave-based societies rooted in patriarchal and aristocratic orders."[138]

One of the earliest codified forms of corporal punishment in ancient China was castration. Under Emperor Shun in 2281 BC castration was approved as a punishment for certain crimes (i.e., adultery).[139] Ernst Faber suggests castration may have been sanctioned as early as 1100 BC. To support this, he notes the presence of eunuchs in courts of the Chow dynasty.[140] In a later work, Faber states that the "Five Punishments," of which castration is one, were adopted in 2282 BC. The other four were: branding on the face; cutting off the nose; cutting off the feet; and death.[141] Werner notes that under some circumstances, these punishments might be commuted in favor of banishment.[142]

As in most places, prevailing sentiments in China changed over the course of time. As John Head and Yanping Yang observe, by 167 BC castration was used not only as a primary punishment, but as an alternative to death sentences.[143] The Emperor Wen ushered in a wholesale reform of punishments by abolishing all mutilations. During the Han Dynasty, crimes that once would have garnered the amputation of a foot or the nose were supplanted by beatings and the wearing of leg irons.[144]

By AD 624 one sees a fuller integration of Confucian principles into traditional Chinese laws. This transformation is best exemplified by the wide promulgation of the Tang Code. The Tang Code contained more than 500 articles divided into twelve major sections.[145]

The Tang Code was an incredibly complex system of legal thought. It was based around two general concepts: fixing a specific penalty to a specific crime and modulation of the penalty based on the relational distance between offender and victim.[146] For relatives, this distance was measured by the kind and duration of mourning required to be observed for each degree of kinship. Relations outside the family were defined according to positions in a stratified social hierarchy. Government officials ranked higher than ordinary men. Ordinary men were, in turn, superior to servants. Under this rubric, a slave having committed a crime against his master would be punished more severely than if an ordinary person had committed the same crime. The relational distance/status "multiplier" worked the same way in the other direction. The same offense committed by the master against slave would result in a lower penalty than the same crime committed by a common person.

As above, penalties modulated along these two axes. The range of penalties generally included various flagellations, banishment, penal labor, banishment with penal labor, death by strangulation, or decapitation. Jacques Gernet argues that one of the purposes of the Tang Code was to move the constellation of punishments further away from the mutilations, brandings, and tattooing characteristic of previous eras as a means to match evolving social sensibilities.[147]

Throughout the remainder of the Chinese feudal period one sees a gradual refinement of sensibilities regarding punishment; but as in other parts of the world, old habits die hard. Not until that last gasp of the Qing Dynasty in the late nineteenth century do substantial punishment reforms manifest. Meithe and Lu coin a particularly apt phrase to describe China between the 1850s–1940s, "half feudal, half colony."[148] Plagued by decades of internal turmoil and besieged by external colonial interests, the grandeur of China-past was barely evident near the fall of the Qing government.

At the turn of the twentieth century profound changes took root in China. The year, 1905, saw the complete abolition of amputations as a punishment. Gone, too, were grizzly public spectacles: severed heads on public display, tattooing, mutilations were all banned. Frank Dikotter notes that corporal punishment was slowly supplanted by fines and with the enactment of the Penal Code of 1908, the only permissible punishments were fines, imprisonment, and the death penalty.[149] As in many other nations, legal prohibitions do not appear to have completely eliminated corporal punishment in practice.

RUSSIA

Where this history of corporal punishment has examined other lands since antiquity, the most profitable place to analyze punishment in Russia starts with that nation's feudal era. By extension, any understanding of punishment in feudal Russia must be grounded in a few facts about the social and economic order of the time.

Few nations have ever elevated a single implement of corporal punishment in the way that Russia has the knout. The knout is a heavy whip with many tendrils like a scourge. Often made of rawhide thongs attached to a long handle, the real violence of the knout was found in the wire or metal hooks often fastened to the ends of each lash. The knout along with the gulag are Russia's enduring shrines of torment.

Arcadius Kahan in his book, *The Plow, the Hammer, and the Knout: An Economic History of Eighteenth-Century Russia*, set the stage with a brief passage:

> The [book] title was not chosen for the vividness of its symbols, but because the symbols embody important characteristics of Russian society under conditions of serfdom. The plow stands for the incessant toil of the Russian serfs, the hammer for the new elements of non-agricultural labor, and the knout for the power wielded either by the serf-owners or by the Russian state—most of the time by both. These three set the rhythm for ... life ... The knout determined where, how fast and how deep the plow turned the soil, how hard the plowman had to grip the implement. The knout directed the hand of the smith, often determining whether the piece of iron ... would take the form of a gun barrel or a sickle. Moreover, sometimes the knout sometimes was swinging, hitting and pounding out of habit, for no good reason except inertia.[150]

Abby Schrader further elucidates this point with her observation that a combination of corporal punishment, physical mutilations, and Siberian exile functioned as a type of "penal complex" for late Muscovite and Imperial Russia. Taken together, these systems of punishment helped the wealthier classes establish social boundaries necessary to control the peasantry.[151] As history has shown, elements of this complex were retained well into the modern era.

Even in the face of this pervasive environment of lower class oppression, concerns about corporal punishment were not the sole province of serfdom. Beyond matters of keeping their human chattel well-regulated and subdued, the Russian nobility feared their own vulnerability to the lash. From the beginning of the eighteenth century, the nobility fought vigorously for legal exemption from corporal punishment. In 1754 under Catherine II, a draft code included a passage exempting nobles from corporal punishment and torture. In 1785, the *Charter to the Nobility* formally gave them protection, "Corporal punishment shall not extend to the well-born."[152] Interestingly, the law was subsequently repealed by Paul, and then restored by Alexander I. From this discontinuity of tsarist support, the nobility remained unconvinced of their security.[153]

Other records indicate that the nobles' fears were justified. Semen Sheshkovskii, the notorious head of Catherine's secret police, was a particularly fearsome figure in noble Russia. Sheshkovskii bore the rather ominous nickname, the "knout-flogger." Where his subordinates were given the task of dealing with commoners, Sheshkovskii's skills were reserved for a more genteel clientele. Reyfman quotes exiled Russian author and social critic Aleksandr Radishchev's reflection on Sheshkovskii, "Sheshkovskii . . . bragged that he knew the way to elicit a confession. Namely, he began by hitting the interrogated person under the jaw with a stick, so that his teeth would crack or even fall out . . . He used the knout with extraordinary skill, acquired by frequent practice."[154]

Whatever the nobility might have had just cause to fear, the peasantry suffered the lash with much more certainty. Hiroaki Kuromiya documents repeated public floggings to squelch or punish rioting workers in the coal-rich Donbas region during the 1890s, "The leaders . . . were arrested and subjected to public flogging . . . A military doctor decided . . . how many blows the workers could stand. Appearance was deceptive and some were carried out dead."[155] As Kuromiya observes, this form of public suppression was widely and openly practiced well into the first decades of the twentieth century. Even as the Russian revolution played out in the late teens, periodic anti-Bolshevik restorations also brought back corporal punishment. Miners, industrial workers, and even the rural peasantry were once again viscously beaten, "Striking colliers in Horlivka were . . . flogged to death. Women were flogged. . . . Peasants were flogged by German troops for having taken the lands and estates of former nobles."[156]

As indicated above, women were flogged during the restoration era of modern Russia. The matter of gender is an incredibly complex and uneven matter with regard to modalities of punishment. Schrader's seminal work on punishment in feudal Russia, *Languages of the Lash*, explores the paradoxical view of women as naturally obstreperous and women as a civilizing influence.[157] Muslim women in the 1830s were exempted from corporal punishment by "virtue" of being seen as less civilized. Two decades later, a prominent argument held that all women were biologically weaker and inherently maternal. Therefore, any advanced civilization would afford them due mercy. What results during the Great Reforms is a decision to privatize the corporal punishment of women by exempting them from the lash but not bread-and-water punishments.

Laura Engelstein argues that these apparent changes in attitude toward women contain the seeds not of mercy, but gender-based oppression. She contends that the Edict of 1863, establishing women's exemption from corporal punishment, "functioned, in fact, as a mark of the peasant male's improved standing . . . and reinforcing the wife's private status."[158] She goes on to say that Russian lawmakers, "chose to extend legal protection for women as a sign of cultural progress . . . Yet such attitudes may be said to mark the persistence of their attachment to the traditional social structure."[159] Moreover, Engelstein positions this dynamic not as a solely Russian phenomenon, but one across Europe, "Special treatment for women based on the peculiarities of their physical and, in particular, sexual constitution endorsed their civil subordination at the very moment when the weakening of formal status barriers challenged the legal subordination of lower-class men."[160]

Where the nascent Soviet society may have lurched between old and new punishment models, by mid-century, corporal punishment was fully banned. Where pre-revolutionary Russian law gave parents the right to use physical discipline at home to correct disobedient or recalcitrant children, the revolution ushered in a new era of family governance. In particular, laws were enacted that forbade corporal punishment of children and made it punishable as a criminal offense.

Solomon Teitelbaum characterizes this change as, "part and parcel of the untrammeled 'progressive education' popular in the early period of the Soviet regimes as well as of the general concept of Soviet law which considers any form of corporal punishment inadmissible."[161] One sees this reflected in Section 4 of the *Principles of Penal Legislation of the USSR*, published on October 31, 1924, "All measures of social defense must be fitting nor should they have as their purpose the infliction of physical suffering humiliation or indignity."[162] Here again, though, one sees an oft-repeated truth regarding the persistence of old ways. As Teitelbaum states, "But child-beating which like wife-beating, was wide-spread among the uneducated masses in Czarist Russia, could not be entirely eradicated. Soviet children however well know their 'inviolability' and avail themselves of it."[163]

MILITARY DISCIPLINE

No history of corporal punishment would be complete without some consideration of military disciplinary techniques. The detailed, consistent, and pervasive regulation of the individual is a cornerstone of military training. Military leaders have written about the discipline of troops since ancient times. Finding a suitable balance between rewards and punishments has been a central concern at least since the time of Sun Tzu (ca. sixth century BC).[164] Physical ordeals, both as a means of athletic conditioning and mental toughness, have made Roman Legionnaires and U. S. Marines. In addition to the calisthenics and marching incumbent upon military trainees, physical discipline has also meant corporal punishment. As in other spheres, this punishment was often harsh, painful, and merciless.

It is likely an artifact of the profession that physical discipline in the military has often been more austere than in the rest of society. This characteristic rigor appears ubiquitous across time and cultures. Corporal punishment as a means of military discipline dates at least to Greek and Roman antiquity in the West[165] and the Warring States period (fifth century BC) in China.[166]

Harry Ward writing about British military discipline in the middle eighteenth century describes a familiar social stratification of punishments. In particular, he notes that the average British recruit was "from the dregs of society" and whose enlistment was motivated by the promise of free-flowing liquor rations and escape from previous social or legal encumbrances. As a consequence of their troops' presumed indolent and shiftless ways, British commanders felt severe discipline was necessary.[167] Earle confirms this with a quote from a seventeenth century author, "A soldier should fear only God and Dishonor." Earle adds, "The British soldier fears only his officers."[168]

Zealous disciplinary control manifested in predictable ways. Floggings—even into the hundreds of stripes, running gauntlets, "riding" the wooden horse, the drunkard's cloak and, of course, death by hanging or firing squad were commonplace in the British army.[169] Even a young British colonel, George Washington, was a staunch advocate of stern military discipline. As he told one of his lieutenants, "We now have it in our power to enforce obedience ... The men being subject to death as in Military Law."[170]

Although arguably more metered, another founding father, John Adams, serving on the Continental Congress Naval Committee, drafted "Rules for Regulation of the Navy." Under these "Rules" naval commanders could inflict up to twelve lashes on enlisted personnel.[171] In 1797, the U.S. Congress endorsed these same rules for the navy of the newly independent nation. In 1799, Congress, under "Articles for Government of the Navy," authorized flogging for a number of offenses. This subsequent act, while perpetuating the use of corporal punishment, was motivated by a desire to prevent brutality. Between 1800 and 1850, the use of corporal punishment was expanded to include its use as a punishment in court martial proceedings. Under this subsequent "Act for the better government of the navy of the United States," enlisted men could be flogged up to ten times for "oppression, cruelty, fraud, profane swearing, drunkenness or any other scandalous conduct tending to the destruction of good morals."[172] In September 1850, Congress abolished flogging in the navy.

Paradoxically, sensibilities about the propriety of corporal punishment in the military were not universal throughout all British colonies. Lord William Bentinck, governor-general of India, abolished corporal punishment in the sepoy[173] regiments in 1835. As Peers states, "[This change] is a particularly illuminating example of the relationship between colonial priorities, contemporary assumptions about race and the imperatives of military discipline."[174] As Douglas Peers also observes, only in India and only among the sepoys did the British military ban corporal punishment before the middle of the nineteenth century.[175]

Even with the ban on corporal punishment against British soldiers, individuals native to the colonized nations of Africa who served British military commanders were subject to it until 1946. As a general construct, European violence against African subordinates was common well into the twentieth century. The logic used to rationalize vigorous physical punishment was steeped in a Eurocentric sense of superiority and express racism:

> Some who were initially repelled by the idea of beating ... reluctantly accepted that it was a necessary form of coercion. Along with the idea that child-like people needed to be schooled and disciplined with physical force, the stick or whip was convenient, instant and closely related with the offense. It was ... readily understood by Africans; coming from societies that inflicted brutal punishments on offenders, Africans clearly

recognized, and indeed expected, physical abuse as the reward for misdemeanors. And in any case, it was argued, they had an ability to bear pain, 'which the primitive African does not feel.'[176]

Here again, one sees corporal punishment used expressly as a tool of the powerful to viscerally assert dominion over a lower social class. That the class happened to be a colonized people in a foreign land hardly changes much.

The experience of Japanese soldiers and sailors in the twentieth century likewise harkened to military discipline of a bygone era. Corporal punishment, already practiced informally, was institutionalized as part of the squad regulations of 1908. Face slapping, for instance, was a routine part of Japanese military discipline and was designed as a mechanism to spur humility and unquestioning obedience. Hanama Tasaki describes a common scene:

> Five old soldiers went down the line without warning, slapping each soldier soundly on his cheek. Those that could not keep their posture of attention were slapped more than the others. The sergeant then demanded of each recruit why he thought he had been slapped. As each gave what he thought might be the answer, he was soundly slapped again. Finally, one recruit, when his turn came said he didn't know. "That is right!" The squad leader said. "When you are slapped don't give excuses. As His Majesty has been pleased to admonish in his Imperial Rescript, 'Uninfluenced by worldly thoughts and unhampered by politics, guard well your single destiny of patriotism.' Our sole duty is to be patriotic to the Emperor. You need only obey what you are told."[177]

Disciplinary techniques that emphasize the importance of unflinching loyalty and obedience are common and recurrent themes in the historic record of virtually all nations. Given that adherence to the chain-of-command is the backbone of military function, this is understandable.

While military hierarchies are expressly designed to reflect power differentials, the structure of penalties in the Russian military of the eighteenth and nineteenth centuries also reflected civilian class divisions. John Keep in his study of Russian officers notes, "As a wit once put it, Russian society of that time comprised but two classes, those who were beaten and those who beat others; officers belonged to the latter group."[178] Keep also points out an even more important, but perhaps subtler aspect of the difference, "[The] main advantage enjoyed by privileged individuals [i.e. officers] may well have been procedural, not penal, in so far as offenders had their cases adjudicated by the ruler or someone close to him/her—even if they were thereby exposed to the vagaries of the autocrat's temperament."[179] While the precise model varied across tsarist regimes, the basic idea that officers were afforded a different quality of judicial process appears to have remained consistent.

Of course, the Russian military was hardly alone in the fact that the composition of its officer corps mirrored basic social and economic inequalities of the larger society. According to one scholar, historic class distinctions had a very practical strategic application. Louis Puleo asserts that the codified distinction (and policy against fraternization) between officers and enlisted personnel can be traced to King Gustavus Adolphus of Sweden in 1621.[180] Owing to the military standards of the day, battles were fought in a series of choreographed close-ordered drills that required the foot soldier to march into enemy fire. As such, it was necessary for the soldier to fear his officers and the consequences of cowardice more than the enemy. In this respect, discipline under fire was maintained by fear.[181] This fear was instilled both by the threat of corporal punishment and prohibitions against fraternization between officers and enlisted personnel.

The putative bonding and automation of response as a consequence of severe physical discipline espoused by many military leaders is far from a dead tradition. In this context, the physical hazing that is often a part of military training can meet the definition of corporal punishment as outlined in this volume. This is to say, hazing in the context of military indoctrination is a form of ritualized physical pain or ordeal, the primary object of which is to bind the recipient or observers to the rules, norms, or customs of a larger social institution.

James Gillian observes that current U.S. military hazing (as part of ritualized indoctrination or promotion) reflects a complex set of pyscho-social values and assumptions about masculinity, "[It's] a form of initiating men into the standard expected male gender role in patriarchies, namely to become violence objects—people who are expected both to inflict violence and to become subjects of violence inflicted on them. People are willing to sacrifice their bodies in order to maintain the survival of an acceptable sense of their own masculine identity."[182]

Charles Moskos concurs, adding an interesting detail:

> To use sociological jargon, the latent function of hazing is that it differentiates and separates one from, and at the same time makes one feel superior to, whatever mainstream you're defining yourself against. Now my own specialty happens to be the military, and I think it's significant that there was little if any hazing in the armed forces in World War II. It seems like a post-Vietnam-era phenomenon, as the military got separated from the mainstream of society. Insecurity drives hazing. And there are sort of homosexual undertones to much of this male hazing; therefore, you have this sort of irony of going through a kind of homoerotic experience to prove you're not homosexual.[183]

As will be explored later, hazing rituals are hardly the exclusive purview of the world's military organizations. Physical ordeals are often the price for inclusion in many social institutions, particularly (but not exclusively) for men where the aspired-to group holds traditional male roles or the threat of physical danger as a primary value. As Lionel Tiger states, "[If] you look cross-culturally at how human organizations work, you see with exceptional frequency patterns in which young males are subjected to some kind of initiation, either more or less rigorous."[184]

TECHNIQUES OF PUNISHMENT

To this point, the discussion of corporal punishment has been limited to its place as an abstract technique of discipline, coercion, or penalty. Some specific methods have been mentioned, most often the convention of whipping, flogging, or beating. While impact and laceration are historically dominant ways to inflict corporal punishment, they are hardly the only methods to have been widely used. This section briefly outlines a number of corporal punishment techniques from history.

The global history of corporal punishment has been an exercise in finding the tolerances of the human body. The appliances employed to deliver corporal punishment have ranged from the simplicity of the human hand to dramatically complicated machines of terror. Bodies have been whipped. Limbs, digits, ears, noses, eyes, tongues, genitals, and other bodily parts have been amputated. The body has been electrically shocked. It has been pulled apart and compressed, broken and twisted. Its movements have been confined or restricted. It has been starved and drowned. It has been hung and impaled. It has been subjected to extremes of the elements. It has been burned, branded, tattooed, and otherwise marked. Isolation, rape, deprivation of light and air have likewise been used to achieve desired ends. In short, corporal punishment has often relied on a mixture of pain, humiliation, and fear.

Since the nineteenth century, a number of authors have compiled vast illustrated catalogs of punishment techniques.[185] Based on their number and popularity, it is clear that a parade of historical torture strikes a chord with the public. Beyond a prurient fascination with the gore, the variety of torture and punishment methods tell us something about the societies and people that produced them. Moreover, it begs the question as to why humans have gone to such lengths to innovate the delivery of suffering.

Michel Foucault states, "[By] the end of the nineteenth century, the gloomy festival of punishment was dying out. . . . Punishment had gradually ceased to be a spectacle. And whatever theatrical elements it still retained were now downgraded . . . it was as if the punishment was thought to equal, if not exceed, the savagery of the crime itself."[186]

As Foucault correctly asserts, punishment in the nineteenth century underwent a wholesale transformation. Although the reasons for this transformation are the subject of debate—one that will be assailed later in this volume—the fact remains that punishment changed. It was largely removed from the public square, the sharp slide of the guillotine being replaced by the dull thud of a locked cell door. Even as the more spectacular punishments dropped into the recesses of history, their existence bears some reflection.

Shame and humiliation are central elements of meaningful punishment, but elicitation of these feelings requires something no external authority can implant. As the noted Harvard philosopher William Ernest Hocking observed, "Only the man who has enough good in him to feel the justice of the penalty can be punished; the others can only be hurt."[187] Much of history amply documents that simply fomenting pain may have played the part of justification.

As above, the history of corporal punishment is the history of punishment theater. The devices used to inflict pain reflect a vast tradition of pain innovation. Their myriad forms suggest it is not enough to merely engender physical pain but fear as well.

The act of striking is perhaps the oldest form of physical punishment. While one could likely use the empty hand to great effect, cultures since the dawn of humanity have used whips, rods, birches, switches, flails, and their kin to magnify the pain and injury. Whipping is so important to the traditions of punishment, Scott devotes no less than seven entire chapters to the topic in his *History of Corporal Punishment*.[188] Whips are most commonly a long braided length of animal hide. The Russian's great innovation in this regard was the knout, a long, wooden-handled whip made of many rawhide tendrils, the tips of which might be adorned with hooks or bits of wire.

In 1530, King Henry VIII passed the *Whipping Act*. This legislation directed that vagrants should be carried to the town square, "and there, tied to the end of a cart naked, and beaten with whips throughout such market town . . . till the body be bloody by such whipping."[189]

Fast forwarding four centuries to the turn of the twentieth century, the practice of public whipping had been in decline for scores of years. An interesting exception to this is the U.S. state of Delaware. There, the practice was abandoned just prior to World War I, but reinstated in 1932 in Sussex County.[190] On February 13 of that year, five prisoners who had each received a sentence of five lashes were lead to the public square where a whipping post had been erected. The punishment was administered, thus issuing in a renewed use of the practice that would last two more decades.[191] The last public whipping in the U.S. took place in Delaware in 1952. That state finally removed whipping as a possible penalty in 1972.[192]

Although whipping is arguably the most ubiquitous punishment throughout history, there are many others that hold a notable place. Two such punishments were the stocks and the pillory. These devices are quite similar. Both were used to restrain an individual, often in the public square by means of holding parts of the body between to pieces of wood in which holes had been carved. The primary difference between them is that pillories held the hands and head, whereas stocks clamped around the ankles. In a pillory, the offender would be standing, often slightly bent, with their head and hands poking through holes just large enough to accommodate them. In the stocks, one was typically seated with one's feet out in front of them, again, held by holes just large enough to permit it. As an added torment for those sent to the pillory, one or both ears would often be nailed back to the pillory frame. Consequent to its nailing, the ear(s) might be ripped as the subject was loosed from the device.

William Andrews recounts a nineteenth-century verse about a criminal in Ellesmere (UK) where the stocks, pillory and whipping post were all combined in one device:

A tailor here, confined in stocks,
A prison made of wood—a—
Weeping and wailing to get out,
But couldna' for his blood—a—
The pillory, it hung o'er his head,
The whipping-post so near—a—
A crowd of people round about,
Did at William laugh and jeer—a—[193]

Andrews further observes that this kind of combined device was common. This construction was practical as individuals were often subject to multiple kinds of punishment.[194]

Corporal punishments sometimes reflected the nature of the offense. A particularly good example of this is the brank. The brank was known by many names: scold's bridle; gossip's bridle; dame's bridle; scold's helm. While records show myriad variations, the basic theme common to all is a large helmet encasing all of the head. Usually comprised of ribs or slats of iron, branks also contained a spiked or flat tongue that was inserted into the mouth for the purpose of causing pain when the offender spoke or preventing speech all together.[195] As one might infer, branks were commonly used as punishments against women deemed to have used impertinent, gossipy, or otherwise unacceptable speech. Earle tells of a brank from Walton-on-Thames dated 1632 with the following inscription, "Chester presents Walton with a bridle to cure women's tongues who talk too idle."[196]

Another common punishment that appears to have largely focused on female offenders was the Ducking Stool. This apparatus was a large cantilevered arm at the end of which a seat was hung.[197] The device would be positioned at the edge of a water body. The person to be punished would be placed in the seat and the arm lowered such that they were dipped, then held underwater. As with whipping, the sentences typically prescribed the number of times the offender was to be lowered into the water. As with the above punishments, this too was the subject of popular verse, "She in the ducking stool should take her seat. Dressed like herself in the great chair of state."[198]

The purpose of the Ducking Stool was generally twofold. In the first instance, water was thought to have a cleansing effect—on the soul and cooling influence on temperament. Secondarily, the sensation of being drowned reminded scolds (i.e., gossipy women) to literally keep their mouths shut.

There were also a great variety of punishments designed to stretch, impale, or induce a penetrating discomfort. The most famous of these, the rack, has come to occupy a kind of pop culture status. As Erik Rühling states, "No fictional, romanticized dungeon was ever complete without a sturdy rack deployed in the center of the room."[199] It's theatrical value notwithstanding, use of the rack dates back at least to ancient Greece. The rack was a long table on which an individual would be placed lying down. Their hands and feet were attached to ropes or chains that were tightened by use of a crank. The person operating the device would progressively tighten the restraints until such time as desired compliance was gained or the joints were pulled out of socket. As an interesting aside, Rühling attributes the colloquialism of harsh interrogations, "the third degree," as having originated in racking. As he observes, racking progressed through three progressively painful and injurious degrees in accordance with the dictates of the interrogation.

This in itself suggests a point that will be elaborated later: modern notions of discrete interrogation, trial, and punishment are just that—modern. Accordingly, the reader should keep in mind that many of the techniques described in this volume were not reserved solely for the punishment of individuals who had been convicted of a crime. Rather, they were often used to elicit evidence of guilt.

Punishments known variously as the wooden horse, the mule, or the Spanish Donkey were somewhat similar to racking. While describing distinct mechanisms, the basic idea common to all is that the person being punished would be placed astride a wooden beam or wedge. Their feet would then be heavily weighted or strapped down. Depending on construction, the principle intent of the device was to cause intense pain in the region of the perineum, genitals, or anus.

Rühling notes a variation on this theme called a Judas cradle.[200] Instead of a beam or wedge, a large pointed wooden pyramid would be centered beneath the subject. The subject having been bound and suspended over the sharp point would then be variously raised and lowered to similar affect as described above.

Although the preceding list is far from a complete catalog of common punishments, it serves as evidence that great thought has been given to the infliction of very particular pains. Where the whip and birch have the quality of immediate and terrible injury, many of the other devices evoke more primal fears. Drowning, confinement, rending of limb, and impaling of the genitals, each tap a different locus of fear, shame, and pain. So, too, do they say something about the cultures that produced them? Each of them asks us to consider what subtle metaphor of pain each technique of punishment implies.

_____

Religion and Corporal Punishment

> Men never do evil so completely and cheerfully as when they do it from religious conviction.
>
> —Blaise Pascal

ALTHOUGH THE ABOVE quotation of Pascal represents an arguably jaundiced view of religion in society, it is undeniable that religious organizations the world over have used physical pain to accomplish many goals. Accordingly, any examination of global corporal punishment practices would be incomplete without an exploration of how these institutions have employed corporal punishments to solidify the commitment of the devoted and assert spiritual, political, economic, or social control over others.

During the last decade, the intersection of religion and corporal punishment has been given broad coverage by Western media. Rather than providing an objective presentation of historical and cultural contexts, media coverage has tended toward the gruesome and spectacular. This can be seen particularly in the coverage of Islamic *Shari'a* courts and Catholic penance rituals as performed by members of *Opus Dei*.

Although these topics are fit for discussion, they push scholarly examination out of its most profitable center. So too, do proclamations by scholars such as George Scott who contend, "The history of religions is the history of man's cruelty to, persecution of and intolerance to man . . . the religious crusader, fired with proselytizing passion becomes a potential danger to the liberty of people."[1]

Similarly, the novelist, Somerset Maugham once observed, "What mean and cruel things men can do for the love of God."[2] Although such positions may reflect an undeniable historical grimness in certain theocratic methods, a more neutral telling likely advances the cause of objective understanding with greater authority.

To this end, corporal punishment is examined here as an aspect of religious practice and as an element of public policy in those societies strongly influenced or regulated by dominant religious traditions. As will be discussed, religion and corporal punishment have a conjoined history that is both ancient and enduring. Corporal punishment emanating out of religious directive manifests in many ways. It is at once a ritualized confirmation of belief, a bureaucratic tool, and a mechanism of social reproach.

ANTIQUITY

Numerous authors confirm that corporal punishment has been an important part of religious traditions since antiquity.[3] In what may come as a curiosity to the modern reader, self-infliction of physical punishment has an exceptionally deep religious provenance. Self-inflicted punishment, frequently flagellation, may take on many meanings, but most often it is done as a sign of intense devotion or veneration.

Although some may argue that self-inflicted pain or ordeal as part of religious practice does not meet the implied criteria for punishment, recalling the definition of corporal punishment as used in this volume, one sees a good correspondence between the two. To again recount the working definition, corporal punishment is the infliction of ritualized physical pain or ordeal, the primary object of which is to bind the recipient or observers to the rules, norms, or customs of a larger social institution. In this construction, one needs three things: a source of social authority representing collective values (a rule giver); an agent of that authority (someone who visibly reinforces and/or follow the rules); and a subject (sic. person) to receive the reinforcement.

Given that one of the goals of punishment is to instill greater drive for self-regulation, the agent of the authority and the subject of reinforcement could be the same individual. For instance, if the source of authority is taken to be God, the agent of the authority may be a penitent believer. In turn, the penitent believer, seeking to heed what they take to be God's will, inflicts physical punishment on themselves as a sign of their contrition.[4]

This idea is taken up both in Michel Foucault's theological analogy of surveillance (i.e., individuals self-regulate their own behavior because they are aware of an invisible and unverifiable power . . . *God is watching me, therefore, I must behave*)[5] and Friedrich Nietzsche's observation that individuals must struggle against themselves to act according to "truth."[6] As such, there is no express requirement that the punishment be administered by a third party.

An individual guided by what they believe to be the dictates of the larger social institution (i.e., a church or the will of God) could then punish themselves as a sign of their accession to the authority's commands. Global history is rich with instances and institutions predicated on acts of penitence, self-denial, and self-punishment in service to religious beliefs—beliefs that often mirror or facilitate the goals of state.

As early as the fifth century BC, Herodotus describes a sacrifice to the goddess Isis involving self-imposed corporal punishment, "After the previous ceremony of prayers, they sacrifice an ox; they then strip off the skin and take out the intestines . . . the rest of the body is stuffed with fine bread, honey raisins, figs, frankincense and various aromatics; after this process they burn it . . . whilst the victim is burning, the spectators flagellate themselves."[7]

In the first century AD, Plutarch details the Lupercalia festival. Although modern scholars[8] debate the origins, meaning, and content of the festival, Plutarch's account details a pair of naked men, faces smeared with blood, running through the town, striking those in the crowd who had assembled to watch.[9] Readers of Shakespeare may also remember Marc Antony's mention of the Lupercalia in act 3, scene 2 of *Julius Caesar*, "You all did see that on the Lupercal I thrice presented him a kingly crown, which he did thrice refuse."

Plutarch likewise recounts the Festival of Flagellations in Lacedaemon (Sparta). According to a similar telling by Cicero, young boys were brought before the alter of Diana for sustained and brutal whippings. Even though the central intent of the whippings was a nonlethal, ritualized punishment, they frequently brought death.[10] As such, we see that corporal punishment, whether self-inflicted or administered by a third party, was a relatively common feature of religious festivals in the ancient Mediterranean world.

Religious rites such as those described above set the stage for more contemporary practices in both Christian and Islamic traditions. In particular, both faiths contain a strong link between corporeal and spiritual discipline. Whether manifesting as outright formal punishment imposed by a theocratic bureaucracy or simple individualized and internalized regulation of habit, both systems of belief contain strictures for the physical regulation of their followers. Modern practices in both traditions can be better understood through a brief history of each.

CHRISTIANITY

Submission to physical suffering is arguably a cornerstone of Christian belief, if not directly taking on the suffering oneself, at least in the acknowledgment of the torment endured by Jesus. The willful experience of physical ordeal or the acquiescence thereto is modeled by Jesus at several points in the New Testament. One sees this especially in three parallel passages: Matthew 26:36–46; Mark 14:32–42; and Luke 22:39–46.

These accounts each tell the story of Jesus's prayer in the gardens of Gethsemane at the Mount of Olives. Jesus, overwhelmed, sorrowful, and cognizant of his impending crucifixion, prays to God, "My Father, if it is possible, may this cup [of suffering][11] be taken from me. Yet not as I will, but as you will" (Matthew 26:39). In this he prays, not necessarily to be relieved of the suffering, but for himself and his disciples to remain steadfast through the coming pains, if the pains must be endured.

With this as background, it would be difficult, if not impossible to overstate the influence of Christianity on secular government in early Europe. As Norman Tanner observes, "Christianity took over many of the Roman empire's procedures of religious inquiry when it emerged as the official religion of the empire in the early 4th century onwards . . . uniformity of religion, including inquiry and coercion were features . . . of most communities that became predominantly Christian."[12]

Edwin Hofstetter concurs, "Christianity has contributed to theories of human rights, due process and the impartial administration of justice."[13] Even so, as Hofstetter acknowledges, Christian influences over matters of crime and punishment have not always been consistent with modern sensibilities.

Perhaps the best example of this can be found in the early European practice of trial by ordeal. Prior to its abolition by Pope Innocent II in the thirteenth century, the church often presided over a type of judicial hearing where the accused were subjected to painful ritualized exculpatory tests. The purpose of these ordeals was to construct a test to reveal guilt or innocence through the invocation of God's judgment.

The process of discerning *iudicium Dei* (the judgment of God) involved the submission of an accused person to often injurious, crippling, or lethal physical "ordeals." Judgment was derived as a product of the accused party's condition post-ordeal. If one successfully endured the ordeal, it was a sign of innocence. Ironically, these rituals regularly resulted in the death of the accused, in which case, it was thought that their reward would be eternal salvation. Contrarily, death might also be a sign of guilt. As such, the system appears vulnerable to "interpretation" of results. Peter Leeson disagrees. He argues the system of ordeals, "accurately assigned accused criminals' guilt and innocence."[14]

Medieval ordeals often took myriad theatrical and absurd forms. Common ordeals involved swallowing poison, pulling an object from boiling oil, walking bare-footed over burning coals, or being submerged while holding a heavy weight. The accused invariably sustained some injury; and indeed their ability (or inability) to overcome said injury was taken as a *prima facie* indication of their guilt or innocence. It also bears noting that ordeals existed as a kind of judicial option, often resorted to if no other methods of fact finding bore fruit.

Corollary to these ordeals, the accused might be subjected to trial by battle (e.g., ordeal by combat). This practice was introduced to England by the Normans. Unlike other ordeals, trial by combat was typically reserved for noblemen suspected of crimes. In most scenarios the accused would have the option to either fight their accuser directly or pay a champion to battle on his behalf. Whoever emerged victoriously from the melee was declared to be correct, innocent, and so on. Again, this stemmed from the belief that the result of the ordeal was a reflection of God's judgment. As in the case of trial by ordeal, the defeated combatant was often dead by the end of the fight.

Soon after Innocent II's abolition of ordeals, another papal decree, by Pope Gregory IX in 1231, set events in motion that would culminate in the Spanish Inquisition. In 1252, Pope Innocent IV authorized the use of torture to elicit confession and information from subjects of inquiry. As Tanner states, "Penalties ranged from mild penances to imprisonment, scourgings and the ultimate sanction [burning at the stake] . . . usually reserved for obstinate or repeat offenders."[15] Tanner also makes the point that the church and secular officials frequently worked in close cooperation as their aims were often well aligned. The Inquisition as a formal enterprise survived the Reformation and was consolidated under centralized Roman authority by Paul III in 1542. The last vestiges of the Spanish Inquisition were formally abolished in 1834.

Although certainly less spectacular than the legendary exploits of fifteenth-century Inquisitor General of Spain, Tomas de Torquemada, another manifestation of corporal punishment was perhaps more pervasive in medieval Christendom. As Scott reports, acts of self-flagellation became commonplace in convents and monasteries of the time, "[I]n many cases the priests genuinely believed that self-punishment, being a form of sacrifice, would propitiate the god they worshiped."[16] Scott goes on to substantiate that both men and women engaged in the practice, "The fair sex, too, adopted flagellation as a means of securing absolution. Maria Magdalena, a Carmelite nun, flogged herself nearly every day as well as submitting to flagellation by others."[17]

Some modern Catholics who are also members of a lay organization, Opus Dei, practice physical self-punishments as part of their regular devotion. Opus Dei, founded in Spain in 1928 by Josemaria Escriva de Balaguer, espouses what they term, "corporal mortification." As the *1982 Statutes of Opus Dei* state:

> This [practice] rests upon the faithful and perpetual sense of humility, external and instrinsic, not only individual but also collective . . . on the familiar and noble plan of activity . . . on work, self-denial, sobriety, acts of sacrifice and on performing established exercises of corporal mortification every day and week, according to each one's age and condition.[18]

The leaders of Opus Dei quickly dispute popular cinematic representations of their rituals, such as those in the 2005 film, *The DaVinci Code*. They assert that the film's gory scenes misrepresent the organization's prescribed observances, "*The DaVinci Code*'s bloody depictions of mortification are grotesque exaggerations that have nothing to do with reality . . . the movie makers were looking for shock value . . . In reality . . . There is no blood, no injury, nothing to harm a person's health, nothing traumatic. If it caused any harm, the Church would not allow it."[19]

Perhaps the most curious manifestation of Christian church-sanctioned flagellation is described by Scott. The act, termed "grave whipping," was a ritual to restore excommunicated individuals to the good graces of the church, "When it was resolved that the dead party should be restored to the communion of the saints, it was ordered that the body should not be disentombed, but that the graves shall be whipped, and while the priest whips the grave, he shall say, 'by the authority which I have received I free thee from the bond of excommunication . . . ' "[20] Although Scott cites a nineteenth-century source for the practice, its broad use or authenticity is not apparent in the literature. With such weak historical provenance, such claims must be accepted with considerable caution.

Perhaps paradoxically, a very small number of modern American Protestants in the Pentecostal tradition also practice strident corporal mortification rituals. Adherents to the teaching of George Wesley Hensley, a charismatic early twentieth-century clergyman, use ritualized physical danger to express their faith. This typically manifests in the handling of venomous snakes or fire and drinking poison.

These practices owe to two passages in the New Testament: "And these signs shall follow them that believe: In my name shall they cast out devils; they shall speak with new tongues. They shall take up serpents; and if they drink any deadly thing, it shall not hurt them; they shall lay hands on the sick, and they shall recover" (Mark 16:17–18); and "Behold, I give unto you power to tread on serpents and scorpions, and over all the power of the enemy: and nothing shall by any means hurt you" (Luke 10:19).

Because a number of people in these "holiness" churches have been severely injured or killed as a result of these practices, several states enacted bans on snake handling beginning in the 1940s.[21] More recently, snake handlers have faced legal problems related to child custody.[22] These child custody cases are representative of a larger body of related cases in which church members defend their position as one of religious freedom, while opponents tend to focus on the dangers.

Dialectics of this sort are not exclusive to Christian corporal mortification rituals. Just as there are many historical as well as modern variants of Christian belief and practice, so too are there myriad Islamic traditions. Perhaps nowhere is this more evident than in application of Shari'a laws.

ISLAM

To many Western readers, Islamic beliefs and practices are an alien subject. In the wake of fundamentalist terrorism and resultant wars, the long history of this religious tradition can become obscured or reduced to exaggerated media stereotypes. Because so much of the present media discussion (at least in the Western world) tends toward dramatic and unrepresentative violence, many readers may find an extended explanation of Islamic justice useful in deepening their appreciation for the cultures in which it is the dominant religious force. Furthermore, because the basic precepts and form of Islamic justice are likely alien to many Western readers, a considerable exposition is necessary to properly understand how Islam often supports the use of corporal punishment.

Early Islam derives much of its character from the region and people that gave rise to it. The Arabian peninsula, although well placed as a locus of East-West trade, had few recognized natural advantages before the development of the petroleum industry. In fact, the expansive desert interior of the peninsula was commonly known as the Rub'al Khali', which literally translates as the "Empty Quarter."[23]

Throughout most of human history, residents of this region were nomadic tribes and clans who moved in regular circuits.[24] As Terrence Miethe and Hong Lu describe, dispute resolution and conflict conformed to certain persistent regional sensibilities, "Retaliation in the form of blood feuds within and between tribes was the primary response to personal injury. However, because of traditional notions of collective responsibility, feuds persisted over time as perpetual retaliatory acts against offended parties on both sides of the dispute."[25]

Multiple sources confirm the importance of Mecca as an early center of trade and worship.[26] The city of Mecca is situated in a rocky valley with few agricultural resources. Even so, in the centuries immediately preceding the promulgation of Islam, it developed into a place of great prosperity. Its success owed to two principal influences. Mecca was a large trading post on the caravan route from the Indian Ocean to the Mediterranean as well as being a nexus for Byzantine and Persian trade. Prior to Muhammad's birth in AD 570, Mecca was already well established as a center of worship for the pagan religious traditions common among the nomads of the region.

Muhammad was born into a merchant family of the Quraysh tribe in Mecca. Although his family was prosperous and influential, Muhammad's father died before he was born, followed by his mother's death when he was only six years old. As a consequence of his parents' death, he was entrusted to the care of a Bedouin nurse. Muhammad spent much of his youth among nomads, accompanying the caravans on Arabian trade routes. By age twenty-five Muhammad had amassed riches and acquired considerable status, primarily through his marriage to the widow of a wealthy merchant.[27]

According to tradition, the archangel Gabriel appeared to Muhammad on Mount Hira. Muhammad described how a luminous being grasped him by the throat and commanded him to repeat the words of God. From about AD 613 Muhammad began preaching in Mecca.

Despite Mecca's centrality as a site of religious worship, adherents to the indigenous pagan traditions did not immediately embrace all of Muhammad's teachings. In fact, he met with increasing hostility from the traders and merchants of Mecca. Much of this owes to his revelation that there is but one God. This assertion contradicted the dominant polytheistic culture of worship (and perhaps more importantly, the related commerce) that emanated from pilgrimages to the Ka'aba, a large cubic structure in the center of Mecca. The Ka'aba, now the most sacred structure in all of Islam, was at that time the place where the devout came to worship a profusion of pagan religious idols. The ire focused against Muhammad came to a head in AD 622, when a plot to assassinate him was discovered. In response, Muhammad fled with his followers to the town of Medina.[28]

Muhammad's escape to Medina represented a watershed moment in the global expansion of Islam. Muhammad's teachings found much greater acceptance in Medina than they had in Mecca. Similarly, Muhammad's reputation as a mediator between rival factions elevated his public status. As an outgrowth of his skillful arbitration, Muhammad's instruction found purchase with a growing body of followers. Meithe and Lu describe the transition among clans as one where, "Muhammad's teaching ... deeds and faith replaced blood as a social bond."[29] According to An-na'im[30] the Medina period was especially consequent in world Islamic history as the *Qur'an* (the principal Muslim holy book) and the *Sunnah* (a collection of Muhammad's teachings and traditions)[31] became increasingly used to establish new social, political, and legal prescriptions for early Muslims.

Meithe and Lu contend the Medina period is also important, as it is there where one sees the initial patterning for a Muslim theocratic state.[32] Matthew Lippman, Sean McConville, and Mordechai Yerushalmi similarly suggest that Medina is where political authority, previously the sole purview of tribal leaders, is first subordinated to the revealed wisdom of Allah through his Prophet, Muhammad.[33] As Meithe and Lu state, "The consolidation of the religious and political authority provided a unified front for the purposes of social control and regulating all aspects of the human condition."[34] Within a decade, Muhammad's teachings had spread sufficiently throughout Arabia that he and his followers marched back into Mecca unopposed. By the time of his death in AD 632, the majority of the Arabian peninsula had been converted to Islam.

The period from Muhammad's death to the twentieth century was a time of great, but often uneasy, expansion of Islam. Muhammad's immediate successors waged a campaign of ambitious territorial expansion. By the closing days of the Umayyad period in AD 750, the Muslim empire covered the majority of the Middle East including the area of modern Iran, Iraq, Palestine, Syria, Egypt, and Turkey. Muslim conquests stretched from India in the east to Spain in the west. Despite these successes, Muslim leaders faced the problem encountered by all great conquerors: Conquest may come easily, but continued rule often proves challenging. Because many of the conquered societies were just as advanced technologically and as politically and culturally complex as the Muslims, a very particular response was required to assert Islamic hegemony.

The systematic Muslim response to the challenge of ruling a diverse empire became known as the process of "Islamization." As Meithe and Lu observe, "[D]isperate groups became a coherent and integrated Islamic 'whole' through the adoption and adaption of pre-Islamic norms and institutions of both Arab and non-Arab segments of the Muslim population."[35] Islamization provided a unified system of cultural values through which formal social controls and expectations could be communicated. A central element of this process was the effective and thorough dissemination of religious prescriptions for correct (i.e., Islamic) living.

As above, the basis of Islamic beliefs derives from the teachings of the Prophet Mohammad, who Muslims regard as the messenger of Allah (God). The five central tenets or "Five Pillars of Islam" are: Faith (i.e., there is no God save for Allah); Prayer; Giving of alms to the poor; Fasting; and Pilgrimage.[36] In turn, the basis for formal social regulation in Islamic societies is known as Shari'a. Often referred to as Shari'a law, the literal translation of the term is "the path to follow." Shari'a provides a rubric for dealing with those who neglect their duties, abandon their faith or violate community laws.[37] That said, local understandings of Shari'a are influenced by sectarian, regional and ethnic traditions or custom.

Paradoxically, even given the noted variation, Shari'a is viewed by many Westerners as being "relatively inflexible to changing social conditions" and "far more inclusive of all aspects of social and economic life of the individual."[38] Be that as it may, Shari'a provides directives for regulation of virtually every sphere of public and private life. In this respect, it shares much with Christianity and indeed many other global religious traditions.

Shari'a is derived from a number of sources. The two primary sources are the Qur'an and the Sunnah. Approximately 200 of the 6,000 verses in the Qur'an deal specifically with legal matters. These two sources were the sole authority for Islamic law during the early period of Islamic practice. As the religion expanded and developed, other sources have been included to shape and inform Shari'a.

In the fourteen-hundred years since Muhammad's death, Islamic law has adapted to resolve perceived conflicts between the Qur'an and Sunnah. In specific, these conflicts have been addressed by bringing additional sources into the canon. According to Lippman, McConville, and Yerushalmi, these include the *hadith* (a collection of Muhammad's sayings), *ijma* (literally "to determine" or "consensus"), *oiyas* ("analogies"), *ijtihad* ("independent judgments), *istislah* ("public good"), ravayat (sayings of the Imams), and *urf* (customs and usage).[39]

Of these, the *ijma* has been particularly important in the development of Islamic law. As Amad Hasan states, "According to the orthodox view, *Ijma* is the unanimous agreement of the community or of the scholars."[40] Hasan further observes, "[*Ijma*] played a vital role in the integration of the Muslim community. In its early phase it manifested itself as a general average opinion, a common feeling of the community, and as a binding force of the body of law against unsuccessful and stray opinions. In the classical period it developed with its complex theory and ramifications. It became a decisive authority in religious affairs. All religious doctrines were standardized through *Ijma*."[41]

Islamic scholars draw an important distinction between *ijma* and other holy documents. As Mohammad Kamali states, "It must be noted . . . 'that unlike the *Qur'an* and *Sunnah*, ijma does not directly partake of divine revelation. As a doctrine and proof of *Shari'a*, ijma is basically a rational proof. The theory of *ijma* is also clear on the point that it is a binding proof."[42] Kamali also speaks to the centrality *ijma* has in providing both an infallible and historically informed judgment:

> Only *Ijma* can put an end to doubt, and when it throws its weight behind a ruling, this becomes decisive and infallible. *Ijma* has primarily been regarded as the instrument of conservatism and of preserving the heritage of the past. . . . *Ijma* enhances the authority of rules that are of speculative origin. Speculative rules do not carry a binding force, but once an *Ijma* is held in their favor, they become definitive and binding.[43]

As such, one sees that Shari'a is derived from a number of interwoven sources. Even so, not all sects (e.g., the Shia) accord the same weight to the authority of consensus.

Islam, like many other world religions, has faced the specter of social change at odds with its teachings. As Lippman, McConville, and Yerushalmi indicate, inclusion of additional sources has helped Islamic legal systems cope.[44] Such inclusions often take the form of heeding local customs, assessments of public interests and jurists' desires to achieve equitable results using nontraditional rules, as well as the use of secular, non-Shari'a courts.

An important set of points made by M. M. J. Nader and echoed by Meithe and Lu regards a number of consistent Shari'a features, found across most Islamic social contexts.[45] As they state, the basic elements of Shari'a that are commonly distributed irrespective of culture include:

- The idea that Shari'a is not given by a ruler, but has been revealed by Allah.
- Shari'a has been amplified by Muslim scholars and jurists across time.
- It is valid regardless of state recognition.
- The fundamental principles originate, not in culture, but only in the divine revelation of Allah.
- It is comprehensive and pervades all the judgments and decisions of life, law and society.
- Shari'a should not be construed as a rule of things that "should be," rather it reflects divine truths that simply "are."

With this brief orientation to the basic principles of Islam and Shari'a, a sufficient background is established to discuss their spread and influence in history. As stated above, since the seventh century, Islam has spread across the Middle East, Northern Africa, Central Asia, and into most nations around the world. Globally, there are approximately sixty nations in which Islam is the dominant or majority religion. According to the U.S. Central Intelligence Agency, there are over 1.2 billion Muslims in the world today.

ISLAMIC PUNISHMENT

Although predominantly Christian societies have included corporal punishment in their repertoire of formal sanctions (and to a lesser degree as a demonstrative instrument of personal conviction or faith), it may be argued that predominantly Islamic societies have also done so, but in a qualitatively different way. Whereas in many predominantly Christian societies religious values may be held up as an abstract basis for formal justice or governmental process, in predominantly Islamic societies, notions of justice and process are wholly inseparable (and directly emanate) from religious prescription. Even in societies with a nominally secular government, the role and extent of government are strongly dictated by religious belief. Accordingly, any discussion of corporal punishment as an aspect of Islamic belief necessarily flows into a discussion of governance. To fully understand how this manifests, a brief explication of Islamic legal philosophy and practice is required.

By way of background, it is important to recognize that Islam, like Christendom, is composed of sects, each with unique and particular beliefs. The primary distinction in Islam is that of *Sunni* and *Shi'a* Muslims. The split between these two sects dates back to the death of Muhammad over the question of who was his rightful successor. The larger of the competing groups, antecedents of the modern Sunnis, chose Abu Bakr, a close companion of Muhammad, as the caliph (leader). His ascension was accepted by a majority of the community who viewed the succession in terms that were more political than spiritual. A smaller rival group, the forerunners of modern Shi'a Muslims, believed Muhammad's son-in-law and cousin, Ali, should be caliph. Their claim rested on the contention that Muhammad had appointed Ali as the rightful heir to his legacy, in both political and spiritual terms. Ultimately, Abu Bakr was appointed first caliph.

Although this explanation does not explore the numerous other distinctions between the sects, it sets up that the world community of Islam contains variation in belief and practice. Sunni Muslims make up the majority (85%) of modern Islamic followers. Even so, Shi'a Muslims comprise the majority in modern Iran, Yemen, Azerbaijan, Bahrain and Iraq. Large Shi'a communities can also be found in Syria and Lebanon.[46]

The legal traditions of Islam are even more diverse. Between the seventh and nineteenth centuries, as many as nineteen separate schools of Islamic law existed. Of these, four remain today. The Sunni legal schools are the Hanaji (predominant in the Middle East), the Maliki (North and Western Africa), the Shafi'i (Indonesia and Malaysia), and the Hanabali, a minority sect in Saudi Arabia dating from the Wahhabi reform movement during the nineteenth century.[47] The Shi'a also represent their own distinct legal tradition within Islam. A key difference with important legal ramifications is that Shi'a differ from Sunni with regard to their beliefs about the infallibility of the transmission of the Sunnah.[48]

To understand how Islamic societies assign punishment to offenders, one must examine the five primary types of crime as delineated by Shari'a. The first of these are the hudud offenses. The term "hudud," or "hadd" in the singular, translates to "limit" or "restriction." These crimes are "limited" in the sense that there exist fixed punishments for them. Hudud offenses are seen as acts against God and are dealt with through state-sponsored prosecution. Citing the Qur'an 24:2, Muslims believe that the appropriate punishments for hudud offenses are decreed by God. As Meithe and Lu observe, "They are absolute, universal, non-negotiable and unpardonable."[49] Even so, the evidentiary proof required for a penalty under hadd is an arguably moderating force. For instance, a judge can only impose the hadd punishment when a person confesses to the crime or if there are a sufficient number of witnesses to the crime. The usual number of witnesses is two, but in the case of adultery, four witnesses are required. In the event that the evidentiary standard cannot be met sufficient to merit the pre-scribed hadd punishment, a given offense may be punished as a ta'zir (a lesser category of offense to be discussed in a following section).

The Qur'an specifies a particular penalty for five hudud offenses (when sub-stantiated by certain evidentiary standards). The first of these is consensual extra-marital intercourse (sic. fornication or adultery). According to the Qur'an (Chapter 24), the penalty for this crime is death by stoning if the offender is mar-ried; or one hundred lashes if the offender is unmarried. The Maliki also impose a penalty of a year imprisonment or exile for unmarried male offenders.[50]

Theft is the second hadd offense. A qualification for this offense is that the items stolen must be of a certain minimum value, which appears to vary across cultures. Another category of excepted items are those for idle amusement (e.g., musical instruments, perishable foods). Theft of items meeting the requisite hadd criteria bring different penalties depending on one's criminal history (Qur'an 5:38–39, 50). For the first offense, the penalty is amputation of a hand at the wrist. For the second, the penalty is amputation of a second hand at the wrist. For the third offense, the penalty is amputation of a foot at the ankle or imprisonment until repentance.

The third hadd offense is defamation, specifically the false accusation of adultery or fornication. This crime carries a penalty of 80 lashes for a free man and 40 for a slave (Qur'an 24:4).

Wine drinking is the fourth hadd crime. Innumerable hadith (collected say-ings that inform jurisprudence) depict the consumption of wine (and alcohol, more generally) as the greatest offense. For example, the Imam Shamsu ed-Deen Dhahabi, quotes a hadith reported by Ad-Darqutni, An-Nasa'i, and Al-Baihaq, "Avoid wine, it is the mother of abomination."[51] Like defamation, this offense carries a penalty of 80 lashes for a free man and 40 for a slave. How-ever, the Shafi'i prescribe 40 lashes for a free man.[52]

Highway robbery is the final hadd offense. Here again, there are specific cri-teria that must be met to establish the appropriateness of a hadd punishment. In particular, the robbery must be committed outside of a city. As for the range of penalties, the Qur'an (Chapter 5:33) dictates a number of possibilities. If one is convicted of highway robbery, the punishment is amputation of the right hand and left foot for the first offense; and amputation of the left hand and right foot for the second offense. If a murder also took place during an attempted robbery, the prescribed punishment is death by the sword. If a murder occurred during the course of a completed robbery, the penalty is crucifixion. During said crucifixion, the offender's body is to be hung for three days. Counter to "normal" murder (outside of robbery), where the victim's relatives may choose between retalia-tion, blood money (diya), or pardon of the offender, here the death penalty is mandatory. Furthermore, all accomplices in the crime must be afforded the same punishment. If one of the accomplices is a minor (for example) and therefore cannot be given the hadd punishment, neither can any of the other offenders.

As implied above, there are a number of other serious offenses that likewise carry severe penalties (which are specified in the Sunnah rather than the Qur'an). Many popular sources include these as hadd, perhaps due to the aforementioned penalties, but there appears to be limited scholarly consensus as to whether these crimes are hadd in the strictest sense. These offenses include murder, homosexuality, apostasy from Islam (i.e., the disassociation from or voluntary renunciation of Islam) and making war on Islam. It also bears note that several sources suggest "more liberal" Muslim scholars do not now treat wine drinking as a hadd.

This point in itself speaks to an often errant supposition by Western writers that casts Islamic justice as inflexible. As Mohammad Madkoar observes, "Judges under Islamic Law are bound to administer several punishments for a few very serious crimes found in the *Qur'an*, but they possess much greater freedom in punishment for less serious (non-*Hadd*) crimes ... Judges under Islamic Law are free to create new options and ideas to solve new problems associated with crime."[53] This flexibility can be readily seen with regard to a lesser category of offenses known as the *tazir*.

The term, "tazir" comes from the verb, "azzara," which means to stop or bring something to a halt or alternatively "to help."[54] Tazir offenses are those for which the Qur'an (or Sunnah) does not prescribe a specific punishment. Rather, tazir punishments are determined at the discretion (ijtihad) of the ruler or judge (Qadi). Apart from correction of the individual offender, tazir crimes are typically punished with a particular regard for instilling a broader social sense of rectitude. To this end, Mahfodz Madkoar observes, "*Shari'a* Law places an emphasis on the societal or public interest. The assumption of the punishment is that a greater 'evil' will be prevented in the future if you punish this offender now."[55] Bin Mohamed states that tazir offenses can be divided into three categories: Committing sinful acts (ma'siyah); Transgressing the public interest; Committing [other] minor offenses.

The first of these, commission of sinful acts, can be defined as neglecting obligations or, conversely, performing forbidden acts that cannot be punished otherwise (i.e., under hadd, qisas, or diya). Bin Mohamed provides a few examples, "stealing things that are not kept well or secure ... eating [an animal's] carcass, drinking blood, cheating, corrupting, bribery, gambling ... offences damaging the fasting and ihram activities, cancelling oaths and having sexual intercourse while in the period of menstruation."[56]

The second category of tazir offenses, those against the public good, is more difficult to fully describe. Several sources suggest that these offenses may not actually require the commission of a crime, but instead are situations in which individuals are merely suspected of having done something for which their punishment would have a deterrent effect for the public.[57] A concrete example of this is the story of a man accused of stealing a donkey. He is initially jailed but released when he is found to be innocent. The "public interest" at issue in this case is that the man's jailing under suspicion should serve as a deterrent for other would-be thieves. A more general admonishment of this kind is found in the Qur'an (49:6), "O you who have believed, if there comes to you a disobedient one with information, investigate, lest you harm a people out of ignorance and become, over what you have done, regretful."

The third category of tazir, minor offenses, is the subject of some scholarly disagreement. In a debate spanning several centuries, a number of Islamic scholars argue that minor cases should not to be considered as offenses, thus the individuals involved should not receive any punishments, while others view them as offenses deserving of formal sanction.[58] According to Mas'od Al-Kasani, the key element of this debate centers around a distinction between acts that are makruh (blameworthy) versus those that are mandub (simply not worthy of praise).[59] One might characterize the difference as one of culpability compared to a benign laxity. As to why some individuals might receive tazir punishment, Bin Mohamed provides perspective:

> Although [some individuals] receive punishments, they are not considered as having committed sinful acts but minor offences . . . The reason scholars give for this . . . is that once Sayyidna 'Umar Ibn Al Khattab punished a man with a *tazir* penalty where his wrong doing was only that he slaughtered a goat with a blunt knife. What the man was doing was/is makruh and still Sayyidna 'Umar punished him.[60]

This passage supports a broader point about tazir. Namely, tazir punishments, unlike those for hadd offenses, are highly variable and owe to the discretion of the presiding judge. Tazir punishments can range from simple advice or admonishment, to fines, imprisonment, banishment, corporal punishment, and even death.

A third type of offense (e.g., prescribed type of punishment) under Islamic codes of justice is a qisas. Qisas is an Arabic term that translates as "retaliation." It emanates from the principle of "an eye for an eye," or *lex talionis*. This concept extends as far back as the Hammurabic Codes. It remerges not only in Islam, but in the Christian Old Testament and later legal codes. The Qur'an (2:178) states:

> O ye who believe! Retaliation is prescribed for you in the matter of the murdered; the freeman for the freeman, and the slave for the slave, and the female for the female. And for him who is forgiven somewhat by his (injured) brother, prosecution according to usage and payment unto him in kindness. This is an alleviation and a mercy from your Lord. He who transgresseth after this will have a painful doom.

Interestingly, the Qur'an also permits the aggrieved to forfeit qisas as an act of charity or for atonement of sins (5:45):

> And We prescribed for them therein: The life for the life, and the eye for the eye, and the nose for the nose, and the ear for the ear, and the tooth for the tooth, and for wounds retaliation. But whoso forgoeth it (in the way of charity) it shall be expiation for him. Whoso judgeth not by that which Allah hath revealed: such are wrong-doers.

Differences exist as to whether qisas may be applied to Muslims who have murdered non-Muslims. The *Sahih Bukhari* states, "No Muslim should be killed in *Qisas* (equality in punishment) for the killing of (a disbeliever)."[61] That said, three of the four modern schools of Sunni jurisprudence expressly prohibit capital punishment for Muslims who have murdered non-Muslims. However, they do permit the payment of diya (blood money). In the Maliki and Hanbali schools of jurisprudence, a non-Muslim's life is assessed at one-half the value of a Muslim. The Shafi'i value the lives of Jews and Christians at one-third of the value of Muslims.[62] The Hanafi school allows capital punishment for Muslims who have murdered non-Muslims, citing a hadith wherein Muhammad ordered the execution of a Muslim who killed a dhimmi.[63]

Briefly defined above as "blood money," the term diya is closely related to qisas. In Arabic, diya translates to "rendering." In the present sense, compensation is "rendered" to an injured party for a serious crime, typically the murder of a family member. Muslim jurists reason that diya serves to console aggrieved family members and that it provides a deterrent for others in society.[64] In a passage from the *Sahih Bukhari* narrated Abu Huraira, the right to diya is set down: "And if somebody is killed, his closest relative has the right to choose one of two things . . . either the blood money or retaliation by having the killer killed."[65]

A final type of offense that bears on the present discussion are those resolved by kaffara (acts of personal penance). According to Sayyed Fadlallah, kaffara "is an act of worship . . . [the term] may have a number of meanings, including 'denial, obliteration, and cover.' Technically, [*kaffara*] means 'what is paid to redress an imbalance or to compensate for commissioning a sinful act, i.e. a kind of punishment or penalty.' "[66]

Kaffara is particularly important to the present discussion as many of its forms have a corporal element. As Fadlallah goes on to clarify, Shari'a defines the associated penalties or expiation in accordance with the type of shortfall or sin. Kaffara might take the form of financial penalties. Common examples are the obligation to feed a specific number of poor people or provide a certain amount of food. Likewise, it could specify clothing the poor. It could also be more personal, requiring a fast or abstention from physical or sensual pleasures, luxuries, and so on. There are also a number of kaffara under which one might be called upon to free a slave.[67]

As with a qisas and other Islamic punishments, there is an express notion of balance at play with kaffara. Often this takes the form of making things right with Allah through a deed of kindness toward others. Where the prescribed recompense in diya addresses a specific wrong to a particular party, this is not necessarily the case with kaffara. In fact, kaffara often requires performing a good work or act of charity toward a neutral party. Feeding the poor as kaffara for failing to meet a spiritual obligation (i.e., deliberately breaking a vow to Allah) is a typical example.

Fasting is also an acceptable mechanism of penance under kaffara. As above, failure to meet a spiritual obligation (i.e., breaking one's fast during Ramadan) would be rectified by a number of possibilities, fasting among them. As Fadlallah states, "The [kaffara] for flouting the rules and breaching one's fast could take one of three forms: a) emancipating a believer [i.e. freeing a slave]; b) fasting for two months; or c) feeding sixty poor people."[68]

Fasting is a particularly rich concept in many religious traditions. Discussion of it provides a bridge between acts of penance and a constellation of renunciation acts designed to promote spiritual growth or refinement. Yudit Greenberg provides a particularly interesting assessment of the ascetic dimensions of Islam:

> Three of the 'five pillars' of Islam involve asceticism to some degree. *Zakat*, or alms giving, is a form of renunciation of material possessions for the greater good. *Sawm*, or fasting, especially during . . . Ramadan is a particularly rigorous practice . . . [that] includes abstaining from food, water, tobacco and sexual activity from sunrise to sunset. *Hajj*, or the pilgrimage to Mecca, also has a strong ascetic component. Pilgrims enter a special ritual state called *ihram* [also a reference to the white gowns of the same name, worn during the *Hajj*]. The pilgrims refrain from sexual activity and do not cut their hair or nails. The effect of this asceticism is not only to represent a special ritual state, but also to express an egalitarian religious vision in which all Muslims are equal before God.[69]

Greenberg also documents the ascetic devotions of wandering Islamic beggars who practice rituals of corporal mortification and denial.[70] Beyond these ascetic rights, there exists a noteworthy corporal mortification associated with the annual Mourning of Muharram.[71] The event, which takes place in the first month of the Islamic calendar (i.e., Muharram), marks the anniversary of the Battle of Karbala. This battle is a significant moment in Islamic history as it is where the Shi'a Imam Ali ibn Hussain, the grandson of the prophet Muhammad, was killed by armies of the Umayad caliph, Yazid I.

During the commemoration, mourners gather for poetic recitations in memory of the fallen imam and to study Islam teachings. The mourning reaches its climax on the tenth day, known as Ashura. Many mourners engage in a corporal mortification ritual known as matam. During matam, mourners pound their chests in remembrance of Hussain. Two other ritual mortifications are found during this commemoration. The first is known as zanjeer zani. This is the ritual flailing of oneself with chains. Second, in a practice known as tatbir, mourners cut their heads with swords.

Just as the corporal mortifications practiced by the sect, Opus Dei, spark controversy in Christendom, so too does matam within Islam. Opponents of its continuation often cite a passage from the *Sahih Bukhari* narrated by Abdullah: "the Prophet said, 'He who slaps his cheeks, tears his clothes and follows the ways and traditions of the Days of Ignorance is not one of us.' "[72]

Even so, the ritual is known to persist in many nations. Several Islamic scholars have issued fatawa (religious opinions issued by an Islamic scholars) supporting these rituals. Typical of them is this fatawa issued by Ayatollah al-Udhma al-Seyyid al-Seestani, "[Tatbir] is permissible, and in fact this is regarded as one of the best means of seeking nearness to Allah, since it is upholding and honoring the *Sha'a'er* of Allah Almighty."[73]

From the preceding discussion of Shari'a justice and punishment, a number of differences between Islamic and Christian societies become evident. One especially remarkable distinction is the relative commonness of corporal punishment as a criminal sanction among Muslim countries. Approximately half of all Islamic countries permit the use of corporal punishment against convicted criminals. That said, the frequency with which corporal punishments are actually assigned remains an elusive figure.

Ali Mazrui asserts that corporal punishment is relatively rare, "In reality, most Muslim countries do not use traditional classical Islamic punishments. These punishments remain on the books in some countries but lesser penalties are often considered sufficient."[74]

This said, generalizations such as Mazuri's are difficult to substantiate. Just as the societies of Asia, Europe, and North America have distinct and often conflicting sensibilities about punishment, it is more probable the commonness of corporal punishment is similarly variable between different societies of the Islamic world.

Meithe and Lu make a distinction between flogging and more severe punishments such as amputations. Although they report individuals being assigned thousands of lashes as well as large groups of individuals being subject to the lash, they also state that data do not support the widespread or common use of amputations. In a similar vein, they also draw lines between nations. As they properly assert, nations vary dramatically between having the technical availability of corporal punishment as a possible sanction and the actual application of it.[75]

These distinctions further lead into a discussion of perception versus reality. Shari'a has perhaps wrongly earned a reputation in some Western eyes as a draconian and cruel form of justice. The specter of a public stoning, beheading, or flogging is sufficient to set Western media fully aflame, even though these events are exceedingly rare. As Muzari states, the fascinated horror is not an exclusively Western response, "While infrequently used, these punishments make headlines— and alarm even some Muslims."[76]

Perhaps what really sets Shari'a punishments apart from those delivered in non-Muslim nations is their visible delivery. Not so long ago, public hangings were a routine part of American criminal justice. For a constellation of complex reasons, the United States no longer conducts executions in an openly public forum. They are always witnessed, but more often those in attendance are small in number. Were this trend reversed and the media allowed to publicize lethal injections, firing squads, or the electric chair, some of the value judgments about Shari'a might be less easily made.

In the preceding sections devoted to corporal punishment in the Christian and Islamic religious traditions, the topic of asceticism was only briefly covered. Because asceticism has been an important aspect of many world religious systems, it was deemed appropriate to give it fuller explication as a separate, but closely related matter. In the following section, the ascetic dimensions of Christianity, Islam, Hinduism, Jainism, and Buddhism will be discussed.

ASCETICISM

At the most general level of explanation, the term "asceticism" describes a life characterized by abstinence from a variety of physical, sensual, and otherwise worldly pleasures as a means of spiritual development. Many of these pursuits might not meet a strict understanding of punishment that dictates the involvement of a third party.[77] Because they are ritualized practices of physical denial or trial (some of which do involve pain, discomfort, or danger) as a means of transforming self, they merit discussion.

As Michel Foucault indicates, most nations of the modern era have transitioned their punishment models from one based in corporal punishment to one based in carceral (i.e., imprisonment) punishment.[78] This shift in regulation can also be seen in certain religious practices, particularly among religious communities dedicated to ascetic life (i.e., priesthood and monasticism). To fully appreciate shifts in punishment, it is important to recognize the interconnectedness of religious practice and social control. The ebb and flow of ascetic practice provides perspective for that endeavor.

Although it represents only one element of a much larger picture, the decline in formal ascetic practice in Western culture is reflected in phenomena such as the dwindling number of priests and members of monastic orders in the American Catholic church. According to Georgetown University's Center for Applied Research in the Apostolate, in 1965 there were approximately 35,925 diocesan priests and a combined 192,225 religious brothers and sisters, serving 48.5 million persons who self-identified as Catholic.[79] In contrast, by 2010, there were 27,182 diocesan priests and a combined 62,234 religious brothers and sisters, serving 77.7 million persons who self-identified as Catholic. Although Catholicism itself appears to be flourishing, those willing to take on the mantle of formal ascetic service are in steep decline. This apparent contradiction suggests further analysis is necessary. Accordingly, asceticism holds the seeds of a much larger discussion about the goals and function of religious life; and by extension, why so many of the world's religious traditions have embraced asceticism as a means toward spiritual goals.

A classic treatise on the ideals of asceticism is found in the introductory passage of Nietzsche's essay, "What is the Meaning of Ascetic Ideals?":

> What do ascetic ideals mean? . . . among the clergy they are the foundation of their priestly faith, their best instrument of power, and also the most important of all permits for their power; finally among the saints they are a pretext for hibernation, their *novissima gloriae cupido* [most recent desire for glory], their repose in nothingness

('God'), their form of insanity. However, the fact that generally the ascetic ideal has meant so much to human beings is an expression of the basic fact of the human will, its horror *vacui* [horror of a vacuum]. It requires a goal—and it will sooner will nothingness than not will.[80]

In this quote from *The Genealogy of Morals*, Nietzsche explores how an embrace of asceticism has endured across time and cultures. The fundamental question posed by Nietzsche is one of paradox. Specifically, how a life of denial is transformed by the ascetic into a life affirmed. Nietzsche resolves the paradox with the assertion that asceticism is born of spiritual sickness. For Nietzsche, ascetic practice, addresses spiritual sickness by extinguishing individual "will" through meditation and work but also through "orgies of feeling," that manifest in the consciousness of sin and guilt, the end of which he describes as "Triumph precisely in the ultimate agony."[81]

Although Nietzsche's analysis of the phenomenon is hardly neutral, it positions asceticism as a vehicle for spiritual adaptation. Without assenting to his larger assumptions on religion generally, the fundamental proposition of triumph through agony is a fitting place to expand present concerns. As previously discussed, ascetic practice is an enduring feature of many religious traditions, some of which have been presented in detail. There are, however, a few other prominent religious schools whose ascetic practices deserve elaboration.

Christian Asceticism

Within Christianity (and for that matter, most religions), one sees that asceticism is not equally embraced among all adherents. The Catholic Church, Eastern Orthodox churches, Oriental Orthodox churches, and some Anglican churches place considerable value in asceticism, while the majority of Protestant denominations practice asceticism with much less centrality. To be clear, congregational ascetic observances among the more orthodox denominations are more apt to take the form of fasting, abstinence from particular foods, drink, or sensual pleasures (i.e., the Lenten Season). Among their clergy, ascetic rites such as celibacy, cloistered living, and so on are more common. As mentioned previously, only among sects like Opus Dei does one regularly see use of corporal mortification instruments such as the cilice and flail.

In the Christian Gospels both asceticism and worldly pleasures are spoken of positively. The juxtaposition seems to indicate a proper time and place for each, or perhaps a balance thereof. John the Baptist is described as a desert-dwelling ascetic consistent with the images typical of an Old Testament prophet, "Clothed in camel's hair, with a leather belt around his waist. He fed on locusts and wild honey" (Mark 1:6). Likewise, Jesus's forty-day fast in the desert as well as his experiences of worldly temptation are consistent with this narrative (Luke 4:1–13). Furthermore, Jesus is shown, to the scandal of some, eating and drinking with not just his followers but also sinners. These practices lead his followers to question, "They said to him, 'John's disciples often fast and pray and so do the disciples of the Pharisees, but yours go on eating and drinking.' Jesus answered, 'Can you make the guests of the bridegroom fast while he is with them? But the time will come when the bridegroom will be taken from them; in those days they will fast' " (Luke 5:33–35). The enduring interpretation of this exchange suggests that after Jesus's death his followers should practice fasting, at least on occasion.

In his epistles, Saint Paul discusses his own practices, drawing a distinction between "true" and "false" asceticism. In particular, he writes of disciplining his body like an athlete, in subordination to reason in the service of the Gospel, "Everyone who competes in the games goes into strict training. They do it to get a crown that will not last, but we do it to get a crown that will last forever. Therefore, I do not run like someone running aimlessly; I do not fight like a boxer beating the air. No, I strike a blow to my body and make it my slave so that after I have preached to others, I myself will not be disqualified for the prize" (1 Corinthians 9:25–27).

Marina Miladinov suggests as an outgrowth of these teachings the early church experienced a burgeoning movement of hermits in which the deserts of the Middle East were host to thousands of ascetic practitioners.[82] Notables include the likes of St. Anthony the Great, Paul of Thebes, and Simeon Stylites. According to the *Catechism of the Catholic Church*, hermits "devote their life to the praise of God and salvation of the world through a stricter separation from the world, the silence of solitude and assiduous prayer and penance."[83]

Generally speaking, Christian monasticism emerged during the Late Empire period of the Roman Empire (ca. 180–476) with the appearance of solitary monasticism in the Eastern Empire. Couched rigorous asceticism, the first Christian monks lived alone in whatever ruins or caves were available to them. F. J. Bacchus states that Pachomius (ca. 292–348), a contemporary of St. Anthony, organized the first formal cenobite (i.e., monastic) community. Although monastic communities had existed prior to Pachomius, they were more loose associations of eremitic (i.e., individual hermit-type) monks who came together for prayer and communion.[84]

The father of modern monasticism in Western Europe was Benedict of Nursia, an Italian monk who founded more than a dozen religious communities in the areas of Subiaco and Monte Cassino in southern Italy during the sixth century. The organization and guiding precepts of the Benedictine order became the most influential model for subsequent orders throughout Europe.[85]

Islamic Asceticism

Perhaps the most prominent manifestation of asceticism in Islam is found in the adherents of Sufism or *ta awwuf*.[86] Sufism is an introspective, esoteric variant of Muslim theology with elements of mysticism. In a *fatawa*, the Egyptian cleric, 'Abd al-Halim Mahmud stated the following about Sufism:

> The ascetic is one who turns away from the goods of the world and its pleasant things. The worshipper is one who is careful to observe the acts of worships, such as getting up [to prayer at night] (al-qiyam), canonical prayer (al-salat), and similar things. The Sufi is both an ascetic and a worshipper. Thus the Sufi abstains from the world, since he is beyond the point where anything can distract him from God.[87]

Sufism is in many ways reminiscent of the Gnostic tradition in Christendom, in that the primary intent is a closeness with God. Muslims use the term *fitra* to describe this perfect accord with the wishes of God.

The origins of Sufism speak to the persistent debate over its legitimacy within Islam. Adherents claim that Sufism merely emulates the example of Muhammad. Whereas opponents argue Sufism is *bid'ah* (i.e., reprehensible innovation), counter to the teaching of Muhammad and his companions.[88]

Sufism experienced a sustained period of growth and refinement near the close of the first millennium. During that era, two foundational documents for Sufi practices were set down. These were the *Risâla* of Qushayri and the *Kashf al-Mahjûb* of Hujwiri. Between the thirteenth and sixteenth centuries Sufism spread throughout the Islamic world. Today Sufism is found commonly throughout the Middle East and Africa.

During the eleventh century, the highly influential Muslim cleric, Al-Ghazali, described Sufi worship habits as dominated by solitude, silence, sleeplessness, and hunger.[89] Continuation of this ascetic tradition can be seen in the three most common elements of modern Sufi practice.

Dhikr is a devotional act done in remembrance of God. It may take many forms, but the element of repetitive action is a common motif. Recitation of the 99 Names of God or passages from the Qur'an and other sacred texts are typical subjects. During these recitations, Muslims may use *misbaha* (strings of prayer beads) to keep track of their recitations while performing dhikr.

Perhaps the most widely known form of dhikr is a ceremony performed by the Mevlevi Order of Sufis from Turkey. Known as Dervishes, they are mendicant ascetics who have taken a vow of poverty.[90] Their particular practice of dhikr is coupled with a moving meditation that takes the form of a multistaged and exceptionally vigorous whirling dance (hence the term "Whirling Dervish"). The object of this ceremony, known as *sema'*, the Arabic word for "listening," is to create a clarified awareness of God's presence through "annihilation" of the ego.[91]

A second form of ritualized Sufi practice is *muraqaba*. Muraqaba is a system of deep meditation; like sema', it is designed to distance the practitioner from corporeal attachments, the ego, even time and space, as a mechanism to become fully attuned to God's presence and watchfulness.[92]

A last devotional practice of Sufism is that of pilgrimage to venerated shrines and other spiritually rich places such as the tombs of saints, Islamic scholars, and other holy figures. Typical examples of this would be journeys to the shrine of Moulay Idris II Zawiya in Fez, Morocco[93] or the shrine of Hazrat Lal Shahbaz Qalandar in Sehwan, Pakistan.[94]

Moving geographically eastward, the Indian subcontinent has been the historical locus of three religions each heavily influenced by an ascetic tradition. Ria Kloppenborg provides a valuable historic perspective on the twined development of Hinduism, Jainism, and Buddhism:

> Since the earliest times, ascetics who leave society to evade the hindrances of worldly ties and to search for insight into reality and salvation have been mentioned as one of the most typical characteristics of Indian religions. The *Rg-Veda* mentions a class of holy men distinct from the *brahmins*, the *munis*, who are said to possess supernatural powers, especially the ability to fly through the air and to read other people's thoughts. This asceticism seems to have developed among different groups or individuals along a similar line, and shows similar characteristics of practice and circumstances: a solitary life outside the community, residence in forests or on the outskirts of towns and villages, dressing in clothes of bark or of rags, living on begged food or plants, shaving the hair, etc. Some of these ascetics lived in isolation, others in groups; still others wandered in groups or alone, begging for alms, preaching their doctrines to those who wished to listen ... They formed a religious group distinct from the orthodox sacrificial priests and developed their own culture and style of living. ... The sense of freedom from worldly cares and ties has been one of the main themes in the religious literature of India, Hindu, [Jain] and Buddhist.[95]

Understanding the interconnectedness of these three traditions lends a firm place from which to explore the specific incarnations of ascetic ritual, corporal mortification, and renunciation as vehicles for individual spiritual practice. Hinduism, Jainism, and Buddhism each contain ascetic traditions that have been important in the formation of Indian and many other Asian cultures.

Hindu Asceticism

Within Hinduism one sees a very large community of ascetics. Dolf Hartsuiker contends as many as 5 million *sadhus*, or wandering mendicant monks, may exist today.[96] To Western eyes, the ascetic traditions of Hinduism may appear to be among the most physically demanding and extreme on Earth. Sadhus are *sanyasi*, or renunciates in the final stage of *ashram*, who have left behind all material and sexual attachments to live in the caves, forests, and temples of India and Nepal. Hartsiker says of them, "Spiritual adventurers, ascetic warriors, devout mystics, occult rebels or philosophic monks, the sadhus are revered by Hindus as representatives of the gods, sometimes even worshipped as gods themselves."[97]

There are many variations of practice within the sadhus. Generally, their asceticism owes to a codified set of observances known as the *yamas* and the *niyamas*. These could be characterized as the proscriptions and prescriptions for belief and activity (i.e., things to avoid and things to pursue). Although all are central to sadhu life, the tenth *niyama*, *tapas*, is of particular interest for the present discussion. Tapas, is performed by ardent worship, intense meditation, pilgrimage, atonement through penance, self-denial, renunciation of possessions, and worldly pleasures.[98]

Becoming sadhu can be an extremely arduous and all-consuming path. Initiates are often guided by a guru, who has a very important role in the spiritual and practical guidance of the sandu. It is the guru who gives the initiate a new name, as well as a mantra (a sacred sound or phrase used in meditation) often known only to the sadhu and the guru.

Sadhu typically practice purification rituals tied to hatha yoga and fasting. For some sadhus, the ritual consumption of hashish or other forms of cannabis is part of their practice.[99] On the extreme end of the sadhu practice are those whose devotions include persistent physical encumbrances such as standing only on one leg for years, perpetually extending an arm above their head, or remaining silent for years. Similarly, there are sadhu who wander naked or nearly so, with long beards and matted hair. Sadhu may exist in solitude or live in communal gatherings.[100]

Jain Asceticism

Where many Westerners may have a nodding familiarity with Islam and Hinduism, Jainism is likely more obscure. To the uninitiated, Jains could easily be confused with the much more dominant Vedic (i.e., Hindu) tradition in India. Although mutually influential and sharing in many practices and coexisting for millennia, Jainism and Hinduism are separate and distinct religious systems. Harry Oldmeadow states, "There is no evidence to show that Jainism ... ever subscribed to Vedic sacrifices, Vedic deities or caste. They are parallel to native religions of India and have contributed much to the growth of even classical Hinduism of the present times."[101]

Jain practitioners constitute only a small percentage of India's population (approximately 4.2 million followers), but their particularly austere ascetic tradition merits their inclusion in the present discussion.[102] Although space will not permit an extended explication of Jain theology, a few key points will suffice.

The core doctrine of Jainism is a broad concern for the welfare of every living being in the universe and for the health of the universe itself. Jains believe all animals (including humans, microbes, insects, etc.) and plants contain living souls. Each of these souls is accorded equal value and, as such, merits respect and compassion. Jains believe in reincarnation. They strive to attain ultimate liberation through which they will escape the reincarnation cycle. In so doing, their immortals soul live forever in a state of bliss. Jains do not believe that any gods or spiritual beings will intercede to help them.[103]

The "Three Jewels" of Jainism, their guiding principles are: right belief, right knowledge, and right conduct. The supreme principle of Jain living is nonviolence or *ahimsa*. In accordance with their pacifism, Jains are strict vegetarians and live so as to reduce their impact on the world's resources. Along with ahimsa, the other four tenets of the *Five Mahvratas* (five great vows) are: nonattachment to possessions, not lying, not stealing, and celibacy. The Jain sacred texts are called the *Agamas*. Jains are divided into two major sects; the *Digambara* or "sky clad" sect and the *Svetambara* or "white clad" sect. Jainism has no priests, per se. The monks and nuns of the respective sects, who lead exceptionally strict and austere ascetic lives, provide religious tutelage.[104]

Of the two sects, the Digambara lead lives of greater deprivation. Digambara monks live completely naked. Nuns are permitted clothing. The Digambara believe they must adhere to a code of extreme deprivation including: no ownership of worldly possessions, not even bowls with which to beg alms; and by demonstrating indifference to earthly emotions, including shame, as demonstrated by their nudity. At least one source[105] suggests the Digambara may own two possessions: a *pichhi* (a peacock-feather whisk-broom used to sweep insects out of one's path) and a *kamandalu* (a wooden waterpot). Digambaras believe that women lack the adamantine body and rigid will necessary to attain *moksa* (i.e., liberation). As such, women must be reborn as a man before moksa is possible.[106]

The Svetambara stand in contrast on a number of frontiers. First, both sexes are clothed. The Svetambara wear simple white clothes and they may have up to fourteen possessions.[107] In contrast to the Digambara's beliefs about women, the Svetambaras hold that women are capable (without reincarnation as a man) of the same spiritual accomplishments as men.[108] Although there are a number of other difference between the sects, the foregoing examples demonstrate that even the relatively more "relaxed" standards of the Svetembaras still position them as among the most self-denying and abstemious religious mendicants in the modern world.

Buddhist Asceticism

Approximately 2,500 years ago, Siddhartha Gautama founded the religious tradition now known as Buddhism. The Buddhist monastic (i.e., ascetic) tradition was greatly influenced by the wandering ascetics of India, under whom Gautama (i.e., the Buddha) had studied. That said, Buddhist monastic practice generally lacks the eremitic character common to other religious traditions of the region. Buddhist monasticism is more connected to and dependent on the lay community for provision of necessities. To this end, as with the monastic traditions of most religious systems, Buddhist monks are expected to live with few possessions and eschew many earthly pleasures. Buddhist monasticism order is divided into two assemblies, the male *bhikkhu* assembly, and the female *bhikkhuni*.

The *vinaya* is the regulatory framework for the *sangha*, the Buddhist monastic community (including the laity). The vinaya is based in the Buddhist scripture, the *Vinaya Pitaka*. Although there have been a number of distinct vinaya traditions (i.e., ordination lineages) over the millennia, only three exist today: the Theravāda, Dharmaguptaka, and Mūlasarvāstivāda. Buddhist monastic practices are quite varied and have been adapted to better mesh with local cultures, geography, and sensibilities.

In describing how a Buddhist monk should live, The Buddha Dharma Education Association states, "Solitary, silent and simple could be a fair description of the ideal lodging for a monk."[109] Other prescriptions for proper living conditions include utilitarian furniture or perhaps just a thick mat spread on the floor for sleeping. Monks often make their own robes from cloth that has been given them. Bowing to climate and modernity, the BDEA adds, "The basic 'triple robe' of, the Buddha [can be] supplemented with sweaters, tee-shirts, socks, etc. and these, of an appropriate brown color."[110] Monks may now use other small personal items, such as needles, razors, pens, watches, and so on. Even so, these items must be plain and simple. All costly or luxurious items are forbidden.

Monks are only allowed to collect, receive, and consume food between dawn and midday. They may not consume food outside of this time nor store food overnight. Plain water can be taken at any time, without having to be offered. Although monks live on whatever is offered, vegetarianism is encouraged. At no time does the monk request food. When receiving food, a monk makes himself available in a situation where people wish to give food. Monks are allowed to use medicines if they are offered in the same way as food. Interestingly, once it has been offered, neither food nor medicine should be handled again by a layperson, as their subsequent handling renders it no longer allowable.

Generally, the Buddhist principles of mendicancy prohibit asking for anything, unless ill, without having first received an invitation. Although the vinaya prohibits use or acceptance of gold and silver, modern interpretations have extended this exclusion to bank notes and credit cards. The vinaya also prohibit a monk from having someone else receive money on their behalf. Monks and nuns lead lives of total celibacy that forbid all sexual behavior, speech, implication, and so on.

SUMMARY

In comparison, one sees strong correspondence between the Buddhist, Jain, and Hindu ascetic traditions. That said, there are several elements that extend beyond the traditions indigenous to India, and across Christendom and Islam as well. Indeed, the global, historical account positions rituals of physical ordeal, mortification, deprivation, and suffering as recurrent elements in many of the world's religious traditions.

We see similar themes again and again, not just in the observances of the ascetic and mendicant orders, but within the laity as well. The corporal and the spiritual are clearly entwined in the human collective conscience. Likewise, a relationship between sacrifice and spiritual growth appear indelibly fixed within the human imagination.

Although the preceding chapter is not intended to provide a comprehensive survey of religious observance and corporal punishment, examples drawn from several traditions are sufficient to illustrate the enduring connection between regulation of the physical body and spiritual development. This chapter has presented a summary of beliefs and ritual from several of the larger world traditions, but it is duly acknowledged that many more examples could be given, both from the traditions discussed and the many others that have been omitted. The indigenous religions and spiritual traditions of Africa as well as Central and South America often involve mortifications and ordeals as severe as any offered here. Their absence from this presentation should not imply any value judgment or presumed hierarchy of value other than that described above. Rather, those religious traditions that were selected for inclusion were chosen because they are likely to be among those with which readers are most familiar.

Corporal Punishment in the Home

When a child hits a child, we call it aggression.
When a child hits an adult, we call it hostility.
When an adult hits an adult, we call it assault.
When an adult hits a child, we call it discipline.

—Haim G. Ginott

HAVING DISCUSSED THE use of corporal punishment in historical and religious contexts, the present consideration focuses on corporal punishment in the home. Susan Bitensky defines corporal punishment as, "the gratuitous intentional infliction of pain on children's bodies for the purpose of modifying behavior."[1] Although this is adequately descriptive, Murray Straus and Denise Donnelly provide a more useful and widely accepted definition of parentally administered corporal punishment. They define it as, "the use of physical force with the intention of causing a child pain, but not injury, for purposes of correction or control of the child's behavior."[2]

The use of physical force can take many forms such as "spanking, slapping, grabbing or shoving a child roughly (with more force than is necessary to move the child), and hitting with certain objects such as a hair brush, belt, or paddle."[3] That said, some of these acts wander dangerously into the arena of abuse and, therefore, cannot be considered corporal punishment. As Straus and Donnelly explain, even though cultural norms may permit the striking of a child with certain objects, the risks of injury to the child increases exponentially (over and above striking with an open hand) and could cause the child to require medical attention, making these acts of abuse and not simply punishment.

In an effort to distinguish between corporal punishment and abuse, Elisabeth Gershoff[4] provides a summary of legal definitions of corporal punishment in the United States. Notably, "29 states assert that corporal punishment encompasses the use of 'reasonable' force with some adding qualifiers that it must also be 'appropriate' (AL, AK, AZ, CA, CO), 'moderate' (AR, DE, SC, SD), or 'necessary' (MT, NH, NY, OR, TX, WI). Three states see the need to clarify that corporal punishment is limited to 'nondeadly force' (AK, NY, TX)."[5]

It would seem in a legal sense that corporal punishment encompasses violence that is deemed to be either appropriate or reasonable and does not result in injury. This distinguishes corporal punishment from abuse, which involves actions or behavior (whether intentional or not) that are injurious to the child.[6] Accordingly, the line between corporal punishment as a disciplinary tool and abuse is thin at best, as it is not uncommon for corporal punishment to seriously injure a child. As Tom Heymann observes, approximately 1,157, 270 children are spanked each year in the United States and almost 20,000 of these children sustain a serious injury.[7] Additionally, the World Health Organization (WHO) notes that two increased risk factors for child maltreatment are the approval of physical punishments and the use of physical punishments.[8] As Gershoff states, "Child abuse in any form is a tragedy and deserves our best prevention efforts, and thus the potential for corporal punishment to escalate into physical abuse must be seriously considered at the levels of scientific research and public policy."[9] For this reason, the WHO recommends parents find alternatives to corporal punishment such as distracting or redirecting behaviors, setting a cooling-off period, and the withdrawal of privileges.[10]

ACCEPTANCE OF CORPORAL PUNISHMENT

As established in preceding chapters, the use of corporal punishment has a rich history and accounts of its use can be traced back to Babylon, ancient Greece, and Rome.[11] In terms of parents hitting their children, it is difficult to trace the historical timeline of such acts, but there is little doubt that it has almost always existed in some capacity or another. Leonard Edwards notes, "the Babylonians, ancient Hebrews, ancient Greeks, and Romans all granted fathers a proprietary interest in their children, thus permitting the sale or exchange of children and the right to kill them."[12] Straus and Donnelly report that there are some isolated tribes where children never experience corporal punishment at the hands of their parents, but these are the exception and not the rule.[13] The primary justification for the corporal punishment of children in Western society can be found in Proverbs 13:24: "He that spareth his rod hateth his son: but he that loveth him, chasteneth him betimes" (i.e., Spare the rod, spoil the child). Furthermore, "Martin Luther believed that parents could use extreme measures, even death, when children were disobedient."[14] Indeed, there is still appears to be a strong relationship between the acceptance of corporal punishment as a parenting tool and religion. Gershoff observes that support of corporal punishment tends to be strongest among conservative Protestants and religious conservatives in general.[15]

The acceptance of corporal punishment can vary depending on cultural norms and customs. Straus and Donnelly note that virtually every American believes in some form of the principle, "Spare the rod and spoil the child."[16] Indeed they argue this view is so pervasive that American societal norms encourage (and in some cases demand) parents hit their children.[17] Cultural acceptance of corporal punishment appears to be so strong in the United States that parents who do not use it as a disciplinary tool feel obliged to either lie and say they do or defend why they do not. Carson found that parents who did not corporally pun-ish their children "tended to avoid the problem by recasting things in a culturally acceptable way, for example, by saying that they only spank 'when necessary' and leaving out the fact that they never found it necessary."[18]

In Japanese culture, the "spare the rod" mentality is known as *ai no muchi* or "The whip of love."[19] It is not surprising then to note remarkable similarity in rates of corporal punishment between American children and Japanese children. I. J. Chang, Rebecca Pettit, and Emiko Katsuranda found that 91% of the U.S. college students surveyed indicated they had experienced corporal punishment at some point during their childhood, compared to 86% of Japanese respondents.[20] Despite the similarity in the rate of reported corporal punishment, the form of parental adminis-tered corporal punishment was somewhat different. Specifically, U.S. respondents reported they were typically hit on either the buttocks or the hand, while Japanese respondents indicated that the head and face were the two areas most often hit.[21]

In an examination of parental corporal punishment practices in Yemen, Abdullah Alyahri and Robert Goodman found that corporal punishment in the home was both more prominent and more severe in rural areas than more urban locations.[22] Specifically, "hitting with a belt, stick or other object was almost three times more common in rural than urban areas (58% vs. 23%)."[23] Other forms of corporal punishment were somewhat rare, such as tying children up or locking them in a room; however, two rural mothers reported pinching their chil-dren and one reported biting her child. It is interesting to note that the authors of this study classified such acts as "harsh corporal punishment" and not child abuse (as they might be classified in North America or other industrialized Western nations).[24] This suggests perceptions of what constitutes appropriate corporal punishment can vary greatly from country to country.

CORPORAL PUNISHMENT IN THE INTERNATIONAL COMMUNITY

Despite the fact that the UN Convention of the Rights of the Child has called for a complete ban on the use of corporal punishment against children as a formal sanction and has stated that children have a "right to protection from corporal punishment and other cruel or degrading forms of punishment," there are many nations where the practice is legal within the home. The UN convention is very explicit in its condemnation of corporal punishment, going so far as to say:

> Parties shall take all appropriate legislative, administrative, social and educational measures to protect the child from all forms of physical or mental violence, injury or abuse, neglect or negligent treatment, maltreatment or exploitation, including sex-ual abuse, while in the care of parents, legal guardians or any other person who has the care of the child.[25]

Citing incompatibility with the Rights of the Child, the UN "[proposes] the revi-sion of existing legislation, as well as the development of awareness and education campaigns, to prevent child abuse and the physical punishment of children." Given this, it can be readily assumed that corporal punishment within the home is not appropriate by international standards, even if cultural norms find it permissible. Some have cited a contradiction between Article 19 and Article 5 of the convention that states:

> Parties shall respect the responsibilities, rights and duties of parents or, where applicable, the members of the extended family or community as provided for by local custom, legal guardians or other persons legally responsible for the child, to provide, in a manner consistent with the evolving capacities of the child, appropriate direction and guidance in the exercise by the child of the rights recognized in the present Convention.[26]

What then of those cultures that deem corporal punishment acceptable because it is customary? To this the UN answers:

> It must be borne in mind, however, that article 19 of the Convention required all appropriate measures, including legislative measures, to be taken to protect the child against, inter alia, physical violence. A way should thus be found of striking the balance between the responsibilities of the parents and the rights and evolving capacities of the child that was implied in article 5 of the Convention. There was no place for corporal punishment within the margin of discretion accorded in article 5 to parents in the exercise of their responsibilities.[27]

As of 2012, only 32 nations had prohibited corporal punishment in the home, leaving 166 countries where the practice is still legal.[28] Expressed as a percentage, in 83.8% of countries it is legally permissible for parents to administer physical punishments to their children. Figures vary, but some researchers find that between a quarter and half of children report severe physical abuse (e.g., being beaten or kicked by parents) and most of these incidents were intended to serve as punishment.[29]

Sweden was one of the first countries to implement a total ban on corporal punishment. In the 1920s, corporal punishment was widespread throughout Sweden. Moreover, it was common for students to receive severe beatings in educational settings.[30] To address the growing concern over corporal punishment, Sweden banned its use in grammar schools in 1927, followed by a ban in elementary schools in 1958, and a total educational ban in 1962 by the Education act.[31]

Despite the ban in educational settings, corporal punishment remained legal in home settings. Even so, early legislation attempted to address physical punishment in the home by replacing the word "punish" with the word "reprimand." Examples of these changes can be seen in the 1949 Parents' Code and Penal Code.[32] In 1957 and again in 1966, both codes were revised. Under these revisions, parents were no longer permitted to use physical punishment against their children.[33] Despite changes in the law, confusion about the legality of corporal punishment remained. A poll conducted in 1965 found that 53% of Swedish citizens still approved of the use of corporal punishment.[34] A subsequent poll conducted in 1971 found that 60% of Swedish citizens were unaware that corporal punishment was not allowed.[35]

By 1979, Sweden became the first country to prohibit the corporal punishment of children in all settings. This ban was precipitated by a court case involving a father who assaulted his three-year-old daughter.[36] The child was beaten so badly that she had to be taken the hospital, where it was found that she had bruises all over her body.[37] Despite the injuries, the father was acquitted and the court noted that he had not "not exceeded his right to chastise his daughter."[38] Finally a ban was enacted in Chapter 6 of the Parenthood and Guardianship Code, which prohibits physical and degrading punishment.[39] The statute, which was amended in 1983, states, "Children are entitled to care, security and a good upbringing. They shall be treated with respect for their person and their distinctive character and may not be subject to corporal punishment or any other injurious or humiliating treatment."[40]

Soon after the Swedish ban was enacted, Finland abolished the corporal punishment of children in 1983, followed by Norway (1987), Austria (1989), and most recently South Sudan in 2011. The table 3.1 lists the countries with full abolition of corporal punishment, as reported by the Global Initiative to End the Corporal Punishment of Children.[41]

Table 3.1 Countries with Full Corporal Punishment Abolition

Abolished	Country	Statute
2011	South Sudan	Transitional Constitution of the Republic of South Sudan, 2011, article 17, section 1
2010	Rep. of Congo	Law on the Protection of the Child, 2010, article 53
2010	Kenya	Bill of Rights, article 29
2010	Tunisia	Law No. 2010-40 of 26 July 2010, amending article 319 of the Penal Code
2010	Poland	Article 2 of the Law of 6 May 2010 "On the Prevention of Family Violence" amends the Family Code, 1964
2010	Liechtenstein	Children and Youth Act, article 3
2008	Luxembourg	Law on Children and the Family, 2008, article 2
2008	Rep. of Moldova	Family Code, amended 2008, articles 53.4 and 62.2
2008	Costa Rica	Family Code, amended 2008, article 143; Code on Children and Adolescents, article 24bis
2007	Spain	Law 54/2007, article 34
2007	Venezuela	Law for the Protection of Children and Adolescents, amended 2007, articles 32-A and 358
2007	Uruguay	Code for Children and Adolescents, amended 2007, in force 2008, articles 12bis and 16f

(continued)

Table 3.1 (Continued)

Abolished	Country	Statute
2007	Portugal	Penal Code, amended 2007, article 152
2007	New Zealand	Crimes Act, amended 2007, section 59
2007	Netherlands	Civil Code, amended 2007, article 1:247
2006	Greece	Law on the Combating of Intra-family Violence, 2006, article 4
2004	Hungary	Act on the Protection of Children and Guardianship Administration, 1997, amended 2004, article 6.5
2004	Romania	Law on the Protection and Promotion of the Rights of the Child, 2004, articles 28 and 90
2003	Ukraine	Family Code, 2003, article 150.7
2003	Iceland	Children's Act, 2003, article 28
2003	Bulgaria	Child Protection Act, 2000, amended 2003, article 11.2
2000	Germany	Civil Code, amended 2000, article 1631
2000	Israel	Removal of the "reasonable chastisement" defense from criminal law
1998	Croatia	Family Act, 1998, article 87
1998	Latvia	Law on Protection of the Rights of the Child, 1998, articles 9.2 and 24.4
1997	Denmark	Parental Custody and Care Act, amended 1997
1994	Cyprus	Family (Prevention and Protection of Victims) Law, 1994, prohibition reiterated in Act on Violence in the Family, 2000
1989	Austria	General Civil Code, 1989, section 146a
1987	Norway	Parent and Child Act, amended 1987, article 30
1983	Finland	Child Custody and Rights of Access Act, 1983, in force 1984, article 1.3
1979	Sweden	Parenthood and Guardianship Code, amended 1979, article 1

Source: The Global Initiative to the End the Corporal Punishment of Children

Perhaps one of the more interesting examples of corporal punishment legislation can be found in Cyprus's abolition in 1994. The Family Law of 1994 made the corporal punishment of children illegal and provides sentencing enhancements because corporal punishment involves violence directed at a family member.[42] Another unique characteristic of the legislation is a provision that bans any violence in the presence of children, which effectively makes domestic violence a form of child abuse.[43]

The case of Southern Sudan represents another example of banned corporal punishment. Passed when Southern Sudan was not yet an independent state, the

Child Act of 2008[44] outlined several protections for children and a prohibition against corporal punishment is among them. Notably, section 22 of the Act provides that:

> Every child has the right to be protected from the following types of treatment and abuse while in the care of parents, legal guardians, teachers, police or any other person who has care of a child—

(a) all forms of physical or mental violence, injury, abuse, negligent treatment, maltreatment or exploitation;
(b) abduction and trafficking, for any purpose or form, by any person including parents or guardians;
(c) sexual abuse, exploitation and harassment including, but not limited to rape, incest, inducement or coercion of a child to witness or engage in a sexual activity; the use of a child in prostitution or other sexual practices; and
(d) the use of a child in pornographic performances and materials.

Despite the apparent legal protections from corporal punishment that children seem to have in the aforementioned countries, with the exception of Cyprus, sanctions for noncompliance with corporal punishment laws are virtually nonexistent. For example, in the case of Sweden, there are technically no sanctions for violating the law, because the law was passed as "social engineering, rather than as a measure to intrude upon family privacy or haul parents before courts."[45] This does not mean that parents cannot receive punishment, however.[46] Though the ban on corporal punishment falls under civil law, it is the criminal code that determines whether an offense has occurred. Typically, parents will not receive sanctions unless the incident meets the same criteria as assault.[47] However, if the physical punishment is deemed assaultive, parents could be incarcerated for up to ten years.[48]

The laws in many other abolitionist countries are similar, in that they are more for parental education than actual punishment. Even without the threat of criminal sanctions, the ban in Sweden appears to be largely effective. In 1965, approximately 53% of Swedish citizens favored the use of corporal punishment but by 1994 support dropped to just 11%.[49] Additionally, rates of child abuse also seem to have dropped in Sweden as "referrals to St. Göan's Hospital in Stockholm, which receives all child maltreatment cases, had declined by 1989 to one-sixth of the 1970 rate."[50]

Despite the abolition of physical punishment by parents, corporal punishment remains legal in the vast majority of nations. In Canada, for example, section 43 of the Criminal Code provides, "Every schoolteacher, parent or person standing in the place of a parent is justified in using force by way of correction toward a pupil or child, as the case may be, who is under his care, if the force does not exceed what is reasonable under the circumstances."[51] A 2004 Canadian Supreme Court ruling (*The Canadian Foundation for Children, Youth and the Law v. The Attorney General of Canada*) examined the legality of the code and concluded that corporal punishment in the home was legal.* In the 6-3 decision, the court stated that "under Section 43, criminal law does not apply when force 'is part of a genuine effort to educate the child, poses no reasonable risk of harm that is more than transitory and trifling, and is reasonable under the circumstances.' "[52] The court did note that corporal punishment by parents was not permissible against children under age two or over age twelve.[53] In defining appropriate limits for corporal punishment, Chief Justice Beverley McLachlin stated:

> Corporal punishment of children under two years is harmful to them, and has no corrective value given the cognitive limitations of children under two years of age. Corporal punishment of teenagers is harmful, because it can induce aggressive or antisocial behaviour. Corporal punishment using objects, such as rulers or belts, is physically and emotionally harmful. Corporal punishment, which involves slaps or blows to the head is harmful. These types of punishment, we may conclude, will not be reasonable.

In response to this case, a bill (Bill S-209) was introduced in the Canadian legislature as an effort to eliminate section 43. The bill, when eventually passed, did not eliminate section 43 (thereby eliminating corporal punishment), but did reduce a caregiver's ability to use corporal punishment only in very specific circumstances, such as a small smack to prevent the child from engaging in dangerous behavior.[54] The bill was passed by the Senate but was never approved in the House of Commons.

With the exception of Israel, all countries in the Middle East permit the use of corporal punishment in the home. In Tunisia, article 319 of the Criminal Code explicitly states "correction inflicted on a child by those having authority over him is not punishable."[55] The Code of Child Protection, amended in 2006, does protect children from ill treatment, which is defined as "subjection of the child to torture, repeated violations of his physical integrity, or his detention, or the habit of depriving him of food, or committing any brutal act which is likely to affect the emotional or psychological well being of the child," but this is not a provision against corporal punishment.[56]

FREQUENCY OF USE

Although it is somewhat simple to determine how many countries allow the use of corporal punishment against children in the home, determining the actual frequency of use by the entire international community is a different matter. In the United States, the National Family Violence Surveys from 1975 and 1985 show that more than 95% of young children in the United States experienced corporal punishment in 1975 and 90% in 1985.[57] Gershoff notes that most parents believe

---

*The implications for educational settings will be discussed in the next chapter.

corporal punishment is most appropriate for children under the age of five (because children are assumed to lack the cognitive ability to respond to verbal reasoning) and support tends to decrease as children age.[58] Despite the negative association between age and corporal punishment, such methods of correction appear to persist throughout childhood and into adolescence.[59] When asked to recall how often their parents hit them during adolescence, about half (49.8%) of respondents of the National Family Violence Survey in 1985 indicated that they were hit at least one time a year.[60] Other research indicates that even by age seventeen, one out of four children in the United States are still hit by their parents.[61]

Virtually all American children have at least some experience with corporal punishment, however, the actual administration of corporal punishment appears to be somewhat infrequent. Murray Strauss and Julie Stewart report that parents use corporal punishment approximately 1.5 times per month until children are two years old; but by age twelve, parents administer corporal punishment less than once a month.[62] The age of the child also influences how severe the punishment will be, with more severe forms of corporal punishment being used on children ages 5 to 8, compared to less severe forms that are meted out for children ages 0 to 4 and 9 to 17.[63]

Official statistics on the use of corporal punishment by the international community are extremely difficult to obtain, as official data are not compiled in most countries. This is not particularly surprising as many parts of the world have been arguably slow to recognize international standards or develop their own for the appropriate treatment of children. For example, it wasn't until 1981 that Hong Kong developed formal guidelines on the handling of child abuse cases.[64] Likewise, Japan started its first association for the prevention of child abuse quite recently in 1996.[65] However, limited research on the use of parental corporal punishment does reveal that children in most retentionist countries experience corporal punishment at fairly high rates.

As stated previously, approximately 86% of Japanese college students reported being hit by their parents.[66] A study of punishment in Turkey revealed 34.7% of mothers hit their children.[67] One largely qualitative study of punishment in Jamaica revealed that virtually all of the children who participated in the focus groups experienced harsh corporal punishment, "including beatings with objects such as belts, rulers, garden hose and boards."[68] Finally, Uma Segal notes that the corporal punishment of children in India is both prevalent and accepted. Interviews with 319 college-educated parents in India revealed that over half (55.8%) had engaged in "normal" violence toward their children (defined as slapping or smacking), less than half (41.1%) had engaged in "abusive" violence (defined as kicking, biting, punching, and using objects), and the remaining 2.8% had engaged in extreme violence (burning, using a knife, etc.).[69] Finally, a study of corporal punishment in Egypt revealed more than a third of the study participants had experienced corporal punishment, with beatings being the most common form of punishment.[70] Taken together, findings from these studies suggest that the corporal punishment of children is anything but rare in most parts of the world.

THE EFFECTS OF CORPORAL PUNISHMENT

The use of corporal punishment in the home is a particularly controversial issue. Advocates of corporal punishment maintain it is an essential tool in the discipline of children. However, opponents site the detrimental impact on psychological and emotional development that can result from its administration.[71] As many as 70% of family doctors and 59% of pediatricians support the use of corporal punishment in some cases and an estimated 42% of pediatricians recommend the use of physical punishments under specific circumstances.[72]

It is curious to see so many medical professionals recommend the use of physical punishment because virtually all of the existing empirical literature cites emotional and developmental problems among the children exposed to corporal punishment. The American Academy of Pediatrics cites a multitude of negative consequences stemming from exposure to physical punishments and recommends that parents be encouraged to use disciplinary techniques that do not involve corporal punishment.[73]

A variety of studies have examined the various negative effects of parental corporal punishment. Some of these effects include: deterioration of the parent-child relationship, aggression in childhood, future spousal abuse or child abuse, developmental defects, depression and other mental health problems, and detrimental effects on brain development. Given the multitude of consequences thought to emanate from parental corporal punishment, each of these will be explored below.

Deterioration of the Parent-Child Relationship

As Gershoff notes, "The painful nature of corporal punishment can evoke feelings of fear, anxiety, and anger in children; if these emotions are generalized to the parent, they can interfere with a positive parent–child relationship by inciting children to be fearful of and to avoid the parent."[74] Straus and Donnelly explain that it can be especially traumatic for young children to experience corporal punishment at the hands of someone they love, trust, and are wholly dependent upon for survival.[75] They argue these early experiences can have devastating effects on the parent-child relationship. Moreover, there is considerable evidence that the effects of corporal punishment last well into adulthood.

Aggression in Childhood and Adulthood

There is some evidence to suggest corporal punishment contributes to an increase in aggressive behavior in childhood and later in life. Minor use of corporal punishment has been linked to a reduced ability to feel empathy for others and inhibited moral development.[76] This could be due, at least in part, to an inability of the child to see past the immediate consequences of their actions. Consequently, "the child may be unable to experience feelings of empathy and guilt, and thus may create a system of values to limit him/her from experiencing and expressing empathy."[77] Recent research from Jennifer Lansford et al. found that children who experienced high levels of physical punishment at age five and six were more likely to display antisocial behavior in later adolescence.[78] The argument that corporal punishment encourages violence makes intuitive sense because hitting a child for misbehaving simply teaches them that violence is an appropriate course of action when dealing with problems.[79]

There is a wide body of evidence that suggests victims of abuse are more likely to commit abuse against animals (in childhood) and possibly other human beings during adulthood.[80] The link has also been explored between corporal punishment and future victimization. Some scholars believe there is an intergenerational transmission of violence that is handed down to children from their parents.[81]

Essentially, "dysfunctional parents become role models for their children regarding the appropriateness of using anger and aggression to deal with stressors and frustrations when interacting with their intimate partners."[82] The idea that violence is passed down from parents to children is strongly rooted in Albert Bandura's cognitive social learning theory, which holds that observational learning is fundamental in the process of learning.

Bandura notes that modeling of behavior can produce three different responses.[83] First, a person can learn new behaviors simply by watching others engage in the behavior in question (this is called the observational learning effect). Second, previously learned behaviors can be weakened or reinforced based on observations. Finally, observations of others can serve as cues to engage in an already learned behavior (e.g., an individual starts clapping when the audience applauds a performer).

Modeling violent behavior is most likely the product of the observational learning effect and subsequent observations or experiences of violence during childhood could reinforce the notion that violence is an appropriate response to certain stimuli. For example, Clifton Flynn examined the link between animal cruelty and corporal punishment and found, "males who committed animal cruelty in childhood or adolescence were physically punished more frequently by their fathers, both as preteens and teenagers, than males who did not perpetrate animal abuse."[84] Childhood animal abuse is frequently explained as a scapegoating process, whereby victims of abuse or those who witness abuse will injure innocent pets, who are generally the weakest members of the family.[85] There is also evidence to suggest the violence may not stop at family pets, as numerous studies point to correlates between corporal punishment and a propensity to engage in spousal abuse and child abuse later in life.[86]

In a study of intergenerational violence, Joseph Carroll found that over a third of couples who had experienced harsh punishment as children were more likely to cite violence as a problem in their adult families.[87] Further, individuals who were raised in families with low parental warmth and high levels of punishment were more likely to have problems with violence in their own families.[88] This suggests a propensity toward violence as a tool of discipline or emotional coping is passed down through family generations.

More recently, Murray Straus and Carrie Yodanis examined the relationship between corporal punishment as a child and negative outcomes in later life.[89] They found individuals who experienced corporal punishment were at an increased risk of marital conflict, depression, and approval of spousal abuse. All three of these factors compounded and made physical assault against a spouse more likely. These findings remained consistent when controlling for age, socioeconomic status, ethnic group membership, and witnessing violence between parents.

In their examination of the intergenerational transmission of violence, Jennifer Wareham, Denise Boots, and Jorge Chavez administered surveys to adult male batterers who were participating in a court-ordered batterers' intervention program.[90] The survey included a variety of measures of violent experiences during childhood (e.g., corporal punishment and abuse) as well as violence perpetrated as adults. Regarding corporal punishment in particular, findings revealed that batterers who experienced high levels of maternal corporal punishment were not necessarily more inclined to engage in violence later in life. In fact, mother figure corporal punishment reduced the odds that batterers would later engage in interpersonal violence. However, when maternal corporal punishment was combined with associations with others who engaged in high amounts of interpersonal violence, the likelihood that the men would engage in interpersonal violence increased markedly.[91] Among those men in which corporal punishment was meted out primarily by a father figure, there was a high likelihood that they would commit acts of minor interpersonal violence.

Depression and Mental Health

Straus and Donnelly find, "regardless of sex, socioeconomic status, drinking problems, marital violence, or whether children witness violence between their parents, the fact is the more people were hit by their parents in their early teens, the higher their scores on the Depressive Symptoms Index and the greater percent who thought about committing suicide."[92] Straus and Donnelly explain the linkage between corporal punishment and depression as a response to the stress of being hit by parents over an extended period of time. Exposure to extreme levels of stress can change hormonal levels and can alter brain development,[93] which may explain the relationship.

Greven (1991) offers a somewhat different explanation of the link between corporal punishment and depression by describing it as a delayed anger response "from being physically hit and hurt ... by adults ... on whom he or she depends for nurturance and life itself."[94] The link could also be explained as a response to feeling helpless and powerless in a situation,[95] and corporal punishment likely reinforces out of balance power dynamics between parent and child. There are no doubt complicated relationships at play and depressive symptoms may be some combination of all three explanations.

In addition to depression and suicidal ideation, corporal punishment has been linked to a decrease in feelings of confidence and assertiveness and an increase in feelings of humiliation and helplessness.[96] The consensus in the literature appears to indicate that corporal punishment has severe psychological consequences for children and these consequences persist throughout the life course.

Brain Development

Related to the issue of mental health is the effect of corporal punishment on brain development. Akemi Tomoda et al. observe that forms of abuse, such as physical abuse and sexual abuse, in childhood have been linked to changes in brain development.[97] To study this, they performed brain scans on victims of harsh corporal punishment (e.g., being hit with an object). They found there was a significant reduction in gray matter volume in the right front medial gyrus and a possible reduction in gray matter volume in the left medial front gyrus and the right anterior cingulate gyrus.[98] These areas are significant because other research has linked them to addiction, suicidal behavior, depression, post-traumatic stress disorder (PTSD), dissociative disorders and depression. It is important to note that this study examined severe corporal punishment and not corporal punishment in general. It is still unclear whether there is a relationship between more common (and less severe) forms of corporal punishment and brain development. However, given that previous research has noted a link between low levels of corporal punishment and depression, antisocial behavior, and moral development, it is reasonable to believe that these results may be generalizable to lesser forms of physical discipline.

Conclusion

Corporal punishment in the home is ubiquitous, found in almost every country and every culture worldwide. The use of corporal punishment by parents has a long history that dates back millennia. With the exception of 32 nations, it persists even today. Physical punishments are still used as a disciplinary technique despite the myriad demonstrated negative effects that manifest in childhood and can last a lifetime. Children exposed to corporal punishment are more likely to exhibit aggressive behaviors than can lead to violence against family pets in childhood and intimate partner violence in adulthood. Further, children who experience corporal punishment are also more likely to suffer from depression and other mental health disorders compared to those children who are not punished corporally. Finally, extreme corporal punishment can lead to deficiencies in brain development. Despite these negative consequences, corporal punishment in the home will likely persist and continue to be a fact of life for children worldwide.

Corporal Punishment in Educational Settings

O ye! who teach the ingenuous youth of nations,
Holland, France, England, Germany, or Spain,
I pray ye flog them upon all occasions,
It mends their morals, never mind the pain

—Lord Byron
"Don Juan" Canto the Second (ca. 1819)

IN DEFINING CORPORAL punishment in educational settings one can generally rely on the same definition provided in the discussion of physical discipline in the home. To restate it, corporal punishment in these contexts is defined as "the use of physical force with the intention of causing a child pain, but not injury, for purposes of correction or control of the child's behavior."[1] The primary difference between corporal punishment administered in educational settings and corporal punishment in the home lies in the person responsible for its administration. In school settings an administrator typically metes out the punishment, but teachers, teachers' aides, or other school personnel may also administer physical discipline. The question of who holds this responsibility is dependent on many factors including school policy, applicable laws, and societal custom.[2]

Applying a comparative approach to the study of corporal punishment in educational settings presents considerable difficulty for many of the same reasons comparative studies are generally more complicated. However, study of educational settings is further impeded by the nonuniversality of definitions. Some studies rely on the definition above (or some variation thereof), while others use a much broader definition. For example, Sara Humphreys includes anything from the caning of a student as punishment for a violation of the rules, to a teacher slapping or punching a student out of anger.[3] Humphreys also includes physical labor (e.g., cleaning) in her definition.[4]

The broad range of definitions raises an interesting question: When is a punishment corporal punishment and when is it assault? A recent U.S. case from the state of Indiana, *State of Indiana v. Paula Fettig*,[5] addresses that question. The case involves a fifteen-year-old student enrolled in Paula Fettig's physical education class. Though accounts of the incident differ, the student (S.D.) gave the following account to law enforcement:

Fast Facts: Corporal Punishment in Educational Settings

- Corporal punishment in educational settings dates back to ancient Greece.
- One of the earliest legal challenges to the use of corporal punishment in educational settings can be found in the 1889 English case of *Gardiner v. Bygrave*.
- In the United States, corporal punishment has been banned in 30 states but remains legal in 20 states.
- The U.S. Department of Education reports during the 2006–2007 school year, 223,190 students received corporal punishment at least once.
- Worldwide, 88 countries still legally permit corporal punishment in school settings.
- In a survey of 5,754 Malaysian students, 52% reported that caning was a common occurrence in their schools.
- Limited research in this area finds that corporal punishment in schools is linked to school bullying, school shootings, school violence, lower academic achievement, and higher school dropout rates.

That she was in gym class when one of her classmates hurt her ankle during a play. [S.D.] remembered that while she was checking on the classmate's welfare, her gym teacher [Fettig] slapped her on the face telling her to "go play" and that the slap stung. [S.D.] went on to explain that there were [four] to [five] students in the immediate area who may have seen or heard the slap to the face.[6]

Fettig was charged with assault, but the charges were dismissed by the trial court and again by the state appellate court. In a 2-1 ruling, the Indiana Court of Appeals ruled Fettig was protected by Indiana's corporal punishment statute and by Indiana code that states teachers, "may take any action that is reasonably necessary to carry out or to prevent an interference with an educational function that the individual supervises."[7] This case helps to underscore the difficulty in differentiating physical punishment for the purposes of behavior modification from assault emanating out of frustration or anger.

The administration of corporal punishment in educational settings can take many forms, but in American schools, the most common form involves the hitting of a student's buttocks or upper thigh with "a wooden paddle, approximately 15 inches long, between two and four inches wide, and one-half inch thick, with a six-inch handle at one end."[8] However, in some Texas schools, shaved down baseball bats have been used to administer corporal punishment.[9]

HISTORY

As indicated previously, the corporal punishment of children in educational settings has a history dating back to ancient Greece.[10] In the United States, corporal punishment has been administered in schools since colonial times and is governed by a single common law principle, "Teachers may impose reasonable but not excessive force to discipline a child."[11] Both historically and presently, educators have the right to discipline a child in a manner consistent with punishments that a parent or guardian might administer.

Corporal punishment has long been regarded as an important element of the educational system. Throughout the eighteenth and nineteenth centuries, it was widely believed that the threat of punishment was "a quick and effective, and thus desirable, form of motivation."[12] The idea of physical punishment as educational motivator has a much longer history, as references to its use can be found as early as the twelfth century when educationist Henry Bompas Smith stated the "average schoolboy should accept that it was the teacher's business to make him obey orders 'even if you have to resort to unpleasant methods of compulsion.' "[13]

If *"spare the rod, spoil the child"* is the primary justification for corporal punishment in the home then the following quote by Egerton Ryerson, the superintendent of Canada West schools in 1864, encapsulates the justification for corporal punishment in schools, "The best Teacher, like the best Parent, will seldom resort to the Rod; but there are occasions when it cannot be wisely avoided."[14] These ideas are not unique to Western society and persist in many parts of the world.

One of the earliest legal challenges to the use of corporal punishment in educational settings can be found in the 1889 English case of *Gardiner v. Bygrave*.[15] In this case, a parent alleged that a teacher had committed assault against their child for corporal punishment that was administered in the school. On appeal, the High Court concluded, "caning upon the hand was a perfectly moderate and reasonable form of punishment and that a teacher could expect to punish a child in this way, regardless of the wishes of a parent."[16] This case helped set the stage for the continued use of corporal punishment in England. Elsewhere, the use of corporal punishment has an equally long history, though many countries have moved to full abolition in school settings.

The United States exists in a middle ground, because corporal punishment has been banned in 30 states, but remains legal in 20 states. The first U.S. state to abolish corporal punishment in educational settings was New Jersey in 1867. It would be another 100 years before a second state, Massachusetts, would institute a similar ban.[17]

INTERNATIONAL PREVALENCE

According to the Global Initiative to End the Corporal Punishment of Children, 109 countries prohibit corporal punishment in educational settings, leaving 88 countries where the practice is still legal. Among the countries allowing corporal punishment in school are: Brazil; The Bahamas; Chile; France; Lebanon; Malaysia; Morocco; Niger; Saudi Arabia; and the United States.

Even in countries with provisions against the use of corporal punishment, it is often difficult to tell whether the law is enforced or merely exists on the books.

Kenya, for example, restricts the use of severe corporal punishment, but it is still used routinely.* As a consequence, there remains some difficulty in classifying countries as retentionist or abolitionist. To date, there is no clear mechanism in place for monitoring the use of corporal punishment in many countries.

In Malaysia, for example, students are caned quite frequently. One survey of 5,754 students revealed "52% agreed that caning commonly happened in their schools, more often in rural schools than urban schools; around 80% of cases occurred at technical schools; 79.5% of teachers and 71.8% of administrators agreed that persistent offenders should be caned."[18]

In India, corporal punishment is the norm in educational settings. A 2004 study of 350 students from public and private schools found that "over 75% said they received punishment at school, and nearly 60% said the most frequent form of punishment was caning or hitting with a ruler. It was common for the whole class to be punished (66%). A third (33%) reported cases of severe injury due to punishment."[19]

In many countries school-based corporal punishment often eclipses the boundaries of rational discipline. There have been reports of severe injuries and in some cases death from the administration of corporal punishment in Nigeria, Ethiopia, Kenya, Tanzania, Botswana, and Egypt.[20] Despite having banned the practice in schools, corporal punishment is still fairly widespread in South Africa, China, Japan, and Zambia.[21] In the following sections, the school-based corporal punishment practices of several nations will be discussed in detail.

The United States of America

Corporal punishment is still routinely used in American schools in 20 states. The laws vary state to state because there is no federal ban on the use of corporal punishment in educational settings. The issue was examined in the 1977 U.S. Supreme Court case *Ingraham v. Wright.*[22] The case involved junior high students from Florida who alleged that they and other students had been subjected to corporal punishment by their teachers in violation of their Constitutional rights. The students argued the punishments they received violated the Eighth Amendment's protection from cruel and unusual punishment and the Fourteenth Amendment's due process clause.

Regarding the Eighth Amendment claim, Justice Powell, writing the opinion of the court, stated that the Eighth Amendment applies only to those convicted of criminal offenses and therefore does not protect children from being paddled for the purposes of maintaining discipline in the classroom. Powell commented

---

*Plan International (2010) recounts the story of one Kenyan child who "along with eight other children in his class . . . was whipped with an electric cable for not completing his English homework. He was injured on his back, arm and abdomen. As well as reporting the teacher to the police (despite being told not to by the headteacher), [the child's] father took his son to a clinic."

further, "the schoolchild has little need for the protection of the Eighth Amendment."[23] With regard to the alleged Fourteenth Amendment due process violations, Powell noted that while there were possibly Fourteenth Amendment issues in the case, the students were ultimately protected by Florida law. Signaling a hesitance to interfere with school matters, the court stated:

> In view of the low incidence of abuse, the openness of our schools, and the common-law safeguards that already exist, the risk of error that may result in violation of a schoolchild's substantive rights can only be regarded as minimal. Imposing additional administrative safeguards as a constitutional requirement might reduce that risk marginally, but would also entail a significant intrusion into an area of primary educational responsibility.[24]

Justice White, Justice Brennan, Justice Marshall, and Justice Stevens dissented. Writing for the minority, Justice White stated:

> If there are some punishments that are so barbaric that they may not be imposed for the commission of crimes, designated by our social system as the most thoroughly reprehensible acts an individual can commit, then, a fortiori, similar punishments may not be imposed on persons for less culpable acts, such as breaches of school discipline. Thus, if it is constitutionally impermissible to cut off someone's ear for the commission of murder, it must be unconstitutional to cut off a child's ear for being late to class.

In addition to possible Eighth Amendment violations, the use of corporal punishment also violates international human rights regulations. The United States has signed the *International Covenant on Civil and Political Rights* and the *Convention against Torture and Other Cruel, Inhuman, or Degrading Treatment or Punishment*. Corporal punishment violates these treaties because it can be viewed as a degrading form of punishment that violates the basic human right to be free from physical violence.[25]

The U.S. Department of Education reports during the 2006–2007 school year, 223,190 students received corporal punishment at least once. While the number of students being corporally punished seems quite high, the numbers appear to be declining. During 2002–2003, 301,016 students received physical punishments and 10 to 20 years ago nearly 1 million students in the United States received physical punishments.[26] These numbers should be regarded with some caution as they count only the number of students and not the number of times corporal punishment is administered.[27] Additionally, not all schools are aware they are supposed to report when they administer corporal punishment.

The majority of states still employing corporal punishment are located in the South. The state of Texas administers corporal punishment more than any other state, with almost 50,000 students receiving such punishments annually.[28] Interestingly, students with disabilities receive corporal punishment at rates disproportionate to their representation within the student population. Of the 223,190 students who received corporal punishments in 2006–2007, 41,972 were students with disabilities.[29] In Tennessee, for example, students with disabilities are 2.1 times more likely to receive corporal punishment than students without disabilities; and in Georgia disabled students are 1.7 times more likely than nondisabled students to receive corporal punishment.[30]

In many cases, students with disabilities are punished because they are acting out in a manner consistent with their disability. For example, children with autism can receive punishment for rocking back and forth, a behavior that is symptomatic of the disorder.[31] In an interview with the ACLU one mother of a son with Tourette's syndrome recounted the punishments that her son would receive:

> One of his tics was balling up his fists . . . that was seen as aggression and he would get in trouble with it . . . He would try to explain it was a tic, and he couldn't control it, but they see that as him escalating it. So now they have him in restraints and then they're giving him sedatives and calling for me to come pick him up. They had a closet and he would go in there and that's where he was hit.[32]

In addition to the disproportionate punishment of children with disabilities, corporal punishment is also meted out against African American children at rates that exceed their representation in the student population.[33] African Americans make up 17.1% of the population in public schools, yet they represent approximately 35.6% of those students paddled.[34]

Although the United States is out of sync with much of the Western world regarding corporal punishment, steps are being taken to bring the United States more in line with growing international sentiments. On April 15, 2010, the U.S. House of Representatives Education and Labor Subcommittee on Healthy Families and Communities held a hearing that focused on the use of corporal punishment in U.S. schools. A representative from the ACLU urged Congress to pass the *Positive Behavior for Safe and Effective Schools Act* (H.R. 2597), which would provide federal funding to schools who implement Positive Behavior Supports (PBS). The goal of PBS is to teach children why their behavior was errant and give them tools to modify their behavior.[35]

Canada

A large number of countries have banned corporal punishment in schools, which stands in stark contrast to a relatively small number of countries that have deemed corporal punishment in the home illegal. This disparity can be partially explained by a general reluctance among lawmakers and policymakers in several countries to intervene in private family matters[36]; thereby dictating what punishments are appropriate. Even so, the same reluctance does not appear to apply where educational settings are concerned.

In 2004, Canada abolished corporal punishment in all of its schools. The path to abolition throughout the country was anything but swift. In 1971, the

Toronto Board of Education abolished corporal punishment in its schools, but the practice persisted across Canada for over thirty years. In 2004, the Supreme Court of Canada released its opinion in *The Canadian Foundation for Children, Youth and the Law v. The Attorney General of Canada*,[37] which led to the abolition of corporal punishment in Canadian schools. Writing the majority opinion for the court, Chief Justice Beverley McLachlin stated:

> Contemporary social consensus is that, while teachers may sometimes use corrective force to remove children from classrooms or secure compliance with instructions, the use of corporal punishment by teachers is not acceptable. Many school boards forbid the use of corporal punishment, and some provinces and territories have legislatively prohibited its use by teachers. ... This consensus is consistent with Canada's international obligations, given the findings of the Human Rights Committee of the United Nations noted above. Section 43 will protect a teacher who uses reasonable, corrective force to restrain or remove a child in appropriate circumstances. Substantial societal consensus, supported by expert evidence and Canada's treaty obligations, indicates that corporal punishment by teachers is unreasonable.[38]

United Kingdom of Great Britain and Northern Ireland

The United Kingdom was similarly late in banning corporal punishment in educational settings. As with Canada, the path to abolition was long. In 1986, Parliament passed the Education (No. 2) Act, which prohibited corporal punishment in all publicly funded schools.[39] The passage of this act stemmed from a court case brought before The European Court of Human Rights for incidents that occurred in two Scottish schools in the 1970s.

The *Case of Campbell and Cosans v. The United Kingdom*[40] involved Gordon Campbell, a student attending a parochial school in Strathclyde that used corporal punishment. His mother expressed concerns that she did not want Gordon subjected to corporal punishment, but the school made no assurances he would be exempt. It is noteworthy that Gordon never actually received corporal punishment during his time at the school.

The second petitioner in the case was Jeffrey Cosans, who attended school in Fife. In this instance, Cosans violated school rules by taking a shortcut through a cemetery to get home. He was told to report to the Assistant Headmaster the following day to receive corporal punishment, but he refused to comply with this request. Cosans was told that failure to comply with the punishment would result in school suspension. Several meetings between school administrators and the child's parents followed in which they were told that their son would have to receive corporal punishment or he would not be permitted to return to school. Once Cosans turned sixteen (the age past which compulsory attendance is required in the United Kingdom) he never returned to school.[41]

Both parents alleged that corporal punishment was a violation of Article 3 of the European Convention for the Protection of Human Rights and Fundamental Freedoms, "No one shall be subjected to torture or to inhuman or degrading treatment or punishment."[42] Because neither child was actually subjected to corporal punishment, The European Court did not find the schools to be in violation of Article 3. However, the court did state, "provided it is sufficiently real and immediate, a mere threat of conduct prohibited by Article 3 (art. 3) may itself be in conflict with that provision. Thus, to threaten an individual with torture might in some circumstances constitute at least 'inhuman treatment.' "[43]

In addition to Article 3 violations, both parents alleged the schools were in violation of Article 2, Protocol No. 1 of the Protocol to the Convention for the Protection of Human Rights and Fundamental Freedoms, which states, "No person shall be denied the right to education. In the exercise of any functions which it assumes in relation to education and to teaching, the State shall respect the right of parents to ensure such education and teaching in conformity with their own religious and philosophical convictions."[44] The court agreed that such a violation had occurred. Regarding the case of Jeffrey Cosans specifically, the court stated:

> The suspension of Jeffrey Cosans—which remained in force for nearly a whole school year—was motivated by his and his parents' refusal to accept that he receive or be liable to corporal chastisement (see paragraphs 10–11 above). His return to school could have been secured only if his parents had acted contrary to their convictions, convictions which the United Kingdom is obliged to respect under the second sentence of Article 2 (P1-2) (see paragraphs 35–36 above). A condition of access to an educational establishment that conflicts in this way with another right enshrined in Protocol No. 1 cannot be described as reasonable and in any event falls outside the State's power of regulation under Article 2 (P1-2).[45]

Eventually, the corporal punishment ban was extended to private schools in England and Wales in 1998 and finally to Scotland and Wales in 2000 and 2003, respectively.[46] Despite the apparent ban, the issue of corporal punishment in schools was not completely resolved, as there were a number of loopholes that allowed the physical punishment to continue in certain educational settings. For example, schools where lessons were taught for 12.5 hours or less per week were exempt from the corporal punishment ban and certain religious schools were also exempt.[47] The loopholes were finally closed and at present no educational institution is permitted to use corporal punishment against students. The chief advisor on child safety, Sir Roger Singleton stated, "Banning physical punishment outside of the family home sends a straight forward message that it is entirely unacceptable in any form of care, education or leisure."[48]

Japan

The word *taibatsu* is commonly used to describe corporal punishment in Japan, but according to Shoko Yoneyama and Asao Naito, the translation is not entirely accurate. They state:

> The Japanese word *taibatsu*, which literally means 'physical punishment', is quite different from what is normally understood as corporal punishment in the West

where it is expected to be used only in a highly regulated manner. *Taibatsu* is often nothing but an arbitrary use of violence by teachers.[49]

Nevertheless, corporal punishment, whether arbitrary or regulated, has been prohibited in Japanese educational settings since 1947. Article 11 of the School Education Law prohibits the use of corporal punishment, which is defined as hitting, kicking, and other nonphysical punishments such as forcing students to sit or stand for extended periods of time.[50] However, a 1981 ruling by the Tokyo High Court suggested the taibatsu ban did not preclude the use of all forms of corporal punishment.[51] Despite the apparent ban, it would seem corporal punishment is still present in some Japanese schools.

There are examples of extreme cases, such as the 1990 case in which seven teachers buried two middle school children in sand up to their necks as a punishment for intimidating others.[52] There was also the well-publicized case of Toshinao Takahashi who was accidentally killed by his teacher while on a school trip in an instance of corporal punishment gone too far. Ken Schoolland recounts the incident:

> At the hotel where the group was staying, Takahashi had been caught breaking a school rule that forbade the use of electric hair dryers. Kazunori Amamori, the teacher on duty summoned Takahashi in order to have him apologize for the infraction. With a number of students looking on Amamori scolded Takahashi, but the boy showed no remorse and refused to apologize. This enraged the teacher, and he started beating Takahashi on the head and kicking him in the stomach. The youngster dropped to the ground and, kneeling in front of his teacher, attempted to apologize. But the kicking and punching continued until the boy fell unconscious. Takahashi was taken to the hospital where officials reported that he died of head and stomach injuries and shock.[53]

At trial, Amamori claimed that he was pressured by his colleagues to be tougher and felt that he had no option but to administer physical punishments. In the end, Amamori was convicted of involuntary manslaughter and received a three-year sentence.[54]

Although the two previous cases are no doubt extreme examples of corporal punishment, there is evidence to suggest public support of corporal punishment is strong in Japan and physical punishments are still routinely meted out in Japanese schools. Aaron Miller argues that while corporal punishment may be discouraged in some schools, it is actively encouraged in others.[55] Further evidence for the permissive attitude toward corporal punishment can be found in the low rate of punishment for teachers that use it. Miller estimates that only 30 to 40% of teachers caught corporally punishing students are ever punished.[56] While it is impossible to get accurate statistics pertaining to how frequently corporal punishments are used in Japanese schools because there are severe levels of under-reporting, for many Japanese students corporal punishment is a frequent occurrence.

The Republic of Kenya

In Kenya, it is believed that corporal punishment is necessary because pain is seen as being fundamental in the process of learning.[57] The law regarding corporal punishment is explicit, stating that "only the head teacher is permitted to administer corporal punishment, and he or she must use a cane or strap of regulation size, hitting boys on the buttocks and girls on the palm of the hand. The head teacher may give no more than six strokes as punishment, and must keep a written record of all the proceedings."[58] Strictly speaking, however, corporal punishment need not always involve hitting the child as any punishment designed to cause physical discomfort can be labeled corporal punishment. Therefore, the use of restraints, certain body holds, and solitary confinement could also fall under the umbrella of corporal punishment.

People's Republic of Bangladesh

Until 2010, corporal punishment in schools was a frequent occurrence in Bangladesh. UNICEF Bangladesh conducted a survey of children (n = 3,840) to measure their perceptions of corporal punishment in the school system. The vast majority of children (91%) reported corporal punishment was frequently employed at their school.[59] The children most likely to receive corporal punishments were boys between the ages of 9 and 13, as well as children living in poverty.[60] Children also reported that corporal punishment tended to manifest as hitting the palm with ruler/stick; standing in class; hitting other body parts with ruler/stick; slapping; ear, hair, or skin twisting; and kneeling.[61]

This situation changed drastically in 2010, when the government of Bangladesh banned corporal punishment in schools amid reports of the suicide of a 10-year-old boy who was severely beaten by his teacher.[62] Another contributing factor was the well-publicized case of eight students who were hospitalized after they were caned by their teacher for forgetting to bring colored pencils to class.[63] Because the ban is so recent, it remains to be seen whether teachers will receive extensive retraining as to how the government will handle violations of the ban.

Republic of India

As stated previously, corporal punishment was historically prevalent in Indian schools, but the situation could be changing. In 2000, the Indian Supreme Court stated that children should not be subjected to corporal punishment in schools and that children have a right to be free from fear.[64] However, it was nearly a decade before a ban on corporal punishment actually took place. In 2009, corporal punishment was banned in schools through the Right to Free and Compulsory Education Act. Article 17 of the act states, "(1) No child shall be subjected to physical punishment or mental harassment. (2) Whoever contravenes the provisions of sub-section (1) shall be liable to disciplinary action under the service rules applicable to such person."[65]

The act was not fully implemented, however, until the passage of The Right of Children to Free and Compulsory Education Rules, which imposed procedures for monitoring the ban as well as procedures for dealing with violations of the act.[66] The penalties for violating the ban are stiff and include up to one year in jail and/or a fine of 50,000 rupees for the first violation.[67] In the event of a second violation, the penalties increase up to three years incarceration and a fine of 25,000 rupees.[68] However, because the ban is new, it is difficult to tell what (if any) effects will be seen in the Indian educational system.

EFFECTS OF CORPORAL PUNISHMENT IN EDUCATIONAL SETTINGS

Compared to the empirical research documenting the negative side effects of the parental use of corporal punishment, the literature detailing the consequences of its use in school settings is surprisingly sparse. Although there exists a doubtless overlap in the consequences of parental and school use of corporal punishment (for example anger, depression, suicidal ideation, substance abuse, and future child and spousal abuse), there are also unintended consequences unique to the school environment.

There is the obvious risk children will receive serious injuries as a result of corporal punishment, because it is very difficult to regulate the force with which a school administrator will administer it. In a study of Nigerian school children, Bernice Adegbehingbe and Ajite Kayode found that corporal punishment contributed to an alarming number of students' ocular injuries.[69] The sample consisted of 186 children who were patients at the Obafemi Awolowo University Teaching Hospital's eye clinic. Of these children, 89 (47.8%) had ocular injuries and 27 (30.3%) had sustained those injuries due to corporal punishment.[70] About half of the children received the injuries while at school and roughly one-third received them in the home. Sticks were the most common implement to cause the injury (48.2%), followed by straps (18.5%), whips (14.8%), stones (11.1%), kicks (3.7%), and shoes (3.7%). The injuries ranged from a moderate degree of visual impairment (48.2%) to blindness in the affected eye (14.8%), and at the three-month follow-up period three children, or 11.1% of the sample, were blind.[71] Ocular injuries occur during the administration of corporal punishment because as the authors note, "during the application of corporal punishment, usually no part of the body is spared and as such it is very easy to inflict injury on the face, head, and especially the eyes while the child is struggling to beg for pardon/mercy from his assaulter."[72]

While it is almost impossible to separate the effects of corporal punishment that is meted out in the home from that which is administered in school settings, the limited research in this area suggests some important conclusions. Whatever short-term gain might be achieved through the use of corporal punishment is often overshadowed by long-term problems such as school bullying, school shootings, school violence, lower academic achievement, and higher school dropout rates.[73] Doreen Arcus examined the relationship between corporal punishment and school shooting fatalities, while controlling for poverty, religion, and other confounding variables.[74] She found students are more likely to lose their lives in schools that permit corporal punishment versus those schools where the practice is prohibited.[75] Although meting out corporal punishment against students is not the only factor that should to be considered, Arcus notes, "the sanctioning of violence toward children as an acceptable means of socialization and discipline in public institutions seems to contribute to the likelihood that such incidents will occur."[76]

The theorized link to higher rates of aggression in school (e.g., bullying and other forms of violence) is easy to understand because corporal punishment in this context legitimates violence and helps to create an environment where resolving conflict through violence is deemed permissible. Further, the administration of corporal punishment may create more anger in students.

In an interview with the ACLU, one teacher notes, "students rarely think they did anything wrong . . . couple that with physical [punishment], that will elicit anger [from the student]. I have seen students acting out in their aggression for receiving corporal punishment."[77]

Corporal punishment has also been linked to higher dropout rates. In a study of corporal punishment in Pakistan, conducted by UNICEF, all 3,582 children surveyed indicated that they had received corporal punishment at school.[78] Concomitantly, Pakistan has one of the highest school dropout rates in the world, with nearly 50% of students dropping out within the first five years of education.[79] Although corporal punishment is certainly not the only reason Pakistani children drop out, the Islamabad-based Society for the Protection of the Rights of the Child, a local NGO, estimates that 35,000 students drop out of school annually for reasons relating to corporal punishment.[80] Similarly, in Nepal, nearly 14% of students cite being afraid of their teacher as a primary reason for dropping out of school.[81]

Finally, no discussion of corporal punishment in educational settings would be complete without a consideration of its economic ramifications. Plan International, a child welfare organization, has calculated the financial impact of school violence in terms of lost social benefits and estimates all forms of violence (corporal punishment, bullying, and sexual violence) to cost almost $60 billion in just 13 nations. In India alone, school violence, manifesting primarily in the form of corporal punishment, was estimated to have cost almost $7.4 billion per year.[82] This research, "found that children who experience violence at school are likely to earn less, be in greater need of healthcare and other services, and long-term, contribute less to their countries' economies."[83]

ROLE OF RELIGION

Although covered in some detail previously, the influence of religion (particularly as a justification or catalyst for certain disciplinary traditions) bears brief restatement. Given that scriptural prescription is one of the main authorizing authorities for the use of corporal punishment in Western society (i.e., *spare the rod*), it should not be surprising that there is a relationship between the support of corporal punishment and religion. Harold Grasmick, Carolyn Morgan, and Mary Kennedy found that religious affiliation was a strong determinant of support for corporal punishment, with fundamentalist Protestants being the more likely than nonfundamentalist Protestants, Catholics, and those with no religious affiliation to favor its use.[84] While empirical research in this area is limited, there are many anecdotal accounts of corporal punishments in parochial schools. In a recent *Newsweek* article, David Noonan recounted his personal experience with corporal punishment in Catholic school. He writes:

> The nuns who smacked me and my friends at our small elementary school in New Jersey were Sisters of Charity, a cheap bit of irony that always draws a chuckle when I talk about being on the receiving end of those holy rights and lefts. And let me say right here that not every nun I encountered in the early '60s resorted to physical violence. Most didn't, in fact, but the ones who did established a pervasive atmosphere of low-grade dread that still taints my memories of those years.[85]

Noonan's experience is certainly not unique to Catholic education in the United States. Tom O'Donoghue notes that there were reports from Australian Catholic schools in Melbourne where the teacher-to-student ratios were 70:1.[86] Corporal punishments became prevalent in these overcrowded classrooms, not necessarily because teachers were motivated by religious concerns to instill discipline in the students, but because the teachers needed an effective crowd control technique.[87] Teachers simply turned to corporal punishment because it was "the only control mechanism they knew."[88]

While there appears to be widespread support of corporal punishment among the general population in the United States, this support drops among clergy members. Margaret Vaaler, Christopher Ellison, Karissa Horton, and John Marcum examined support for corporal punishment among Presbyterian clergy members and found only limited support for its use.[89] Regarding support for corporal punishment, Vaaler et al. note, "Most clergy members express significant reservations about this practice; this hesitancy is especially marked among specialized clergy, rather than those who are engaged in parish ministry."[90] In addition to the opposition of specialized clergy, females and non-Hispanic clergy members were also less likely to support the use of corporal punishment. Although this study examined only Presbyterian clergy, the results are somewhat surprising and lead to questions about the support of corporal punishment among clergy in other Christian denominations, as well as other religions.

Within the Islamic faith, the issue of corporal punishment in madrasahs is a point of debate. Madrasah is an Arabic term that means "place of instruction" and any institution of learning that focuses on Islamic subjects (e.g., the Qur'an, hadith, or fiqh) falls under the umbrella of a madrasah.[91] In Morocco and elsewhere, early madrasahs (circa 1900) focused on rote memorization of the Qur'an and used corporal punishment extensively.[92] Corporal punishment was seen as a necessary component of education,[93] but there is some debate about whether that view persists. In an examination of madrasahs in India, Hartung and Reifeld note that they observed corporal punishment on only a handful of occasions during their visits to the schools, and teachers' views about the use of corporal punishment were somewhat divided.[94] Some teachers felt that the threat of corporal punishment was the only method that would ensure a smooth and functional classroom environment, while others favored verbal reprimands over physical punishments.[95]

ROLE OF GENDER

As with religion, one cannot overlook gender issues in the administration of corporal punishment. Humphreys notes that in Sub-Saharan Africa females are often punished as a way to regulate sexual behavior. In some cases male teachers will administer physical punishments to girls that have rejected their advances.[96] In Botswana corporal punishment is administered differently depending on the gender of the student receiving the punishment. The guidelines are specifically outlined in the Education Act regulations of 1978. They state that male teachers are not permitted to administer physical punishments to female students (only a male headmaster is permitted) and girls are not to be beaten on the buttocks, but instead are to be beaten on the backs of the calves or on the palm of the hand.[97]

Although corporal punishment may take a different form or is justified for different reasons among female students, it appears male students are more likely than their female counterparts to receive physical punishments in school. In the United States boys make up 78.3% of those paddled. In some cases gender disparity is exacerbated because educators in U.S. schools will often give children an option between corporal punishment and another sanction, such as suspension.[98]

When this "devil's bargain" is offered, male students may be more inclined to select corporal punishment because of the societal expectation that they should be able to "take it like a man."[99] One former teacher interviewed by the ACLU stated, "there's a certain amount of bravado that comes with it, you want to take your licks like a man, not crying or anything. With boys it's a badge of courage to choose corporal punishment over in school suspension."[100]

ROLE OF POSTCOLONIAL LEGACY

As the preceding discussion of corporal punishment in educational settings has demonstrated, the use of physical punishments by teachers is strongly conditioned by the cultural setting as well as other factors such as gender and religion. However, those countries included in this discussion are also countries that were once colonized by the British Empire (i.e., Kenya, India, and Bangladesh).

Harber notes that colonialism is a major factor in explaining the prevalence of corporal punishment in educational settings around the globe.[101] Harber goes on to state, "In Africa, for example, it has been argued that although corporal punishment is now justified on the grounds that it is 'part of African culture', evidence on pre-colonial education systems suggests that is unlikely."[102]

In summary, corporal punishment in schools is less prevalent than in the home. That said, physical punishments in schools are a regular feature of the school day for children across the world. An estimated 200,000 children each year receive corporal punishment in the United States alone. The negative consequences of corporal punishment in educational settings are myriad and include the risk of physical danger for children, as well as an increased likelihood of violence in the school and higher dropout rates. Although 109 countries have abandoned the practice of corporally punishing students, the practice still remains legal in many parts of the world.

Corporal Punishment in Institutional Settings

I consider the chastisement by the whip, the most efficient, and at the same time, the most humane which exists; it never injures the health, and obliges the prisoners to lead a life essentially healthy . . . I consider it impossible to govern a large prison without a whip.

—Elam Lynds

The formal administration of corporal punishment by the criminal justice system encompasses both criminal sanctions for offenders and disciplinary measures for inmates inside correctional institutions. Physical punishments were once a mainstay of order keeping in North American and European prisons, but they are no longer legally permitted inside the prisons or other correctional institutions of those nations. They are, however, still a routine punishment administered to both adult and juvenile correctional inmates in many parts of the world. This chapter discusses the types of corporal punishment used against prison inmates. This chapter also provides an examination of the implications of corporal punishment for the institutional environment and the inmates themselves.

HISTORY

PHYSICAL PUNISHMENTS HAVE a long history in English prisons. When English prisons instituted rules of silence, the incidents of physical punishment drastically increased. Michael Ignatieff notes that punishments for prison offenses went from one out of every 191 inmates in 1825, to one out of every 3.4 inmates in 1835.[1] He further states, "irons, bread and water, the dark cells, and floggings followed every attempt to speak or protest."[2]

During testimony before British Parliament in 1868, Major William Fulford, the governor of Stafford Gaol in England, testified on many aspects of prison operations, including the administration of flogging. Regarding how flogging was administered at the jail, he testified, "the man is tied up as in a military flogging, and I parade the whole of the prisoners, and read the proceedings from the magistrates' minute book, and he is flogged in the presence of all the prisoners

---

Fast Facts: Corporal Punishment in Institutional Settings

- Corporal punishment is illegal inside institutional settings in many countries, including the United States, Canada, and all EU countries.
- In 1955, the First United Nations Congress on the Prevention of Crime and the Treatment of Offenders adopted standard minimum rules for the treatment of prisoners.
- Corporal punishment for disciplinary infractions inside prisons was introduced in Egypt in 1956 and remained legal until the Egyptian parliament banned the practice in 2001.
- Singapore's Prisons Act stipulates women, prisoners sentenced to death, and men over 50 will not be subjected to corporal punishment. All other offenders can receive corporal punishment.
- Amnesty International (2009) reports that approximately 200,000 people are held in prison camps and other secure facilities in North Korea and many undergo especially harsh treatment and torture.
- Corporal punishment is used as a disciplinary measure for adults and children in institutional settings in Bangladesh.

---

and the surgeon."[3] When asked if there were some prisoners for whom corporal punishment was the only way instill discipline, Fulford replied, "No doubt it is so; it is the only thing that they dread."[4]

During testimony before the same committee in Parliament, James Gardner, the governor of the Bristol Gaol, echoed similar sentiments about the use of flogging in prisons. When asked if he would ever be willing to surrender the power of flogging, Gardner responded, "I should not like to see flogging done away with for the purposes of prison discipline. I think if it were used a little more freely, all the gaols in England would be managed better and quieter."[5]

Despite the view that corporal punishment was absolutely essential to the smooth functioning of English prisons, by the end of the nineteenth century the coming change was inevitable. In 1898, the power to flog prisoners was taken away from magistrates and placed solely in the hands of the Home Secretary.[6] The purpose of centralizing physical punishments was to ensure that their administration would be rare.[7]

Henry Salt speaks of the desire to maintain flogging in English prisons despite its abolition in the British Army and the Navy.[8] He writes, "As might have been expected, the very first symptom of a proposal for the abolition of flogging in prison excessively alarmed prison officials and ex-prison officials. Flogging is, in their eyes, almost a sacred privilge (*sic*)—the last species of active bodily torture which it is possible for them to inflict on the bodies of their fellow-creatures, and, as such a desperate effort must be made to cling to it."[9]

Corporal punishment as a judicial sanction was abolished in 1947 with the passage of the Criminal Justice Bill, but remained in place as a disciplinary measure inside prisons for grave offenses. It was not until 1967 that corporal punishment inside English prisons was finally abolished.[10]

The reach of British penal sensibilities did not stop at the English coast. Rather, the English influence can be seen in the penal practices of most former British colonies. This is especially so in the United States.

Given the widespread use of physical punishment in English prison facilities, it should not be surprising that physical punishments were common in U.S. facilities. Though corporal punishments were technically barred at the Walnut Street Jail (one of America's early attempts at the use of incarceration as punishment), inmates were forced to spend hours on a device known as the treadmill, which used inmate leg power to operate a milling machine.[11]

More formal accounts of the use of corporal punishment in prisons can be found in the Auburn and Pennsylvania Penitentiary systems, both of which are considered America's first attempt at large-scale incarceration. Although both systems relied on silence as one of their primary reform mechanisms, the Auburn system allowed inmates to work in congregate (e.g., factory) type settings, while the Pennsylvania system relied on solitary confinement for an inmate's entire sentence. Given that the Auburn system allowed inmates to interact, albeit in a limited manner, violations for breaking the code of silence were somewhat frequent.

Elam Lynds, principal keeper at both Auburn Penitentiary and Sing Sing (both Auburn-type institutions), developed a reputation for being especially cruel.[12] Lynds is reported to have administered beatings on numerous inmates, both the sick and the healthy.[13] In one account, Lynds was reported to have "dragged out of a hospital bed an allegedly ailing and deranged Auburn convict named Louis von Eck. Accusing Eck of shamming sickness, Lynds beat and kicked him."[14] Louis von Eck eventually died as a result of a number of beatings such as these.[15]

Lynds was not unique for administering corporal punishments in the early penitentiaries. Robert Wiltse, warden at Sing Sing from 1830 to 1840, administered beatings to inmates with an arguable frequency. In one case, he administered 100 lashes to an inmate for making noise at night and then gagged the inmate to prevent him from making noise.[16] Whipping with a cat-o-nine-tales (*cats*), was one of the most frequently administered punishments at Sing Sing during the 1800s. It was administered most often as a punishment for talking.

Of the 776 rule violations that took place at Sing Sing during 1845, "362 were punished with the cats, 414 with the shower bath, solitary confinement, and deprivation of food and bedding."[17] Although corporal punishment was probably more prevalent in the congregate system of imprisonment, it was certainly not absent from the more solitary Pennsylvania system. Where the whip was a regular feature of Auburn-type institutions, Pennsylvania-system penitentiaries relied more on straitjackets and the iron gags.[18]

Once the reformatory system was implemented, corporal punishments were similarly used, though they were not meted out with the same regularity as in the penitentiary system. Philip Klein notes, "the Elmira Reformatory included corporal punishment as part of its regular routine though inflicted only in rare cases and then always under the personal supervision and generally by the hand of the superintendent."[19] In keeping with the principles set forth in the 1870 National Prison Congress Declaration, rewards more so than punishments were to be used in reformatories. Corporal punishments were not unique to the experience of male inmates, as they were also used in women's reformatories. John Gillin notes that flogging was used in 14 of the 28 women's reformatories he studied. In these institutions, it was most often applied for running away and "sex perversions."[20] In addition to floggings, "cold water baths, drugs which cause vomiting, playing a stream of water from a fire-hose upon the disturber, and tying up" were also used against female prisoners.[21] Reformatories were found primarily in the northern region of the United States, but that did not mean that female inmates in the South escaped such punishments. Female lessees often received corporal punishments just like their male counterparts, and they were frequently whipped in the presence of males.[22]

Despite America's history of allowing physical punishments in prisons, corporal punishment is no longer permitted for rule violators in U.S. prisons. Two court cases that dealt specifically with matter include the Supreme Court case *Weems v. United States*, 217 U.S. 349 (1910) and the Eighth Circuit case *Jackson v. Bishop, 404 F.2d 971.*

The *Weems* case serves as the basis for interpreting all Eighth Amendment claims. Weems, who was in the Philippines, was convicted of falsifying official records of the U.S. Coast Guard, which resulted in the loss of 612 pesos by the government.[23] Weems was sentenced to fifteen years of hard labor, during which he was required to be in chains.[24] In addition to these punishments, "he lost all political rights during imprisonment, was subject to permanent surveillance after his release, and was fined 4,000 pesetas."[25] The sentence was eventually overturned because it violated the Eighth Amendment provision against cruel and unusual punishment. Conventional thinking holds the requirement that Weems serve his sentence in chains was perceived as being corporal punishment.[26] However, the sentence did not violate the Eighth Amendment simply because of the corporeal element. Rather, the sentence was viewed as excessive due to the combination of punishments—a long period of incarceration in tandem with the hard labor in chains.[27]

The *Jackson* case was far more explicit in its rejection of corporal punishment. The case dealt with inmates of the Arkansas Department of Corrections who alleged that the use of corporal punishments inside state prisons was unconstitutional. Corporal punishments were formally approved in Arkansas in 1962, but they had been used long before their formal approval.[28] It was widely believed that corporal punishment was necessary to ensure the proper functioning of prisons in Arkansas.[29] Initially, prisoners in Arkansas could be whipped up to ten times per day, but as time went on officials introduced other forms of corporal punishment including the insertion of needles under the fingernails, crushing knuckles, and the now infamous "Tucker telephone."[30] "The Tucker

Telephone" was a torture device that was built from a converted crank telephone. The telephone was wired with electrodes that were usually attached to the inmate's big toe or genitals. Cranking the telephone generated electrical current that would run through the inmate's body.[31]

In the *Jackson* opinion, Chief Justice Blackmun noted that many of the points raised by the inmates in *Jackson* echoed issues that had been previously raised in the 1965 Arkansas case, *Talley v. Stephens*. The *Talley* case lead to the creation of detailed guidelines for the administration of corporal punishments, including the provision that corporal punishments were only appropriate for major offenses, including homosexuality, agitation, insubordination, making/concealing weapons, refusal to work, and participation in a riot. Furthermore, corporal punishments were limited to ten lashes with a strap, to be administered by at least two prison officials.[32] Petitioners in the *Jackson* case received whippings in which the inmates were forced to lower their trousers to receive the lashes (this runs contrary to guidelines that state whippings are to be conducted with the inmates fully clothed) and that the inmates sustained deep bruises as a result of the whipping.

Regarding the appropriateness of corporal punishment in view of the Eighth Amendment, the court stated:

> [We] have no difficulty in reaching the conclusion that the use of the strap in the penitentiaries of Arkansas is punishment which, in this last third of the 20th century, runs afoul of the Eighth Amendment; that the strap's use, irrespective of any precautionary conditions which may be imposed, offends contemporary concepts of decency and human dignity and precepts of civilization which we profess to possess; and that it also violates those standards of good conscience and fundamental fairness enunciated by this court in the *Carey* and *Lee* cases.

Paradoxically, these findings applied only to adult inmates. It was not until the late 1970s that the conditions inside many juvenile justice facilities were brought to light in the landmark case, *Morales v. Turman, 430 U.S. 322*. The case involved fifteen-year-old Alicia Morales who had been incarcerated at the request of her father, along with eleven other juveniles who were incarcerated in Gainsville and Gatesville juvenile correctional facilities in Texas.[33] Ten of the plaintiffs testified to cruel and unusual conditions inside the facilities, which prompted the judge to order all of the children currently incarcerated in those facilities to be interviewed.[34] At issue was whether the purpose of juvenile corrections was to punish or rehabilitate and this question was partially answered by the Corporal Punishment Laws of Texas. At the time the law stated:

> Corporal punishment in any form shall not be inflicted upon any boy except as a last resort and then only after evidence has been gathered and presented to the Superintendent and the Chaplain. After an examination by a physician and found to be in good health, the Superintendent and Chaplain shall sign a whipping order ... the boy shall not receive over ten licks with a light strap ... at no time ever have the skin

broken or be struck except as herein provided nor abused or threatened by any guard or employee.[35]

Though the law stated children should not be abused, testimony in the case painted an entirely different picture of the discipline of juveniles in state custody. During an interview, one boy stated that a punishment called "the peel" was the favored form of punishment at Gatesville.[36] In this punishment, "the guard administers blows to the child's bare back with the palm of his hand while the boy kneels with his head between the guard's legs. Running in place puts the youngster in the same position except the guard runs in place. The friction to the sides of the head causes burning and severe headaches."[37] Interviews with other children provided similar accounts of punishments that clearly violated the Eighth Amendment. The case led to sweeping changes throughout the Texas juvenile justice system, including the elimination of corporal punishment.[38]

Corporal punishment is not currently legal as a disciplinary sanction for adults in prison in any U.S. state. The majority of states have laws and/or policies to ban its use in juvenile settings.[39] Furthermore, the American Correctional Association has expressly stated that corporal punishment is not be used in institutional settings. Despite this, there is some evidence it may still be practiced in some institutions (albeit against institutional policy).

In 1993, inmates in Onondaga county jail in New York reported that they were suspended from cell bars by handcuffs and were routinely shackled to their beds.[40] More recently Maricopa County, Arizona, Sheriff Joe Arpaio, who describes himself as "America's toughest sheriff," has made a number of headlines for his rough treatment of jail inmates. In *Graves v. Arpaio* (2010),[41] the Ninth Circuit Court held Arpaio in violation of the Eighth Amendment's provision against cruel and unusual punishment for housing inmates in temperatures that exceeded 85 degrees* and for feeding inmates substandard meals. The court cited testimony from pretrial detainees who stated they were "often given food that is overripe, moldy, and generally inedible."[42] Though not considered in the case, Arpaio's use of chain gangs could also be an Eighth Amendment violation. Inmates on the chain gang work six days a week, performing tasks such as rock breaking in temperatures that can exceed 120 degrees.[43]

USE BY THE INTERNATIONAL COMMUNITY

In 1955, the First United Nations Congress on the Prevention of Crime and the Treatment of Offenders adopted standard minimum rules for the treatment of prisoners. Standards for various aspects of institutional life were set forth including Item 31 that expressly prohibits corporal punishment.[44] Despite this provision, as well as numerous calls from the United Nations to end the use of

---

*Inmates are housed outside in tents at the jail, located in the Arizona desert.

corporal punishment, Manfred Nowak, the United Nations Special Rapporteur on torture and other cruel, inhuman, or degrading treatment or punishment, has provided extensive documentation of ongoing instances of corporal punishment and torture around the world. Nowak states that detainees in many countries are particularly vulnerable to torture while at police stations. Moreover, the likelihood of torture diminishes only somewhat after detainees have been transferred to institutions.[45] However, there are many countries where corporal punishment for rule violations is the norm inside prisons. Nowak cites Equatorial Guinea and Jordan as two countries where corporal punishment while incarcerated is very likely. In Jordan, for example, he states:

> The Al-Jafr Correction and Rehabilitation Centre was in fact a punishment centre, where detainees were routinely beaten and subjected to severe corporal punishment. Detainees who did not 'behave' in other prisons, many of them drug users, were brought to this remote place in the middle of the desert. In order to make them understand the new 'regime' they were thrown down from the vehicle upon arrival and greeted by a 'welcome party', i.e. severe beatings with different instruments by the guards. The overwhelming number of detainees I spoke to in Al-Jafr showed scars and bruises on their backs and other parts of the body. I am grateful to the Government of Jordan that my recommendation was taken up and Al-Jafr was closed in December 2006.[46]

Even if some countries have formally abolished corporal punishment in their constitutions or via statutes, this does not guarantee prisoners are actually free from physical punishments inside prisons. Sri Lanka, Tongo, Indonesia, Moldova, and Kazakhstan have all abolished corporal punishment. Even so, Nowak found evidence of its use against both adult and juvenile inmates.[47] There is also some difficulty in pinpointing which countries use corporal punishment and how often it is used in correctional settings because many countries prefer to remain opaque, at least insofar as human rights abuses are concerned. In the following sections a detailed look at corporal punishment in several countries is provided.

Egypt

Corporal punishment for disciplinary infractions inside prisons was introduced in Egypt in 1956 and remained legal until the Egyptian parliament banned the practice in 2001.[48] The law regarding flogging for disciplinary purposes stated that juvenile offenders (under age 17) could receive 10 blows with a wooden stick, while older inmates could receive up to 36 lashes with a whip for rule violations.[49] In a detailed report on prison conditions in Egypt, Human Rights Watch outlined how the punishments would be meted out:

> The punishment of whipping is applied in all prisons ... by trying up the prisoner, half naked to a wooden structure akin to a cross, which jailers have for a great many

years given the euphemism al-arousa (the bride). The punished prisoner is tied to this structure by the hands and the feet, his face towards it. The lashes then shower upon his back, turning it into a slab of red flesh from which blood flows down [to] the ground under the arousa.[50]

Officials told Human Rights Watch this punishment was typically given only to offenders who committed serious offenses, such as attempting escape or assaulting a guard.[51] However, the report further documents instances of abuse and corporal punishment against pre-trial detainees. One prisoner held without charges for almost a year recounted:

> Every three or four days, they would bring Central Security Forces soldiers for the 'prison search.' They would remove our blankets and clothes and beat us with whips. He said that sometimes a liquid would be sprayed into detainees eyes—'our eyes would swell and we could not see.' He also told HRW that detainees were beaten if they asked for medication for medical problems: 'you cannot complain. If you do, they hit you.'[52]

In addition to the aforementioned abuses, detainees and convicted offenders have been victims of torture including: electric shocks, beatings, whippings, death threats, and sexual victimization.[53] These conditions persisted for decades inside Egyptian prisons despite Article 42 of the Egyptian Constitution, which provides:

> Any person arrested, detained or [has] his freedom restricted shall be treated in the manner concomitant with the preservation of his dignity. No physical or moral harm is to be inflicted upon him. He may not be detained or imprisoned except in places defined by laws organizing prisons. If a confession is proved to have been made by a person under any of the aforementioned forms of duress or coercion, it shall be considered invalid and futile.[54]

Though flogging is now banned inside Egyptian prisons, conditions have not necessarily improved. In a news report about a prison riot in an Egyptian prison, the BBC described prison conditions as "dire and overcrowded, and security personnel have been accused of abusing inmates"[55]

Singapore and Malaysia

There have been reports of serious human rights abuses in prisons in both Singapore and Malaysia. In each country beating and flogging are the two most widely reported abuses, but prisoners also report being forced to stand and sit in various stress positions, and recount incidents of choking and electric shock.[56] Two types of electric shock are used. In the first "an induction coil was used, one electrode being attached to the hand or foot and the other wire applied to various parts of the body. The second kind, apparently more severe, was called the electric table or electric cap."[57]

Singapore's Prisons Act stipulates that women, prisoners sentenced to death, and men over 50 will not be subjected to corporal punishment. Furthermore, corporal punishment is limited to 10 strokes for juveniles and all punishments are to be administered with a medical officer present so that s/he may stop the punishment if the inmate becomes medically unfit to continue. Caning is administered with a rattan that is approximately half an inch in diameter.[58] The prison superintendent may punish any inmate who commits an aggravated offense with up to 12 strokes with a rattan.[59] However, section 74 of the Prisons Act stipulates, "where a prisoner is accused of any aggravated prison offence and the Superintendent is of the opinion that, in the circumstances of the case, the power of punishment which he possesses is inadequate, he shall forthwith report the matter in writing to the Visiting Justice or Justices."[60] In these cases, visiting justices have the authority to punish an inmate with up to 24 strokes. The following twelve offenses are defined as aggravated offenses and thus eligible for corporal punishment:

(1) mutiny
(2) escape or attempt to escape
(3) taking part in any assault or attack on any officer
(4) aggravated or repeated assault on any other prisoner
(5) wilful (*sic*) destruction of prison property
(6) wilfully (*sic*) causing to himself any illness, injury or disability
(7) wilfully (*sic*) making a false or groundless accusation or complaint against any officer or prisoner
(7A) any act constituting a minor prison offence under section 72, committed by one or more members or associates of a secret society in connection with the activities of any secret society, whether or not all the other members of the secret society are present
(8) repetition of any minor prison offence after having been twice punished for the same minor offence
(9) failure by a prisoner subject to a home detention order under section 52 to report to such person and at such times and place as may be specified under the conditions of the order
(10) where a prisoner subject to a home detention order under section 52 is required under the conditions of the order to allow the Superintendent or any person authorised by the Superintendent to enter his place of residence, or any other place or places designated under the order, the refusal by the prisoner to allow the entry, or obstructing or hindering the entry, of such person
(11) any other act of gross misconduct or insubordination
(12) abetting the commission of any aggravated prison offence.[61]

A total of 49 offenses are defined as minor in section 72 of the Prisons Act and inmates can be subjected to corporal punishment if these acts are repeated or committed with members of a secret society. Some of these include:

> talking during working hours, or talking loudly, laughing or singing at any time after having been ordered by an officer of the prison to desist; quarrelling with any other prisoner; doing any act or using any language calculated to wound or offend the feelings and prejudices of any other prisoner; visiting the toilets without permission of an officer or remaining there longer than is necessary; refusing to eat the meals provided; introducing into food or drink anything likely to render it unpalatable or unwholesome; tampering in any way with prison locks, lamps or lights or other property with which has no concern; damaging the trees within the enclosure of the prison; disobeying any lawful order of an officer; and malingering.[62]

Amnesty International reports that 602 prisoners were caned during 1987 and 616 during 1988; of these 234 were foreigners.[63] Although more recent figures are not available, there is nothing in the literature to suggest rates have decreased since the 1980s.

North Korea (The Democratic People's Republic of Korea)

North Korea is perhaps one of the most opaque countries in the world. North Korea is notoriously secretive, making it difficult to properly evaluate its human rights record.[64] However, intermittent reports indicate corporal punishments (as well as deplorable prison conditions) are most likely part of daily life for prisoners. Amnesty International reports approximately 200,000 people are held in prison camps and other secure facilities, many of whom undergo especially harsh treatment and torture.[65] Though conditions are harshest for those inmates who have been labeled as political prisoners, all inmates are subject to hard labor for at least ten hours a day.[66] Amnesty International notes, "forms of punishment include beatings, forced exercise, sitting still for prolonged periods of time and humiliating public criticism."[67]

In a chilling account of incarceration in a North Korean prison camp, Kang Chol-hwan, and Pierre Rigoulot recount experiences from the ten years Chol-hwan spent in Yodok camp from 1977 to 1987.[68] Throughout the autobiography, Chol-hwan writes of abuses suffered and beatings endured at the hands of camp educators and guards.

In another account of North Korean incarceration, one juvenile told interviewers, "some people think kids don't get hit in prison, or that they get hit less. This isn't true . . . Sometimes kids get hit more."[69] Even so, beatings are not the only form of physical punishment that takes place, as one former juvenile inmate told interviewers:

> [My] punishment was sitting in a chair every day for 15 hours. From 7:00 am in the morning until 10:00 pm at night, I had to sit perfectly still in a chair. I wasn't allowed

to move an inch or say a word. They had a surveillance camera on us and watched from another room. If one person moved, everyone was beaten. We were served lunch and dinner in our chairs. That was the only time we were allowed to move.[70]

North Korea is not the only Asian nation with a questionable human rights record where conditions of confinement are concerned. North Korea's larger neighbor, the People's Republic of China, has its own dubious record.

The People's Republic of China

In 1994, China passed the Prison Law of which article 14 stipulates that guards may not "use torture to coerce a confession, or to use corporal punishment, or to maltreat a prisoner; or to beat or connive at others to beat a prisoner." Despite this, Human Rights in China (HRIC) has documented a number of abuses at Chifeng Prison. Abuses include, the use of electric batons by prison guards, "being made to be stand for extended periods in uncomfortable and painful positions, being chained upright to a metal door for excruciating lengths of time, and being sent to a cell with dimensions too small to allow the prisoner lie down."[71] Philip Williams and Yenna Wu note that the frequency of beatings has decreased in China, but they have by no means been eliminated inside many Chinese prisons.[72] Former inmates of Chifeng prison report up to 14 hours a day of hard physical labor was required and beatings were common if an inmate could not make their quota.[73]

Bangladesh

Corporal punishment is used as a disciplinary measure for adults and children in institutional settings in Bangladesh. Provisions for whipping can be found in The Prisons Act of 1894. Section 45 of The Prisons Act outlines various prison offenses (e.g., assault, willful disobedience, immoral behavior, etc.) and Section 46 stipulates that whipping is one of many approved punishments. For adult males, whipping may not exceed 30 stripes, "with a light rattan not less than half an inch in diameter on the buttocks, and in case of prisoners under the age of sixteen it shall be inflicted, in the way of school discipline, with a lighter rattan."[74]

IMPACT ON PRISONERS

Corporal punishment is administered in institutional settings primarily as punishment for rule violations and not to effect any real change on the part of the inmates. Numerous campaigns against the use of corporal punishment in the United States were waged because as Myra Glenn explains, there was a general "belief that corporal punishment was an ineffective means of social discipline and it 'merely' repressed an individual from wrongdoing. This punishment, however, allegedly failed to accomplish the 'true' aim of discipline, namely, the reformation of individual moral character."[75] If corporal punishment fails to achieve more rehabilitative aims, then it is reasonable to explore the long-term effects of corporal punishment versus the short-term gain of rule compliance.

The effects of corporal punishment on prisoners are difficult to evaluate in light of the dearth of existing literature and the aforementioned opacity of many retentionsist nations. Because many view corporal punishment as torture, some comparisons can be made by turning to the literature on torture. Although the comparison may not be exact, there are sufficient parallels to merit consideration.

Though there are many definitions of torture, the United Nations Convention against Torture and other Cruel, Inhumane, or Degrading Treatment or Punishment defines it as:

> any act by which severe pain or suffering, whether physical or mental, is intentionally inflicted on a person for such purposes as obtaining from him or a third person information or a confession, punishing him for an act he committed, or intimidating or coercing him or a third person, or for any reason based on discrimination of any kind, when such pain or suffering is inflicted by or at the instigation of or with the consent or acquiescence of a public official or other person acting in an official capacity.

Given the UN characterizes torture as pain induced as punishment for an act committed, the literature on the effects of torture is likely generalizable here.

Obviously, there are physical effects from corporal punishment that can last anywhere from minutes to years depending on the severity of the punishment. Amnesty International obtained photographs of caning victims where substantial scarring was visible months after the incidents were reported to have occurred.[76] Researchers have also observed a variety of psychological effects stemming from physical forms of punishment.

James Jaranson and Michael Popkin note that the psychological effects of torture can have more consequence for survivors than the immediate physical side effects.[77] Furthermore, there may be some delay in the onset of psychological symptomology. Some scholars have noted the effects can last decades after the event has occurred.[78] Lance Rintamaki, Francis Weaver, Philip Elbaum, Edward Klama, and Scott Miskevics's study of World War II prisoners of war (POW) found that a high percentage still had vivid flashbacks and dreams of their POW experience. Of them, 16.6% met the clinical requirements for a current diagnosis of posttraumatic stress disorder.[79]

Ellen Gerrity, Terence Keane, and Farris Tuma note torture victims experience the same types of symptoms regardless of differences in culture and differences in the type of traumatic event.[80] Some common symptoms include "hyperarousal, reexperiencing the event, avoidance behavior, amnesic episodes, difficulty concentrating, and poor memory."[81] Anne Goldfeld, Richard Mollica, Barbara Pesavento, and Stephen Faraone found that torture victims experience a range of psychological effects including anxiety, depression, irritability, aggression, and social withdrawal.[82] Additionally, victims may also experience cognitive impairment and neurovegetative symptoms (e.g., sexual dysfunction, nightmares, etc.). Given the myriad side effects of physical punishments, it is clear that whatever short-term gains the institution might experience may be off-set by the long-term latent consequences experienced by inmates.

In summary, corporal punishment is still administered for disciplinary infractions inside prison facilities in many parts of the world. Even in countries where laws exist that forbid the use of corporal punishment inside prison facilities, the practice can still be found. This is likely the case because prisoners are removed from public view, many facilities lack the transparency to hold officials accountable for their actions, and others may simply remain willfully ignorant. While corporal punishment might be an effective disciplinary tool in the short term, it is clear the impacts of extreme or protracted physical punishments are detrimental to both the physical and psychological wellbeing of inmates in the long term.[83]

It should be noted, however, that not all forms of corporal punishment are equal. We are mindful of Graeme Newman's argument for corporal punishment and his statement, "[T]here are many different kinds of corporal punishments, and not all have the same physical and mental effects."[84] Even while advocating for corporal punishment under certain conditions, Newman does not support its use in correctional settings. While we certainly agree not all corporal punishments are synonymous with torture (and as a corollary will not always have the same psychological effects), when corporal punishments are administered inside institutions and away from public view the danger for abuse becomes great.

Case Studies: Nigeria, Singapore, and Saudi Arabia

I would say colonialism is a wonderful thing. It spread civilization to Africa. Before it they had no written language, no wheel as we know it, no schools, no hospitals, not even normal clothing.

—Ian Smith Prime Minister of Rhodesia

IN AN EFFORT to provide a more thorough portrait of contemporary practices, this chapter presents a detailed examination of corporal punishment use in the nations of Nigeria, Singapore, and Saudi Arabia. These three countries, which appear on face to be worlds apart in terms of culture and development, all make extensive use of corporal punishment. Each country's history is examined here with a special focus on the role of postcolonial legacy. With this theme as a central focus, a clear explanation emerges as to why corporal punishment has endured in these three nations.

CONTEMPORARY NIGERIA

Geographically, The Federal Republic of Nigeria is relatively small (measuring about twice the size of the state of California). As of July 2011 it has a population of approximately 155,215,573 people.[1] Nigerian society is quite diverse, with over 250 distinct ethnic groups. The Hausa and Fulani constitute 29%. Other major groups are the Yoruba (21%), Igbo (18%), Ijaw (10%), Kanuri (4%), Ibibio (3.5%), and Tiv (2.5%).[2] In terms of religious diversity, Nigeria is made up of approximately 50 percent Muslims, 40 percent Christians, with the remainder practicing either the various indigenous religions or no religion at all.[3]

Nigeria tends to rank low developmentally compared to most other countries. One of the most common measures of development is the Human Development Index (HDI), compiled annually by the United Nations. This index is comprised of several development indicators including life expectancy, school enrollment, and gross national income per capita.[4] Nigeria's HDI value is estimated to be 0.423, which places Nigeria 142 out of 169 nations included in the index. Life expectancy is estimated to be approximately 48.4 years. The less than five (year-old) mortality rate is high, at 186 per 1,000 live births.[5] The adult literacy rate is moderate, with 74.8% of people over age fifteen being able to read.[6]

Finally, the gross domestic product per capita measures approximately $2,289.[7] These measures place Nigeria slightly above other nations in Sub-Saharan Africa, which has a combined estimated HDI value of 0.377.[8]

Within Nigeria, there are 36 states and one territory,[9] all of which operate with a great deal of autonomy.[10] Each state has a governor and a state assembly. The Non-Governmental Organization (NGO), Human Rights Watch observes, "state governors are granted considerable autonomy in many respects and, in practice, the federal government rarely intervenes to challenge their decisions or policies."[11]

Country History

Like many African nations, Nigeria is a relatively new post-colonial country, having gained independence from Great Britain in 1960.[12] The British influence in this region cannot be overstated. Even the name, Nigeria, which stems from the Niger River, the largest physical feature in the country, "was suggested in the 1890s by British journalist Flora Shaw, who later became the wife of colonial governor Frederick Lugard."[13] Three aspects of culture and history have combined to shape contemporary Nigeria in profound ways: the spread of Islam, the slave trade, and the colonial era.[14]

Islam

Islam has a long history in Nigeria, though there is some debate as the exact timing of its emergence. Some argue it was present in the region as early as the seventh or eighth centuries.[15] However, most believe Islam was brought to West Africa by the Uthman Dan Fodio Jihad in 1804.[16] M. G. Smith states the war, lead by Fodio was, "launched against the Hausa chiefs of Gobir, Kano, Katsina, Zaria, Daura, their allies and congeners, in 1804."[17] Lasting a total of six years, the final outcome of this jihad[18] was the unification of northern Nigeria and some parts of Niger and Camaroon under one Islamic state, thus ushering Shari'a law* into the region.

As discussed earlier in this volume, the traditional Islamic legal system specifies punishments that apply to Muslims for criminal and civil infractions. Its customs have been in effect (primarily in the northern region) in Nigeria since the pre-colonial era.[19] Disputes over the dates notwithstanding, Islam has had the greatest impact in the northern region of the country. According to Helen Metz, this influence, "helps account for the dichotomy between north and south and for the divisions within the north that have been so strong during the colonial and postcolonial eras."[20]

---

*"Shari'a, an Arabic word meaning 'the right path', refers to traditional Islamic law, which comes from the Qur'an, the sacred book of Islam" (Anyanwu, 2006: 316).

Most recently, the division between North and South was further cemented in 1999 when twelve states in the northern region integrated Shari'a law into the criminal justice system. As Ogechi Anyanwu states, the practical effect "of the full implementation of Shari'a law in these states has been the imposition of sentences that are either adjudged more severe than those provided for under the Penal Code, or sentences not provided for at all in the code, and the establishment of offenses that are not found in the national penal law."[21]

The precise reasons for adopting Shari'a law in these twelve states is discussed at length in the scholarly literature. Principal justifications include political maneuvering on the part of politicians, as well as a general sense of disenfranchisement with the criminal justice system among the Muslim populace in the regions. The prevailing view among many citizens was that the existing criminal justice system was largely ineffective, corrupt, and unresponsive to the needs of the citizenry in the North.[22] Additionally, "there was the expectation among the general public that Shari'a, with its emphasis on welfare and the state's responsibility to provide for the basic needs of the population, would go some way towards alleviating their plight."[23] Because the punishments prescribed under Shari'a (in particular hudud or hadd punishments) have direct bearing on our discussion of corporal punishment in the Nigeria, they will be discussed more broadly later in this chapter.

The Slave Trade

The slave trade has had a lasting impact on the whole of Africa, and Nigeria in particular. Approximately 3.5 million slaves sent to the Americas are estimated to have originated from Nigeria.[24] Throughout the entire continent, Lovejoy estimates approximately 11,863,000 Africans were imported by colonial powers.[25] These numbers are hotly debated and could range anywhere from ten million to twenty-eight million people.[26] Notably, one of the contributing factors to the internal conflict in Nigeria can be traced directly back to the external influences of the slave trade.

Nigeria played an important role in the slave trade during the nineteenth century, as approximately 30% of all exported slaves came from Nigeria.[27] Furthermore, slavery within Nigeria was common practice during this time and the consequences of this are still evident today. As Metz explains:

> The Sokoto Caliphate, for example, had more slaves than any other modern country, except the United States in 1860. Slaves were also numerous among the Igbo, the Yoruba, and many other ethnic groups. Indeed, many ethnic distinctions, especially in the middle belt—the area between the north and south—were reinforced because of slave raiding and defensive measures that were adopted for protection against enslavement. Conversion to Islam and the spread of Christianity were intricately associated with issues relating to slavery and with efforts to promote political and cultural autonomy.[28]

As the preceding paragraph illustrates, issues of religion and slavery were largely entwined and formed the basis for divisions still seen in present-day Nigeria. A third factor, colonialism, was also important in shaping Nigeria.

Colonialism

When the slave trade collapsed, European demand for other exports, such as palm oil (which had applications in making soap, candles, and some lubricants) increased.[29] Indeed, "palm oil soon supplanted slavery and dominated trade in the Niger Delta," with England creating the largest demand for it.[30] In general, Africa, post-slave trade, became the locus of other forms of exploitation.

A number of European countries with direct economic interests in various parts of Africa (i.e., Great Britain, France, Germany), as well as other countries (the United States, Belgium, Spain, the Netherlands, and Russia), were invited to the 1885 Berlin Conference.[31] Four reasons for the necessity of the conference were cited:

> one, to regulate the conditions most favorable to the development of trade and civilization in certain regions of Africa; two, to assure all nations of the advantage of free navigation on the two chief rivers of Africa flowing into the Atlantic ocean (the Congo and the Niger); three, to obliate the misunderstandings and disputes which might in the future arise from new acts of occupation on the coast of Africa; and four, to further the moral and material well-being of the native population.[32]

The Berlin Conference opened an era of avaricious colonial expansion that Thomas Pakenham describes as, "the Scramble for Africa."[33] The practical outcome of this conference was that "Europeans sat down and savagely carved up Africa" with little regard for tribal, cultural, or social divisions that were already in place.[34] Given their high demand for palm oil, the British were granted control over much of the lower Niger region.[35]

The terms used to describe the external administration of Nigeria and other African nations are typically some variant of colonialism (e.g., economic colonialism, political colonialism, geographic colonialism, etc.). Viviane Saleh-Hanna uses the term "penal colonialism" because in her estimation it captures the violent reality of colonialism, which has "infiltrated and dominated entire social structures in Africa."[36]

The entire colonial period was relatively short, lasting only about 60 years,[37] but it had drastic consequences that persist even in the post-colonial era. Despite the fact Britain implemented a more indirect rule of Nigeria (for reasons of cost and ease), colonialism pervaded every aspect of Nigerian life. Due to British influences, sweeping changes were made to existing economic, political, and social structures.[38] Although there were some marginally positive aspects to these changes (e.g., economic growth through increased exporting), most resulted in increased tensions in the country because the primary beneficiaries of colonialism were the colonizers themselves. The prevailing viewpoint among most Nigerians was that "colonial rule eroded traditional cultures and institutions . . . and exploited Nigerian labor, both manual and intellectual, in a way that profited European firms more than the Nigerians themselves."[39]

The structure of the justice system in Nigeria provides an interesting example of the conflicts that can arise when an institution is imposed upon a colonized people. Unsurprisingly, the Western criminal justice system imposed by the British clashed greatly with the indigenous system already in place.[40] A few aspects of Nigerian justice are discussed below.

Corporal Punishment as a Criminal Sanction in Nigeria

The issue of state-sanctioned corporal punishment in Nigeria came to the forefront in 1999 when 12 northern states adopted Shari'a law into their justice system. However, this was not the first time that the issue of Islamic law had been raised in Nigeria. Anyanwu notes that Shari'a law had been in place during the pre-colonial era in Nigeria, but the British found the system to be too barbaric. As such they, "imposed a Western-style criminal code, and established the 'repugnancy test' system, which permitted the conquered people to punish civil law violations only as long as the punishment passed the 'repugnancy test.' "[41] The repugnancy test, set forth in *Proclamation No. 6 of 1900,* was essentially an allowance for customary punishments to be enforced only in cases where they were not "repugnant to natural justice, equity, and good conscience, not contrary to any official law."[42] Consequently, punishments such as amputation, stoning, beheading, and crucifixion were abolished under colonial rule.[43]

A system of Western-style criminal justice persisted throughout Nigeria, even after independence was gained in 1960. Shari'a law was largely relegated to areas of personal law until October 27, 1999, when the governor of the Zamfara state, Ahmed Sani Yerima, instituted a full system of Shari'a law.[44] The states of Kano, Kaduna, Niger, Kebbi, Katsina, Borno, Sokoto, Jigawa, Bauchi, Gombe, and Yobe soon followed the Zamfara example.[45] While there were concerns by the international community about various aspects of the new system (e.g., lack of due process, lack of judicial training, etc.), the implementation of the hudud (or haad) punishments garnered the most concern and criticism from the international community.

As discussed in Chapter 2, under Shari'a law there are three classes of punishments, hudud, qusa/diya, and ta'zir.[46] Shari'a law, in general, and hudud punishments, in particular, have been implemented in varying degrees in the aforementioned 12 northern states. The Zamfara state enacted the most sweeping changes by giving the Shari'a courts jurisdiction over all matters, criminal and civil.[47] Niger state, on the other hand, took a slightly more measured approach and modified only portions of the penal code and made some procedural changes to conform to some legal aspects of Shari'a law.[48] It is important to note that Shari'a law applies only to the Muslim population in the 12 northern states in Nigeria[49] and there have been no reports of non-Muslims being forcibly tried in

Shari'a courts, though a person could elect to have their case heard in a Shari'a court if they desired.[50]

Shari'a courts in Nigeria have regularly handed down hudud punishments. Osita Ogbu provides a useful overview of many of the corporal punishments meted out from 2000 to 2002.[51] During that two-year period, almost 50 people had been sentenced to punishments ranging from lashings to death by stoning.[52] Persons convicted of crimes such as fornication, consumption of alcohol, and carrying a Muslim woman on a motorcycle all received sentences of lashings.[53] For example, an offender from the state of Zamfara received a sentence of 180 lashes for the crime of fornication and another offender from the state of Sokoto received 80 lashes for consuming alcohol.[54] These punishments are typically carried out in full public view. As Ogbu explains, "Haddi lashing or flogging is intended to expose the offender to public disgrace. For instance, hundreds of jubilant Muslims on 3 April 2002, at Dutse, Jigawa State, witnessed the infliction of 80 strokes of the cane on Idris Ibrahim for drunkenness."[55]

Offenders convicted of theft were routinely sentenced to amputations and Human Rights Watch estimates that at least 60 amputation sentences have been handed down during the four-year period from 2000 to 2004.[56] In one amputation case, the offender (Buba Kare Garki) was convicted of stealing a cow, but did not have legal representation during his trial (HRW, 2004). During an interview with Human Rights Watch, the governor of the Zamfara states:

> admitted that he had given the orders for these amputations to be carried out for political reasons and that his political reputation depended on the outcome of these cases. Referring to the case of Jangebe, he told Human Rights Watch: 'The people at that time really wanted Shari'a, therefore we had to implement the sentence.' He claimed that despite the judge's wish to impose a more lenient sentence, Jangebe had confessed and 'insisted.' He claimed that he had made every effort to provide a lawyer to Jangebe, but he had refused. 'I personally sent several messengers to [him] asking him to appeal. [...] This was a test case for me. I wanted to exhaust all options. But the man said no, I don't want to be a bad Muslim. I sent a lawyer to him for free. The man refused. After thirty days, people were counting the days and saying 'let's see if the governor is serious.' The judges had to implement it.'[57]

A number of death sentences for adultery also have been handed down. These have proven to be extremely difficult tests for the fledgling Shari'a systems. While the international community has been outspoken about all forms of corporal punishment, the punishment of death by stoning has drawn the most criticism.[58]

The Case of Sarimu Mohammed Baranda

In 2002, Sarimu Mohammed Baranda, described as a poor, mentally ill man from the Jigawa state, was sentenced to death by stoning for the rape of a nine-year-old girl.[59] Baranda's case is notable because it represents a departure from most stoning cases, the vast majority of which have involved women accused of adultery.[60] Baranda, who did not have a lawyer to assist him with his case, pled guilty and was sentenced to death by stoning.[61] He later reported that his confession to the rape had been made under duress.[62] Though he initially refused to appeal the case, his family finally persuaded him to file an appeal and the death sentence was overturned due to his mental illness.[63] Human Rights Watch noted that there was genuine concern that Baranda might be publicly executed, in part because he was initially unwilling to appeal, but also because his mental state was so fragile.[64]

The Case of Amina Lawal

Amina Lawal's case garnered international attention in 2002, after she was sentenced to death by stoning for adultery by a Shari'a court in the state of Katsina.[65] At the time, Lawal was pregnant with a child, though her husband had passed away five years previously.[66] Under Shari'a law there are different standards of guilt in adultery cases for men and woman. To be found guilty of adultery a man must be seen committing the act by a minimum or four persons, but for a woman, having a child out of wedlock is evidence enough.[67] Lawal had initially claimed that a neighbor had raped her; however, because she could not produce any witnesses to affirm this assault, the court dismissed the claim. She then confessed to the adultery, but her confession was secured only after vigilantes from her village had raided her home after the birth of her child.[68] Her alleged confession, coupled with her pregnancy, was sufficient to "prove" her guilt for the crime of adultery.[69]

A number of procedural safeguards were absent during Lawal's initial trial. Specifically, the state of Katsina did not have a Shari'a criminal procedure code in place in 2002. Moreover, Lawal did not have counsel and was not informed of her option to have one. Perhaps most importantly, she was never informed that she could withdraw her confession.[70] Despite this, Lawal was convicted and sentenced to death by stoning.

Numerous international and Nigerian human rights and women's rights organizations became involved with the case. The international backlash for the perceived harshness of the sentence was fierce. Soon after the sentence was declared, Lawal secured the help of legal counsel and filed an appeal. On her first appeal, the sentence was suspended for two years so that she could care for her newborn child.[71] Several other appeals were filed and finally in 2003 a Shari'a court revoked her death sentence.[72] A number of reasons were cited for revoking the death sentence. Some involved the aforementioned lack of procedural safeguards (e.g., lack of counsel and inability to withdraw her confession),[73] but the chief reason was more religious than procedural. Lawal's attorney "pointed to phrases in the Qur'an that recognize a husband's paternity over his wife's children for years after his death."[74]

INTERNATIONAL CRITICISM

The international community has been vocal in its criticisms of hadd punishments. In specific, detractors say they violate basic international standards against cruel and inhumane punishments and they violate the Nigerian constitution. Setting aside for the moment whether they are cruel or inhumane, there is evidence to support the constitutional argument. In particular, section 33(1) of the Nigerian constitution states, "Every person has a right to life, and no one shall be deprived intentionally of his life, save in execution of the sentence of a court in respect of a criminal offence of which he has been found guilty in Nigeria."

From this it can be reasonably argued that a sentence of stoning to death for the act of adultery is a violation of the constitution.[75] Freedom of religion, a right that is guaranteed by section 38(1), is another important issue pertaining to Shari'a law because "no Muslim is allowed the right to change his or her religion" and doing so carries a sentence of death by stoning.[76] Furthermore, section 34(1) of the constitutions stipulates, "Every individual is entitled to respect for the dignity of his person, and accordingly—no person shall be subject to torture or to inhuman or degrading treatment." This right is further echoed in the African Charter on Human Rights, Article 5: "Every individual shall have the right to respect of the dignity inherent in a human being and to the recognition of his legal status. All forms of exploitation and degradation of man particularly slavery, slave trade, torture, cruel, inhuman or degrading punishment and treatment shall be prohibited."[77]

CORPORAL PUNISHMENT AND THE JUVENILE JUSTICE SYSTEM

In addition to corporal punishments handed down by Shari'a courts, the practice is likewise found in the secular juvenile justice system. Nigerian laws stipulate under what circumstance corporal punishment may be declared. A report prepared for the Committee for the Rights of the Child notes:

> Art.9 of the Children and Young Persons Law states that: "Where a juvenile charged with any offence is tried by a court, and the court is satisfied of his guilt, the court may (f) order the offender to be whipped;" Art. 11 (2) of the same law stipulates: "No young person shall be ordered to be imprisoned if in the opinion of the court he can be suitably dealt with in any other way whether by probation, fine, corporal punishment, committal to a place of detention or to an approved institution or otherwise." Furthermore, Art. 18 of the Criminal Code (South) states: "Wherever a male person who in the opinion of the court has not attained seventeen years of age has been found guilty of any offence the court may, in its discretion, order him to be whipped in addition to or in substitution for any other punishments to which he is liable."[78]

In addition, "Part 42 of the Criminal Procedure Code governs how caning is to be carried out—up to 12 strokes 'with light rod or cane or birch' (article 386)."[79] Although children are generally protected from capital punishment under Nigerian law, there are some circumstances where a child could receive a hadd punishment in a Shari'a court. Under Shari'a law, "the age of adulthood is defined as the age at which a person becomes responsible for his or her acts. Very often this is considered the age of puberty. If found guilty under the Shari'a penal legislation, Nigerians under 18 could [thus] face the death penalty."[80]

Inside custodial institutions, corporal punishments appear to be routinely administered. E. E. O Alemeka and I. C. Chukwuma report that flogging, kneeling, frog jumping, and tough physical drills are administered inside juvenile institutions on a very frequent basis.[81] Reminiscent of the old "trustee" system in U.S. prisons, inmate-on-inmate violence is tacitly encouraged inside Nigerian juvenile institutions. As Article 18 of the Approved Institutions Regulations states, "Where possible the principal shall arrange that inmates themselves shall be responsible for the maintenance of discipline and obedience to rules and for the *punishment of offending inmates by other inmates.*"[82]

CORPORAL PUNISHMENT IN THE HOME AND IN EDUCATIONAL SETTINGS

Corporal punishment is by no means exclusively used in the adult and juvenile justice systems in Nigeria. Parents are free to use corporal punishment in the home, both in the northern and southern regions of the country. According to the Global Initiative to End the Corporal Punishment of Children, corporal punishment is legal in the home in both regions of the country.[83] Article 55 of the northern penal code states, "Nothing is an offence which does not amount to the infliction of grievous hurt upon any person and which is done: by a parent or guardian for the purpose of correcting his child or ward such child or ward being under eighteen years of age."[84] The penal code in the South (Article 295) is a bit more specific about the use of corporal punishment, stating:

> A blow or other force, not in any case extending to a wound or grievous harm, may be justified for the purpose of correction as follows: (1) a father or mother may correct his or her legitimate or illegitimate child, being under sixteen years of age, or any guardian or person acting as a guardian, his ward, being under sixteen years of age, for misconduct or disobedience to any lawful command . . . (2) a master may correct his servant or apprentice, being under sixteen years of age, for misconduct or default in his duty as such servant or apprentice and (4) a father or mother or guardian, or a person acting as a guardian, may delegate to any person whom he or she entrusts permanently or temporarily with the governance or custody of his or her child or ward all his or her own authority for correction, including the power to determine in what cases correction ought to he inflicted; and such a delegation shall be presumed, except in so far as it may be expressly withheld, in the case of a schoolmaster or a person acting as a schoolmaster, in respect of a child or ward. [85]

The Nigerian government has stated that the Child Rights Act of 2003 outlaws corporal punishment in schools, but it is still widely practiced both in the North and the South. The aforementioned penal codes for the North and the South clearly render corporal punishment permissible in educational settings.

Since the ban, there has yet to be a legal test for the use of corporal punishment in Nigerian schools. Moreover, there appears to be no government enforcement of the Child Rights Act. Several court cases decided prior to the ban bolster the legal argument for its use. The judge in *Ekeogu v. Aliri* declared it is "the public duty" for teachers to use corporal punishment in the classroom, even though the incident in the case involved a severe ocular injury in which the student lost their eye.[86]

Florence Olusa v. Commissioner of Education, Ondo State and Marian Olaniyan centered on a student who was performing chores at the home of her teacher. After a short time, the teacher noticed some of her money was missing and suspected her student had stolen it. In an effort to illicit a confession about the theft, the teacher flogged the student and locked her in the apartment for several hours.[87] The court ultimately dismissed the student's claim, citing the Nigerian constitution of 1979, which, "empowers teachers to deprive students their personal liberty in accordance with a procedure permitted by law for the purpose of the child's education."[88]

THE REPUBLIC OF SINGAPORE

The issue of corporal punishment in Singapore was brought to the forefront of the American consciousness in 1994 when 18-year-old teenager Michael Faye was sentenced to caning for committing vandalism while there. Although this case brought the issue to the attention of international media, the use of corporal punishment in Singapore has a long history, which will be examined in the following section.

Contemporary Singapore

The Republic of Singapore is a relatively small country (approximately 3.5 times larger than Washington, D.C.) located in Southeastern Asia between Malaysia and Indonesia.[89] Singapore was initially founded as a British trading colony in 1819, and gained independence from Britain in 1963. Singapore became a fully independent nation after gaining independence from the Federation of Malaysia in 1965.[90] The population is comprised mainly of persons of Chinese descent (75.2%), followed by Malay (13.6%), Indian (8.8%), and Other (2.4%).[91] The predominant religion in Singapore is Buddhism (42.5%), though 14.9% of the population identify as practicing Islam, 14.8% practice no religion, 14.6% are Christian, and the remaining 8.5% practice Taoism.[92]

Singapore is considered by many as one of the most prosperous countries in Southeastern Asia.[93] By most measures of development, Singapore scores quite high compared to other nations. With a Human Development Index Value of .846, Singapore ranks 27 out of 169 nations included in the index.[94] Life expectancy in the country is high at an average of 80.7 years and the literacy rate is among the highest in the world, with an estimated 95.2% of the population over age fifteen being literate.[95] Finally, the GDP per capita is $50,266.[96] Singapore scores comparatively higher than other East Asian nations, which have a cumulative HDI of .65.

Historical Overview

Historians have rich records of Singapore's history that date back to at least the third century AD. It was not until the seventh century AD that Malay, Thai, Javanese, Chinese, Indian, and Arab maritime traders began to use the area as a trading post and supply point.[97] By the thirteenth century, the Malays ruled the trading post, then known as Temasek.[98] The city of Singapura (or "lion city," after a lion-like creature that was sighted in the area) was founded around 1299.[99]

European influence in the region began in the 1500s when Portuguese explorers captured and burned the port of Melaka in 1511.[100] About 100 years later, in 1613, Portuguese explorers again burned a trading post at the mouth of the Temasek River, causing most of the population to abandon the island.[101] It was another 200 years before extensive planting and settlement on the island resumed.[102]

British involvement in the island nation began in 1819, when Sir Stamford Raffles began looking for a suitable location for an English trading post in the Straights of Malacca.[103] Raffles made an agreement with the local Malay chief to use the area in exchange for 3,000 Spanish dollars per year.[104] The population grew substantially over the next 100 years; by 1911, the island was home to 311,303 people.[105] The British were largely uninvolved in local affairs, leaving much of the governance to the various sultans that ruled the population.[106] This was the case until the 1870s when a number of factors, including piracy, smuggling, and fear of other European competition, led the British to turn the Malay states into protectorates.[107] The British then grew more ensconced in local affairs and British residents began advising sultans in all matters, with the exception of religion and local customs.[108]

British involvement in Singapore is largely responsible for the presence of corporal punishment in the region. When Raffles acquired the island, a combination of British common law and Indian penal code was instituted.[109] These codes specified corporal punishments for a number of offenses, including begging and robbery with violence and others.[110] When Singapore became a Crown Colony, the penal code was once again replaced. From this point, the Straits Settlement Penal Code became the official legal guide. This code expanded the use of corporal punishment. Whippings were the prescribed punishment for crimes such as, "aggravated forms of theft, house breaking, assault with the intention to outrage modesty, second or subsequent offences relating to rape and prostitution."[111] Section 72(b) of the Straits Settlement Penal Code stipulated:

> Whenever by any law in force or to be in force in the Colony the punishments of whipping may be awarded, the number of stripes to be inflicted shall be specified by the Court in the sentence. The punishment of whipping shall be inflicted with a rattan not exceeding half-an-inch in diameter, and shall, in no case, exceed fifty stripes when ordered by the Supreme Court, or forty stripes when ordered by a Court of Quarter Sessions or ordered by two or more Magistrates, or thirty stripes when ordered by one Magistrate.[112]

Per section 72(A) of the penal code, females, offenders under the sentence of death, and offenders sentenced to more than four years of imprisonment or servitude were not to receive the punishment of whipping. When Singapore became a separate Crown Colony, a new penal code was implemented and the use of physical punishments was expanded. With this change, caning became the preferred method of corporal punishment.[113]

Contemporary Corporal Punishment

In many respects, Singapore is a progressive and economically prosperous country, which leads some to question why corporal punishment is still used by the government. Specific punishments are outlined in Chapter 224 of Singapore's statutes and Singapore's Penal Code.[114] Caning is among the possible sanctions for offenses ranging from serious violent crime, such as robbery and kidnapping, to less serious offenses like vandalism and immigration infractions. Similar to the Straits Settlement Penal Code, women, persons over 50, and offenders under a sentence of death cannot be caned. For adults, the maximum number of strokes allowable is 24. For youthful offenders (ages seven to sixteen), the maximum number is 10 stokes and a lighter cane is typically used.[115]

There is no prohibition against torture in Singapore's constitution. Although torture is prohibited by Article 37(a) of the Convention of the Rights of the Child, the government of Singapore does not recognize its use of caning as a violation of the article.[116]

Part of the reason corporal punishment has persisted in the region can be attributed to the shared values of the people of Singapore. In 1991, the government published the Shared Values White Paper that partially explains the government's approach to human rights. The paper stipulates the government's approach to human rights involves each of the following:

> Nation before community and society above self: Putting the interests of society ahead of the individual.
>
> Family as the basic unit of society: The family is identified as the most stable fundamental building block of the nation.

Community support and respect for the individual: Recognizes that the individual has rights, which should be respected and not light encroached upon. Encourages the community to support and have compassion for the disadvantaged individual who may have been left behind by the free market system.

Consensus, not conflict: Resolving issues through consensus and not conflict stresses the importance of compromise and national unity.

Racial and religious harmony: Recognizes the need for different communities to live harmoniously with one another in order for all to prosper.[117]

The constitution of the Republic of Singapore contains few individual rights because "rights are viewed as disruptive to social harmony."[118] Harsh punishment is required, the government reasons, because it helps make Singapore a safe place to live and restore balance back to the community.[119] This emphasis on communitarianism and harmony as the primary justifications for corporal punishment are what sets Singapore apart from other retentionist nations, many of which rely primarily on religious justifications.

Notable Corporal Punishment Cases

In 1987, twenty-two-year-old Qwek Kee Chong pled guilty to four counts of armed robbery. He did not have an attorney at his trial and was sentenced to 10 years imprisonment plus 12 strokes with a cane for each of the counts of robbery (for a total of 48 strokes).[120] The caning took place in one continuous session at the prison. Chang's injuries from the caning were so severe that he had to be hospitalized.[121] This case is problematic because the "Criminal Procedure Code states that in no case shall the caning awarded at any one trial exceed 24 strokes in the case of an adult or 10 strokes in the case of a youthful offender."[122] Chong went on to sue the government for damages resulting from his punishment.[123]

On September 1, 2010, Kamari Charlton, a former Florida State University college football player was detained by authorities in Singapore and charged with overstaying his visa as well as 21 other charges related to money laundering.[124] Overstaying a visa is an offense punishable by caning (3 strokes) and if convicted, it would have marked the first time in 16 years that an American received a caning sentence.[125] Charlton pled guilty to 5 of the money-laundering charges and the remaining 17 charges, including the overstay charge, were dropped (Channel News Asia, 2011).[126] While Charlton might have avoided caning, one need not look very far for numerous instances where the punishment has been carried out.

In 2010, Oliver Fricker, a Swiss citizen, received a sentence of five months in jail and three stokes with a cane for vandalism.[127] His sentence was eventually extended two additional months for trespassing. The judge presiding over the case, Justice Rajah, stated, "[The] laws of Singapore proscribing vandalizing are indeed severe . . . but these are the very laws that are largely responsible for a clean and graffiti-free environment as well as a low incidence of crime involving damage to public property and services."[128]

Corporal Punishment in Other Settings

Given its widespread use throughout the justice system, it should come as no surprise that corporal punishment is legal both in the home and in schools in Singapore. The penal code (Article 89) states:

> [N]othing, which is done in good faith for the benefit of a person under 12 years of age, or of unsound mind, by or by consent, either express or implied, of the guardian or other person having lawful charge of that person, is an offence by reason of any harm it may cause, or be intended by the doer to cause, or be known by the doer to be likely to cause, to that person", provided that it does not cause or is likely or intended to cause death or grievous hurt.[129]

Although family violence is prohibited by Article 64 of the Women's Charter (1961), family violence covers only the following four areas:

> (1) willfully or knowingly placing or attempting to place, a family member in fear or hurt, (2) causing hurt to a family member by such act which is known or ought to have been known would result in hurt, (3) wrongfully confining or restraining a family member against his will, and (4) causing continual harassment with intent to cause or knowing it is likely to cause anguish to a family member.[130]

In short, the physical discipline of children under the age of twenty-one is permissible provided it is done with lawful force and for the purposes of correction.[131]

Corporal punishment is likewise permissible in educational environments, though Regulation Number 88 under the Schools Regulation Act (1957) only permits corporal punishment of male pupils and school officials are only permitted to administer the punishment on "the palms of the hand or the clothed buttocks."[132]

KINGDOM OF SAUDI ARABIA

Arguably, there is no other country in the world more closely linked to corporal punishment than the Kingdom of Saudi Arabia. Based on the ultraorthodox precepts of Wahabbism, Saudi Arabia is estimated to administer more forms of corporal punishment than any other nation in the world.

Saudi Arabia is located to the north of Yemen and borders the Persian Gulf and the Red Sea.[133] The total estimated population of Saudi Arabia is 26,131,703. The overwhelming majority of the population is of Arab descent (90%), with about 10% reported to be Afro-Asian. Saudi Arabia is ethnically homogeneous, as well as religiously homogeneous, with 100% of the population practicing the Islamic faith. About 90% of the population are practicing Sunni Muslims and the remaining 10% are Shi'a.[134] Such homogeneity in religion should not be surprising, as it is illegal to publicly practice any religion other than Islam.[135]

In terms of development, Saudi Arabia has an HDI value of 75.2, placing it above other Arab states (the combined HDI score for other Arab states in 59.0). Life expectancy is high at 73.3 years. The literacy rate is also high (86.7% of adults over age fifteen are literate), but the mean level of education is low (7.8 years).[136] Finally, the GDP per capita is moderate ($24,208).[137]

Historical Background

Though Saudi Arabia is a relatively new country, having gained independence in 1932, people have inhabited the region for 15,000 to 20,000 years.[138] James Wynbrandt and Fawaz Gerges note the indigenous population referred to the area as Jazirate Al-Arab, meaning "Island of the Arabs." Most of the early population is believed to have come from the Assyrians, Babylonians, Egyptians, Israelites, as well as other Middle Eastern civilizations.[139]

Pre-Islamic society was largely clan based, with each clan free to determine and enforce appropriate conduct for its members.[140] The year, AD 570, marks an important beginning in the history of the Saudis and for most others of Arab decent.[141] The birth of the prophet Mohammed in 570 is considered the beginning of Muslim heritage. In contrast, the time preceding Mohammed's birth is generally referred to as "the time of ignorance."[142,143]

The most orthodox form of Islam, known as Wahhabism, has been particularly influential in Saudi Arabia. The rise of Wahhabism began to coalesce between 1500 and 1850. Indeed, much of the reason that corporal punishment remains prevalent in Saudi Arabia stems from the influence of the Wahhabi movement.

Muhammad ibn Abd al Wahhab preached reform of the Islamic religion because he began to grow concerned over the "way the people of Najd engaged in practices he considered polytheistic, such as praying to saints; making pilgrimages to tombs and special mosques; venerating trees, caves, and stones; and using votive and sacrificial offerings."[144] Additionally, Wahhab noted that followers of the Islamic faith were becoming lax in their adherence to the tenants of Islam and Islamic law.

Wahhab in effect advocated for a return to what he construed as the more pure form of Islam. Members of the Al Saud clan (for whom Saudi Arabia is named) were early adherents to the Wahhabi movement.[145] The Al Saud were such strident supporters of Wahhab that "In 1744 Muhammad ibn Saud and Muhammad ibn Abd al Wahhab swore a traditional Muslim oath in which they promised to work together to establish a state run according to Islamic principles."[146]

As a consequence of this devotion, the entire social structure of Saudi Arabia is heavily guided by the tenets of Wahhabism. Its effects can be seen throughout the judicial system, educational system, and political structure.[147] This strict adherence to the precepts of Wahhabism has not been without conflict. As

In December 2011 Australian national Mansor Almaribean was on a pilgrimage to Medina when he reportedly read passages aloud out of a book that insulted the Prophet Muhammad's companion. According to news reports, he was officially found guilty of blasphemy, which is considered a very serious crime in Saudi Arabia. Almaribean was subsequently sentenced to one year in jail and 500 lashes. The lashes will purportedly be administered in seven sessions. Given that there has been substantial international response to this sentence, it is unknown whether it will be carried out.

Blanchard observes, "Wahhabism opposes most popular Islamic religious practices such as saint veneration, the celebration of the Prophet's birthday, most core Shiite traditions, and some practices associated with the mystical teachings of Sufism . . . Indeed, given this strict interpretation of Islam, "even 'orthodox' Muslims could be considered unbelievers in the context of the 'true' faith."[148]

Contemporary Corporal Punishment

It is difficult to estimate how much corporal punishment is actually administered in modern Saudi Arabia because there is no governmental mechanism to collect or disseminate criminal justice data.[149] However, Amnesty International and other NGOs report that corporal punishments are administered with a high degree of frequency. Flogging is perhaps the most common sanction. The number of strokes can vary wildly from just a few to as many as several thousand.[150]

Flogging can be administered by the courts or by the religious police (mutawa'een), who have little oversight. A number of offenses carry the punishment of flogging, many of which are specified in the Qur'an. A recent campaign was undertaken to combat the harassment of women and girls and newspaper accounts estimate that nearly 172 youths have been flogged since the crackdown started in 2001.[151]

Amputations receive perhaps the most media attention, but Miethe and Lu report that they are relatively uncommon. Based on their data, there were approximately sixteen amputations officially reported during the reign of King Abdel azis Al Saud. Furthermore, they note that Amnesty International recorded 82 amputations from 1981 to 1995. However, Saudi Arabia is among the more opaque nations in the world so official reports are to be regarded with a healthy degree of skepticism. Terance Meithe and Hong Lu appear to agree, as they go on to note that anecdotal evidence suggests that amputations may be all too common as the need arose to differentiate criminals who received amputations as a sanction from Iraq war veterans who sustained their injuries in battle. As they state, there was "discussion of modifying these practices (e.g., by also branding criminals' foreheads). Such concern would only arise if limb amputation was not an uncommon punishment for criminals in this country."[152] In the sections that follow, we will explore recent corporal punishment cases that have captured recent media attention.

The Case of Puthen Veetil Abdul Latheef Naushad

Corporal punishment in Saudi Arabia can be administered according to a rather literal reading of retributive law (e.g., eye for an eye). This approach is exemplified in the recent case of Puthen Veetil Abdul Latheef Naushad, an Indian migrant worker. In 2003, Naushad was working at a gas station in Dammam, when he got involved in an altercation with a customer (Nayif al-'Utaibi) over payment.[153]

Human Rights Watch reported that "Naushad told 'Utaibi that he would not be able to obtain a refund once he used the jumper cable he had just purchased. When 'Utaibi demanded a refund after using the cable, Naushad advised him to speak to the shop owner, who was not there at the time."[154] On being told that he would have to wait for the owner, 'Utaibi jumped over the counter and lunged at Naushad.[155] During the ensuing physical altercation, Naushad damaged al-'Utaibi's eye, leaving him blind.[156] In response to this, the court pronounced a sentence of eye-gouging.

Human Rights Watch reported that "Naushad's Saudi employer, Abu Muhammad al-'Umri, . . . offered to pay over $25,000 in compensation, but the offer was refused."[157] At the trial, Naushad testified that he did not intend to injure 'Umri, but his testimony was not admissible in court because Saudi law forbids non-Saudis from testifying in cases that involve Saudi nationals.[158] Naushad was eventually pardoned and the eye-gouging sentence was never carried out. Even so, Saudi courts ordered sentences of eye-gouging on at least three occasions during 2003. It is unknown whether the other two were executed.[159]

Court-ordered Paralysis

In one of the most unusual cases heard by a Saudi Arabian court, officials are purported to have considered damaging the spine of a Saudi national (who remains unnamed). The unknown offender was alleged to have been involved in an altercation with al-Mutairi. During the altercation, the assailant is said to have attacked al-Mutairi with a meat cleaver, causing damage to his spine, which later led to paralysis and the loss of a foot. Rather than receive a form of compensation, "Al-Mutairi asked a judge in northwestern Tabuk province to impose an equivalent punishment on his attacker under Islamic Law."[160] The presiding judge then approached hospitals to determine whether it would be possible to intentionally injure a person's spine. During an interview with the victim's brother, he indicated "that one of the hospitals, located in Tabuk, responded that it is possible to damage the spinal cord, but it added that the operation would have to be done at another more specialized facility."[161] Another hospital was also approached, but they refused to perform the surgery on ethical grounds.[162]

A high court eventually refused to carry out the spinal punishment and instead ordered the victim to receive compensation.[163]

The Case of the "Qatif Girl"

Compared to the standards of the Western world, women's rights are notoriously lacking in Saudi Arabia. The case of the "Qatif Girl" provides an example of gender bias in Saudi justice. The victim in the case has not revealed her identity and is simply known in the media as the "Qatif Girl," after the eastern province in Saudi Arabia where her attack took place.[164] The victim was gang raped by seven men, who received sentences ranging from two to nine years in prison.[165] The victim received 90 lashes as punishment for being with a male who was not a relative. However, after she went to the press with her story, the victim's sentence was increased to 200 lashes and six months in prison.[166] Her lawyer in the case, Abdul Rahman Al-Lahem, was ordered to appear before a disciplinary committee and his license was revoked.[167] The victim was eventually pardoned by the King, "but press reports say King Abdullah's move did not mean the sentence was wrong."[168]

Although all of the aforementioned cases were eventually overturned, one must wonder whether they would have been carried out had they not received such widespread international media attention. For every lashing case or mutilation case that has been overturned, there are doubtless others that have been carried out. One case of corporal punishment that was administered to Muhammad 'Ali al-Sayyid has received extensive media attention after the fact, due to the extreme nature of the punishment.

The Case of Muhammad 'Ali al-Sayyid

Muhammad 'Ali al-Sayyid, an Egyptian national, was convicted of robbery in 1990 and sentenced to seven years imprisonment and 4,000 lashes. Because such a high number of lashes could result in death were they to be administered at once, the punishment was carried out during numerous sessions. Amnesty International reported that he received 50 lashes every two weeks.[169] Not surprisingly, "each flogging session ... reportedly left him with bruised or bleeding buttocks and unable to sleep or sit for three or four days."[170] When the sentence sparked international protest, authorities indicated that al'Sayyid's sentence was actually a lenient one because he should have received amputation.[171]

The Case of Donato Lama

Donato Lama, a Filipino national, was found guilty of preaching Christianity and sentenced to 18 months imprisonment and 70 lashes (to be administered in one session). Donato gave the following account of his experience to Amnesty International,

> I was brought to the whipping area. They tied me to a post. My hands were handcuffed and they also shackled my legs. I was wearing a T-shirt and jogging pants . . . The whip was one and a half metres long . . . with a heavy lead piece attached to the tip. It was terrible. Some fell on my thighs and my back. I would fall when the whip reached my feet but the prison guard would raise me up to continue the whipping. It was terrible. I was amazed to find myself still alive after the 70th lash was given. It lasted about 15 minutes . . . my back was bleeding. I cried.[172]

CONCLUSION

Nigeria, Singapore, and Saudi Arabia all vary widely in terms of development, culture, and history. Yet all continue to use corporal punishment in many spheres of life. Although each nation uses corporal punishment, the reasons for its persistence in each society are quite different. In Nigeria, the intersecting issues of Islam, slavery, and postcolonial legacy largely explain why corporal punishment is still used. In the case of Singapore, postcolonial legacy plays an integral part in the inclusion of corporal punishment in the criminal justice system, but the cultural emphasis on shared values and communitarianism appears more dominant where corporal punishment is concerned. Finally, in Saudi Arabia, the puritanical precepts of Wahhabism largely explain why corporal punishment is so prevalent.

The future of corporal punishment in Nigeria is somewhat uncertain, as some reluctance on the part of the courts to implement more severe forms of corporal punishment has emerged. In the case of Singapore, it seems that corporal punishment will likely persist. Saudi Arabia carries out more corporal punishment than any other country due, in part, to the puritanical nature of Wahhabism, which affects nearly every facet of life in the Kingdom. Although many of the more extreme cases of corporal punishment have ultimately been reduced or overturned on appeal, there are countless other cases of corporal punishments that have been carried out.

7 ———

Case Studies: Bolivia and The Bahamas

Soldiers! I hope you will have humanity and compassion even for your most bitter
enemies. Be the mediators between the vanquished and your victorious arms; show
yourselves as great in generosity as you are in bravery.

—Simon de Bolivar *Letter to his troops, 1821*

IN THE PREVIOUS chapter three distinct societies were presented that currently use
corporal punishment across many spheres of life. Several reasons for the persistence of such punishments were discussed. Among the most influential forces
in Nigeria are those of religious tradition, the slave trade, and post-colonial legacy. In Singapore, one sees similar, yet distinct social forces, namely, postcolonial legacy and communitarianism. Saudi Arabia, in contrast, derives most
of its corporal punishment mandate from an ultraorthodox and homogeneous
religious tradition.

Moving from Africa and the Far East to Latin America and the Caribbean
yields an opportunity to further expand the discussion of corporal punishment
in a social context. Of particular interest are the traditional justice practices in
Bolivia and the more formalized justice system in The Bahamas. Both of these
nations currently permit corporal punishment as a criminal sanction and in other
social realms. Because corporal punishment can be found in many settings
including the home, educational environments, as criminal sanctions, as disciplinary measures in correctional and alternative care settings, these two countries
are particularly good candidates for closer examination.

PLURINATIONAL STATE OF BOLIVIA

Although it may seem surprising to some, corporal punishment is still employed
in four Latin American countries. As of December 2010, the Global Initiative to
End the Corporal Punishment of Children reports that traditional justice systems
in Bolivia, Columbia, Ecuador, and Guatemala mete out corporal punishments
for some crimes.[1] While each of these countries has a unique culture and history,
Bolivia provides an especially rich example of corporal punishment in practice.

Country Background

The Estado Plurinacional de Bolivia is a landlocked country located to the south-west of Brazil in the central part of South America.[2] Its land mass is larger than Texas and California combined, making it the sixth largest country in South America.[3] The estimated population is approximately 10,118,683. As such, it is one of the most sparsely populated countries in the Western Hemisphere.[4] The predominant ethnic groups are Quechua (30%), Mestizo (30%), Aymara (25%), and white (15%).[5] The majority of the population (an estimated 50 to 60%) is comprised of "peoples native to the highland and valley regions of the country as well as the tropical rain forests and lowlands."[6] The predominance of the indigenous population has direct and important ramifications for the use of corporal punishment and will be explored later in the chapter. The majority of the population lives in rural areas (55%), which is unusual among countries in South America.[7] In terms of religion, the vast majority of the population (95%) practices Roman Catholicism and the remaining 5% practice Protestantism.[8]

According to the Human Development Index (HDI), Bolivia is a country of moderate development.[9] Life expectancy at birth is approximately 66.3 years. The mean level of education is 9.2 years. Almost 91% of the population over the age of 15 is literate. The national GDP per capita is $4,502.[10] Taken together, these measures give Bolivia and HDI value of .643, and a ranking of 95 out of 169 nations.[11] Bolivia ranks slightly below other Latin American nations in terms of development, as the combined average HDI for Latin American and the Caribbean is .706.[12] Although development is moderate, economic inequality is quite severe in Bolivia. The World Bank Development Indicators estimate that "the richest 20 percent of the population average 10 times the GDP compared to the poorest 20 percent."[13]

Historical Background

Bolivia's history is a fascinating combination of pre-Columbian heritage and colonial rule.[14] Anthropologists conclude that humans have lived in the Bolivian highlands for 21,000 years,[15] with some Andean cultures inhabiting the area as early as 10,000 to 7500 BC[16] Little is known of these early cultures, but some records suggest farming did not begin in the region until 3000 BC with copper mining commencing about 1,500 years later.[17]

The first great Andean culture rising to prominence was the Tiahuanacan empire, which inhabited the area surrounding Lake Titicaca beginning in 600 BC.[18] The Tiahuanacan empire flourished such that archeologists suggest it may have rivaled the scale of some Incan empires.[19] Tiahuanacan influence was vast and extended from modern-day Ecuador to the Chilean and Peruvian coasts by means of an intricate paved-road system.[20] It has also been suggested that the Tiahuanacan were technologically sophisticated with a knowledge of copper alloys and great agricultural skill.[21] The empire continued to expand until

1000 but suddenly collapsed in 1200 for reasons that remain unclear.[22] Aymara oral traditions make mention of a catastrophic event that wiped out the empire (e.g., flood, earthquake, or feud), but some archeologists suspect a prolonged period of drought may have been to blame.[23]

Following the collapse of the Tiahuanacan empire, seven regional kingdoms of Aymara rose to power, the most influential of which was situated on Lake Titicaca.[24] The Aymara nations had a complex and highly structured system of governments that was "stratified into two separate and unequal internal kingdoms—one high and one low—and each had its own king and its own ruling elite."[25] The Aymara were successful, in part, because they adapted to the climate conditions in the region and increased "their food supply through irrigation and the process of freezing and drying crops."[26] Though successful for a time, the Aymara were eventually conquered by the Quechua (later to be known as the Incas after they took the name of their rulers) in the latter part of the fifteenth century.[27] The Incan civilization was highly advanced, had a rigid social structure, and a large military that aided in the expansion of the Incan empire. Though their empire was vast, the Incans were never able to conquer the tribes of the eastern Bolivian lowlands, perhaps because unlike other Incan conquests, these tribes did not rely on agriculture for survival.[28] Because of this, "the Indian groups of the eastern two-thirds of Bolivia preserved their ways of life to a great extent, even after the Spanish conquest."[29] By the sixteenth century, the Incan empire was weakened by internal strife and civil war, thus opening the door to European colonizers.[30]

The era of conquest and colonial rule in Bolivia lasted from 1532 to 1809, beginning with the Spanish conquest of the Incan empire. As Herbert Klein notes, the Spanish conquistadors were not perceived by the indigenous population to be substantially different from the Incans.[31] They were simply thought of as being a more powerful conquering force than the Incans. He goes on to state, "for this reason, and because of the relatively recent Inca subjugation and the existence of antagonistic non-Quechua groups still not fully assimilated within its borders, the Spaniards initially had an easy time overthrowing the Inca Empire."[32]

The Spaniards not only capitalized on the existing civil war inside the Incan empire, they also employed subterfuge to convince the Incans that they were simply interested in gold and other riches—and did not plan to stay once they obtained said riches.[33] The Spaniards also used local Indians to fight many of their battles. This tactic had the dual advantage of minimizing Spanish losses and reducing the potential pool of indigenous combatants.[34] The ensuing war lasted just about a century, with the Indians bearing the brunt of the casualties. By the time Spanish rule became more stringent, thus drawing the ire of the local population, the indigenous losses were so great as to present only token resistance to the Europeans.

Interestingly, there was an area of Bolivia that did not attract much attention from Spanish colonizers. As Klein explains,

[T]he arrival of the Spaniards in 1532 for their definitive conquest of Peru[35] initially had not been felt in the Altiplano and valleys south of Lake Titicaca. A region rich in peasants, herds, wools, and traditional Indian food crops, it initially contained neither the armies nor the readily available gold and silver so sought after by the Spaniards. The urban centers of the Aymara kingdoms and Quechua colonies were small and relatively less developed by the standards of Cuzo. Also, the region had been intensely loyal to the Huascar faction in the Inca civil war and as a result initially welcomed the Spanish intervention as a victory over their enemies. Because of this loyalty, none of the Quito armies that so concerned the Spaniards in the early years remained in the area, and thus they did not attract Spanish military concern.[36]

This is not to say that the Aymara and Quechua peoples were not oppressed by their Spanish colonizers. Indeed, during the later years of colonization, they were aggressively subordinated. Perhaps paradoxically, they were also able to retain a great deal of their cultural identity, including their notions of justice.[37]

Indigenous Populations and Communal Justice

Andrew Canessa notes, "who is and who is not indigenous and what it means to be indigenous is highly variable, context specific and changes over time."[38] Some claims to indigeneity could simply be described as "we were here before you."[39] However, a framing put forth by Martínez Cobo, Special Rapporteur to the United Nations UN Sub-Commission on the Prevention of Discrimination of Minorities, is more instructive. In his report, Cobo defines indigenous populations: "Indigenous communities, peoples and nations are those which, having a historical continuity with pre-invasion and pre-colonial societies that developed on their territories, consider themselves distinct from other sectors of the societies now prevailing in those territories, or parts of them."[40]

In Bolivia, over 50% of the population self-identifies as indigenous. The Quechua and Aymara are the largest indigenous groups, with many living in the Altiplano area, as well as the cities of La Paz and El Alto.[41] Despite their large numerical presence, the indigenous populations in Bolivia have often been marginalized. This marginalization has typically taken the form of inequities in education, economics, and justice.[42] Vicente Fretes-Cibils et al. note that governmental justice is absent in over half of Bolivia's municipalities, making access to fair legal process a very serious problem for many Bolivian citizens.[43]

In 2006, Aymara Indian Evo Morales was elected as President of Bolivia, marking the first time an indigenous person was elected to the office. During a speech after he was sworn in, Morales stated, "I wish to tell you, my Indian brothers, that the 500-year indigenous and popular campaign of resistance has not been in vain . . . We're taking over now over the next 500 years. We're going to put an end to injustice, to inequality."[44] He followed through on his promise for sweeping changes by giving indigenous populations more self-governance in the newly revised Bolivian constitution. Specifically, the system of indigenous justice or communal justice was formally recognized in the newly adopted constitution. The ability for indigenous populations to administer their own system of justice has direct bearing on the legitimization of corporal punishment in Bolivia.

CONTEMPORARY CORPORAL PUNISHMENT

Although reliable information about the use of corporal punishment in contemporary Bolivia is difficult to obtain, the newly adopted constitution gives the indigenous population broad latitude to administer justice according to traditional ideals. Adopted in 2009, the Bolivian constitution broadens "definitions of property to include communal ownership; allow Indians to mete out corporal punishment under their own legal systems; extend limited autonomy to regional prefects; and reaffirm state control over Bolivia's ample natural gas reserves."[45] The constitution "recognizes the right of original indigenous peasant communities (*naciones y pueblos indígenas originario campesinos*) to administer justice in any civil or criminal dispute arising within their territory, applying their own principles, cultural values, norms and procedures (Articles 190 and 394)."[46] Under these provisions, traditional justice is viewed as being equal to state-sponsored (i.e., more Eurocentric) justice in state courts and is accorded a philosophical and legal parity.[47]

The above rights are afforded to indigenous communities, but within certain jurisdictional limits. It is important to note that indigenous justice applies only to persons living in rural areas and in predominantly indigenous communities.[48] Furthermore, indigenous communities do not have jurisdiction over many criminal infractions including "murder, rape, crimes involving violence against children and adolescents, crimes against state security, war crimes, crimes against humanity, offences involving drugs, corruption and infringement of customs regulations."[49] Additionally, many civil matters (where the state is a party) are excluded from indigenous courts, as are any issues pertaining to "Labor Law, Social Security Law, Mining and Hydrocarbon Law, Forestry Law, Agrarian Law, and International Law."[50]

There have been reports of indigenous communities meting out what is commonly termed "communal justice." According to the Human Rights Foundation, communal justice dates back to Incan civilization. It can involve various divination rituals, such as consultation of cocoa leaves.[51] Finding the exact parameters of communal justice in Bolivia is a difficult enterprise and arguably open to interpretation.[52] Most would likely agree, however, that in instances of communal justice, the decisions are often handed down quickly and corporal punishment is generally among the range of punishments available.[53] Though punishments can vary from community to community they typically include public lashings, physical labor, and burying people alive, among others.[54] Javier Galvan recounts several recent incidents that have been reported by local Bolivian news outlets:

In Potosi, they buried a woman alive in December 2006 for cheating on her husband. In a small community near Illampu, local people killed six young men for the robbery of their cattle. In Bunsillos, Potosi thieves are routinely punishment to public lashings until they confess and apologize. In the poor agricultural community of Humanata, a man who stole farming equipment in 2007 was dragged on the floor for almost 1,500 feet and then hanged from a bridge.[55]

Similarly, the Human Rights Foundation reports that there has been a dramatic increase in physical forms of punishments (some resulting in death) since 2005.[56] In the 2.5-year period from November 2005 to January 2008, "forty-six such cases have been reported in the Bolivian news."[57] In one 2007 case,

Llallagua Potosi's district attorney offices had to be closed after a mob threatened to lynch prosecutors assigned to investigate the death of Javier Charque Choque, who had been stoned, beaten, tied, and buried alive upon communal judges' sentencing in Villa Arbolitos, near Llallagua, on December 29, 2006. Cirilo Gaspar Cruz, the communal leader responsible for the sentence and a participant in the events that led to Charque Choque's death, was freed by the mob and the charges were dropped. Charque Choque had been accused of rape; however, according to Gustavo Calvo, Potosi's district attorney, the victim was not presumed innocent, and did not receive due process.[58]

It is difficult to tell if these are isolated incidents related to a lack of law enforcement in rural areas[59] or if they are part of an existing justice framework in indigenous communities. The opacity of these incidents is hardly the only point of contention they prompt.

Critics vociferously denounce communal justice in Bolivia. Their essential argument posits that the system was developed to appear sympathetic to and inclusive of indigenous notions of justice, but in reality, is little more than another vehicle for more expedient and violent oppression. To this end, the government of Bolivian President Evo Morales worked to make communal justice the only system of law available to indigenous communities, with no right to appeal and no due process guarantees for the accused. The views of Thor Halvorssen, president of the Human Rights Foundation (HRF), reflect this position:

Communal justice entirely disregards due process. In theory, it enables indigenous communities to address their needs in a fair and disinterested manner. In practice, it is judicial terror. It is breathtaking that the Morales government wishes to enshrine such arbitrary and barbaric practices and make them legally unappealable.[60]

Another outspoken critic of communal justice, Maurice Van der Velden, highlights an interesting and perilous chasm between communal justice and the national system:

Bolivia recognizes the jurisdiction of communal justice in indigenous communities; nevertheless, discussion doesn't stop after simply establishing the 'borders' of both systems. What does one do if individuals within the system of communal justice prefer to use the national justice system, and vice versa for people living in the territory that falls under the jurisdiction of the "regular" justice system who prefer to have their case treated by communal justice?[61]

In many ways, the controversy surrounding communal justice in Bolivia is endemic to postcolonial societies around the world. Vestiges of an older indigenous order are manipulated by colonialists or their heirs to create systems that promote class division, social marginalization, economic oppression, and political exclusion.

Rights of the Child

Bolivia has enacted several articles within its newly adopted constitution that recognize the rights of children to be free from violence. Specifically, Article 13 of the constitution states, "Treaties and conventions ratified by the Legislature Multicountry, that recognize human rights and prohibit their limitation in states of emergency prevailing in the domestic. The rights and duties enshrined in this Constitution shall be construed in accordance with international human rights treaties ratified by Bolivia."[62] In addition, Article 62 of the constitution "prohibits and punishes all forms of violence against children and adolescents in the family and in society."[63] Bolivia adopted the Children and Adolescents Code in 1999, which clarifies when abuse has occurred. According to Article 109 of the code, it is considered that the child or adolescent is a victim of abuse when:

> According to Article 109 of the code, a child or adolescent is considered a victim of abuse when the action, Causes physical or mental harm; Fails to respect dignity and integrity; Causes neglect in the areas of food, clothing, housing, education, and health care; Endangers the child's life or health; Places the child in prolonged isolation.

These rights notwithstanding, corporal punishment is not expressly prohibited, and it appears that corporal punishment is still practiced by indigenous communities and that it is permissible in accordance with indigenous justice.

The United Nations Committee on the Rights of the Child raised some concerns that in accordance with the new constitution, corporal punishment could be legal in some instances. On questioning by the committee, the Bolivian delegation assured the UN committee, "In the new Constitution, any form of violence against children in the family or in the society was punished.[64] However such forms of violence were allowed currently and they would have to act in order to bring in line the facts on the ground with the provisions of the new Constitution."[65] Given that indigenous communities operate with a high degree of autonomy and the rights accorded indigenous peoples are both broad and vague, it is unclear whether the Bolivian government would enforce these provisions in rural settings.

Corporal Punishment in the Home and Educational System

Despite the constitutional protection against family violence, corporal punishment is legal in Bolivian homes. The Bolivian Criminal Code (Article 276) provides that, "No aggression will be punished if the victim of the aggression is not seriously hurt and the aggressor is husband or wife, parent or grandparent, child or grandchild, sibling, close relative, political sibling, and if they are living together."[66] Although Article 109 of the Children and Adolescents Code protects children from acts of corporal punishment that may cause harm, a parent would be acting within their legal rights to administer corporal punishment if it stops short of physical harm.[67] This law could be construed as being similar to other nations that permit reasonable corporal punishment for the purposes of correction.

Corporal punishment is technically illegal in Bolivian schools, but it appears to still be in use. Although Article 61 of the Constitution and Article 109 of the Children and Adolescents Code technically bar its use, enforcement is hardly universal. A 2001 study of abuse in Bolivian schools conducted by Child Defense International revealed that 50% of children had received corporal punishments on occasion and 6% reported that they received physical punishments constantly at school (UNICEF Bolivia, 2001).[68] Furthermore, 40% of teachers reported they believed corporal punishment was both necessary and effective.[69] Recently the U.S. Department of State noted that corporal punishment and verbal abuse are still common correctives in Bolivian schools.[70]

Commonwealth of The Bahamas

The next case study in this chapter examines the island chain of The Bahamas. While The Bahamas is perhaps best known as a tourist destination with white sandy beaches, it has an interesting history with regard to corporal punishment in its justice system. Corporal punishment was present in Bahamian justice for a long time, but eventually fell out of favor. In a turn almost without parallel, it was reintroduced in 1991 with the implementation of the Criminal Law (Measures) Act.[71] Despite the legislative revival of corporal punishment in The Bahamas, controversy persists as to its legality.

Country Background

The Bahamas is an island chain located in the Atlantic Ocean, southeast of the U.S. state of Florida.[72] With a total land mass of roughly 13,880 square kilometers, the country is about the size of Connecticut. The population is an estimated 313,312, making it rather sparsely populated.[73] The population is predominantly black (85%) with 12% white, and 3% of Hispanic and Asian descent.[74] A variety of predominantly Christian faiths are represented among the population, including Baptist (35.4%), Anglican (15.1%), Roman Catholic (13.5%), Pentecostal (8.1%), Church of God (4.8%), Methodist (4.2%), other Christian (15.2%), none or unspecified (2.9%), and other (0.8%).[75]

In terms of development, The Bahamas ranks relatively high compared to other Caribbean nations. According to the Human Development Index, Bahamian citizens have an average life expectancy of 74.4 years. The mean years of schooling is 11.1. The GDP per capita is approximately $25,887.[76] Taken together, these measures give The Bahamas an estimated HDI value of .784, which ranks the country 43rd in the world.[77] By way of comparison, other Latin American and Caribbean nations have a combined estimated HDI of .706.[78]

Historical Background

The Bahamas was first "discovered" by Christopher Columbus during his famous 1492 journey in search of better trade routes to India.[79] After extensive study, The National Geographic Society determined that Columbus likely landed at Samana Cay, located on the southeastern region of the island chain.[80] Early records show the island chain was still referred to as being "newly discovered" as late as 1650.[81] This lag in discovery time can likely be attributed to a lack of widespread European involvement in the area. Although Europeans were minimally present in The Bahamas in the period after Columbus made landfall, a permanent colony was not established until 1649.[82] In 1649, Puritans from the English colony of Bermuda formed a settlement on The Bahamas known as Eleuthera (which is Greek for "place of freedom").[83] The goals of the colonists were similar to those of Puritans who had established colonies in the Northeast region of the United States—religious freedom.[84]

By 1666, other English colonists arrived on the islands and established New Providence.[85] This effort at colonization was short lived, however, as the English colonists were attacked by the Spanish in 1682. Owing to attacks by combined French and Spanish forces, the English were driven out of the area by 1703.[86]

Following the defeat of the British during the American Revolution, English loyalists, along with their slaves, fled to The Bahamas. By the 1780s, the population of New Providence had nearly tripled.[87] The Spanish once again took control of the island in 1781, "but it was retaken in 1783 by some American Loyalists under Colonel Deveaux, and by the treaty of Versailles in 1783 it was finally restored to Great Britain."[88]

Given The Bahamas's status as a British colony, it was governed by English law, including the English Penal Code, which had provisions for corporal punishment. Corporal punishment remained as a legacy of colonization, until eleven years after The Bahamas gained their independence, when bodily punishments were abolished.[89]

THE CRIMINAL LAW (MEASURES) ACT

Corporal punishment was abolished in 1984 but was reinstated just seven years later in the Criminal Act of 1991.[90] A principal reason for the abolition of corporal punishment was that 1984 marked the 150th anniversary of the end of slavery in The Bahamas.[91] The abolition of corporal punishment on that particular anniversary allowed politicians to "garner goodwill and enforce the PLP's [Progressive Liberal Party] image as the liberator of blacks from the oppression of white colonialists by officially eliminating from the law that obsolete, but nonetheless symbolic vestige of slavery, the cat-o'-nine tails."[92]

Corporal punishment was reinstated seven years later in 1991. The reinstatement was in part a response to the rising Bahamian crime rates of the 1980s.[93] Where mounting crime in places like the United States resulted in three-strikes and other increased prison sentences, The Bahamas returned to corporal punishment.

In 1991, Prime Minister Pindling (the same Prime Minister who had called for an abolition of corporal punishment in 1984) introduced a bill to reinstate corporal punishment in The Bahamas.[94] The public was largely supportive of the measure, as were women's groups and religious groups who called for a return to retributive justice.[95]

The resulting law, Part II of the Criminal Law Act, specifies how corporal punishment is to be administered, as well as what types of offenders are eligible for such punishment. With regard to how floggings are to be administered, article 4 states:

> (1) Whenever an offender is sentenced to undergo corporal punishment, such punishment shall be inflicted privately either by flogging or whipping in accordance with the provisions of this section.
> (2) Flogging shall be administered with a cat or rod of a pattern approved by the Governor-General and, when with a cat, on the back of the offender and when with a rod on his buttocks, and in either case only after an examination by and in the presence of a medical officer.[96]

As stipulated later in the section, floggings are reserved for adult males only, but this does not mean that children cannot receive physical punishment. Rather,

Article 4(4) states that when a child is found guilty of an offense that would normally carry a punishment of flogging,

> in lieu thereof he may be sentenced to be whipped. Whipping shall be administered with a light cane of a pattern approved by the Governor-General on the buttocks, by or in the presence of a parent or guardian (if he desires to be present) or by such other person as the court may approve. In New Providence a sentence of whipping shall be administered only after an examination by and in the presence of a medical officer.[97]

Article 5(2) further stipulates:

> the maximum number of strokes which may be administered at any one time shall be twelve in the case of a flogging and six in the case of a whipping and no person who has been flogged or whipped shall be again flogged or whipped within fourteen days.[98]

Finally, female offenders are generally spared from corporal punishments as article 6 states:

> No sentence of flogging or whipping shall be passed upon a female of any age; but in lieu of such sentence, where a female is convicted of an offence for which corporal punishment may be inflicted on a male, the court may sentence her to solitary confinement or to any other such additional punishment as the law for the time being permits to be inflicted on a female for an offence against the rules of the prison in New Providence.[99]

Somewhat problematically, the 1991 Criminal Law Act conflicts with the Bahamian Constitution. Article 17(1) states, "No person shall be subjected to torture or to inhuman or degrading treatment or punishment."[100] The court of appeals directly addressed this conflict in the Andrew Bridgewater case as discussed in the next section.

CONTEMPORARY CORPORAL PUNISHMENT CASES

Corporal punishment is most often prescribed in cases of rape or other sexual offenses.[101] Although many cases have not received widespread attention, it appears corporal punishments have been administered in some cases. As with many nations, even those that are relatively more developed, precise statistical counts from The Bahamas are not available.

That said, Amnesty International provides details of the first two corporal punishment cases since the reinstatement. In 1995, Leavon Williams, convicted of rape and armed robbery, was sentenced to 12 strokes (six with a "cat-o'-nine-tails" and six with a rod), in addition to 25 years imprisonment.[102] Concerns arose in this case because Williams did not have legal representation at his trial and, while he had up to 21 days to appeal his sentence, the first portion of the flogging was carried out prior to his appeal.[103]

In July 1995, Melvin Saunders, also convicted of rape, as well as assault and armed robbery, was sentenced to corporal punishment and 25 years imprisonment.[104] Like Williams, Saunders appealed his punishment. However, it remains unclear whether the flogging was actually carried out.

More recently, Alutus Newbol was sentenced to eight strokes, as well as 24 years imprisonment for the burglary and the attempted rape and assault of an 83-year-old woman after he broke into her home in 2004.[105] Newbol won an appeal for the flogging sentence. While corporal punishment was not administered in this case, it sparked more international debate as to the appropriateness of its use.[106]

The issue of judicial corporal punishment was once again brought to the forefront in the case of *Bridgewater v. Regina*.[107] On December 13, 2006, Andrew Bridgewater pled guilty to the rape of a six-year-old girl and was subsequently sentenced to a seven-year prison term and ten strokes with a "cat-o'-nine-tails."[108] Bridgewater appealed the corporal punishment, stating that is was excessive because:

> (1) the appellant had no previous conviction for any offence of a similar nature; (2) he was slightly retarded; (3) the girl's caregiver had allowed the girl to go with the appellant; (4) the appellant was in terrible state, physically, when he was arrested for this offence; and (5) the appellant has shown remorse for what he did.[109]

The court upheld the seven-year prison sentence, but took issue with the corporal punishment sentence. They cited inconsistencies in the Bahamian Constitution, Penal Code, and Criminal Law. Notably, section 118 of the penal code reads, "Notwithstanding anything to the contrary in this or any other law, *no form of corporal punishment shall be imposed as a penalty under any law in respect to the commission of a criminal or disciplinary offence*" (emphasis added in the original).[110] Clearly, this passage stands in direct conflict with the 1991 Criminal Law (Measures) Act that was previously discussed. The court summed up its position by stating, "Insofar, therefore, as the Criminal Law (Measures) Act, purports to extend corporal punishment to persons convicted of an offence under section 10(1) of the Sexual Offences and Domestic Violence Act, it is in conflict with Article 17(1) of the Constitution and is not saved by either Articles 17(2) or 30 of the Constitution and is therefore invalid."[111]

In 2008, during the Universal Periodic Review by the United Nations, the Bahamian government stated that they intended to repeal the corporal punishment laws, but to date this has not taken place.[112] The legality of corporal punishment is clearly in flux and will remain that way until inconsistencies in the law are addressed.

Corporal Punishment in the Home

The Bahamas ratified the Convention on the Rights of the Child and as such is obligated to "ensure the protection of children from all forms of maltreatment by parents or caretakers" (Article 19). Furthermore, The Bahamas is "obligated to establish appropriate social programs for the prevention of abuse and the treatment of victims, and under Article 34, to protect children from sexual exploitation and abuse, prostitution and pornography."[113]

These rights notwithstanding, corporal punishment is permissible in home settings in The Bahamas. Parents and guardians are permitted to "correct his or her legitimate or illegitimate child ... for misconduct or disobedience to any lawful command," and "no correction can be justified which is unreasonable in kind or in degree."[114] During the University Periodic Review by the United Nations, The Bahamas was questioned about the corporal punishment of children. In particular, "Germany enquired into the difference between permitted corporal punishment and physical abuse, to which Mr. Barnett [Attorney General and Minister of Legal Affairs of The Bahamas] responded that 'wounding someone or drawing blood' would be considered abuse."[115] In response to these queries, the Bahamian government requested assistance with human rights education and training.[116] To date, there is no information about the type of assistance/training that may have been provided, but corporal punishment remains a mainstay in the home.

There is a paucity of research about the prevalence of corporal punishment in Bahamian homes. Shane Brennan, William Fielding, Marie Carroll, Janice Miller, Latanya Adderlay, and Mary Ann Thompson represent one of the extant few studies in this area.[117] Their survey of 933 people in New Providence revealed that "children were spanked in 77% of homes with children, pets were hit in 25% of homes with pets, and domestic violence was found in 23% of homes."[118] Of the 422 respondents who indicated they spanked their children, 37% said children were spanked only when "very naughty." In addition, 27.5% reported sometimes spanking their children. 25.8% indicated they rarely spanked their children, and 9.7% reported that they often administered spanking. The research also contained more detailed case studies and of the ten respondents who were responsible for the care of children, all but one punished their children and six used violence during the course of the punishment.[119]

Corporal Punishment in Educational Settings

Corporal punishment is legally administered throughout the Bahamian school system. During the Universal Periodic Review by the United Nations, the country's representative stated corporal punishment is administered by school officials (principal, vice principal, and senior master/mistress) in accordance with standards set forth by the Department of Education.[120] In 2005, the Committee on the Rights of the Child expressed, "concern at the fact that corporal punishment is still widely practiced in the family, in schools, and in institutions, and that domestic legislation does not explicitly prohibit its use" and recommended provisions be made to prohibit its use.[121] Numerous years have passed since that recommendation and there does not appear to be any change in the legal status of corporal punishment.

Corporal Punishment as a Disciplinary Measure

The legality of corporal punishment as a disciplinary measure inside prison facilities is not clear. Chapter 208 (14–16) of the Bahamian statutes details when, how, and on whom corporal punishment may be inflicted.[122] Specifically, article 14(1) states:

> Corporal punishment may be inflicted on male prisoners for such prison offences as may be prescribed by the rules.
>
> (2) Every infliction of corporal punishment with the cat shall be attended by the Superintendent of Prisons or such other prison officer as may be delegated by him and the medical officer.
>
> (3) The medical officer shall give such orders for preventing injury to the health of a prisoner on whom corporal punishment is inflicted as he may deem necessary and it shall be the duty of the Superintendent to carry them into effect and the Superintendent shall enter in the punishment book the hour at which the punishment is inflicted, the number of lashes and any order which the medical officer may have given on the occasion.
>
> **15.** (1) Corporal punishment for a prison offence in the case of a male prisoner of or over sixteen years of age shall be inflicted with a cat or rod and in the case of a male prisoner under that age with a rod. (2) The cat and rod shall be of patterns approved by the Minister.
>
> **16.** The number of lashes inflicted for a prison offence on a prisoner of or over sixteen years of age shall not exceed twenty-four and on a prisoner under that age, eighteen.[123]

However, a footnote has been added to these rules citing Chapter 84 (118) of the Penal Code, which reads, "Notwithstanding anything to the contrary in this, or any other law, no form of corporal punishment shall be imposed as a penalty under any law in respect to the commission of a criminal or disciplinary offence."[124] The inconsistencies in the laws make it very difficult to definitively ascertain the status of corporal punishment in Bahamian prisons.

CONCLUSION

In sum, Bolivia and The Bahamas represent two countries in the Western Hemisphere where corporal punishment is used in many spheres of life. Although corporal punishment is not used in the formalized justice system in

Bolivia, it is practiced in traditional justice systems. Corporal punishment has a long history in communal justice, as the practice possibly dates back to the Incan empire. While the Bolivian government asserts that they value human rights (as well as the rights of the child), they also recognize the rights of indigenous populations to govern themselves. This recognition extends to some matters of jurisprudence and punishment. The basic human right to be free from degrading punishments needs to be balanced against the rights of the indigenous populations.

The case of The Bahamas helps illustrate one of the difficulties of cross-national research. Although corporal punishment is legal and has been administered in several cases, Bahamian courts note inconsistencies between the Criminal Law Act, which makes corporal punishment legal, and the country's Constitution and Penal Code, which prohibits corporal punishment. Several years ago, the Bahamian government indicated an intent to repeal the modern corporal punishment provision, but to date this has not occurred. These legal inconsistencies make it hard to state with certainty whether corporal punishment will actually be employed in the future. It may well be that the corporal punishment law will stay on the books, but corporal punishments will not be carried out. This would make The Bahamas abolitionist in practice, but still technically legal.

8

Explaining Current Global Trends

> All human actions have one or more of these seven causes: chance, nature, compulsions, habit, reason, passion and desire.
>
> —Aristotle

OUR DISCUSSION OF corporal punishment up to this point has tended toward a descriptive treatment, positioning the institution either as an artifact of history or as an element of certain contemporary cultural settings or institutions. This chapter represents a move from a largely descriptive to a more analytical assessment of the topic.[1]

As has been well established, corporal punishment is one of humanity's most enduring cultural institutions. A complex web of shifting social relationships promotes the use of corporal punishment in one society and retards it in another. We see that corporal punishment has been used across continents, time, and social contexts. The detailed retrospective presented heretofore provides a necessary predicate from which we can base a deeper look at the modern phenomenon. In specific, the goal of this chapter is to move from questions of "who," "how," and "where" corporal punishment has been used to the much more controversial and difficult question of "why" its use continues.

Explaining "why" a given society continues to permit corporal punishment is an especially complicated proposition. In order to assail the topic with due detail, we have limited the focus of this chapter to a consideration of corporal punishment as a sanction against convicted criminal offenders. By limiting discussion to this one context it is possible to glean a deeper understanding of the institution. While this approach suffers in its generalizability to other spheres, it nonetheless may provide useful insights for further study.

The basic notion that undergirds all punishment is control of others. That said, punishments do not arise or persist as atomized social phenomenon. They have a context. They are shaped by the cultures and priorities of the people who employ them.

As efforts to understand complex, historically nested social issues tend to be, the analysis presented here is but a first step on a much longer road. The theories and explanations proffered below should not be taken as a last word on the topic but rather as guideposts to further exploration.

To the preceding point on the difficulties endemic to this kind of discussion, a brief word is warranted on the nature of macro-sociological analyses motivated by a conflict or critical approach (such as is presented here). Alan Liska provides an instructive caution to scholars who employ a conflict perspective in their research. He contends conflict theorists have generally failed to properly operationalize and connect concepts such as "ruling class interests" and "threat" with the phenomenon they purport to explain.[2] Corollary to this, he notes that this kind of problem extends throughout the literature. As he states, "Because the critical causal variables are not well defined, theoretically and operationally, and are not clearly linked to each other in the form of propositions or a causal model, the relevant research literature is also not well defined and integrated."[3]

Conscious of Liska's concerns, the following discussion of corporal punishment and its social correlates is perhaps best considered in a context similar to that offered by Irma Adelman and Cynthia Morris in their multinational study of economic development. As they state, "[These findings] suggest the existence of a systematic pattern of interaction among mutually interdependent economic, social and political forces, all of which combine to generate a unified complex of change in the style of life of a community."[4]

Following their basic approach, the social conditions discussed below should be regarded similarly. Taken together, these factors suggest a set of social relationships that bear on the nature and modality of punishment that a given society is likely to employ. What emerges is a constellation of social connections and dynamics that, while highly predictive of certain punishment modalities, necessarily falls somewhere short of an idealized statement of linear causality.

BACKGROUND

As has been well established throughout this volume, corporal punishment as a sanction for criminal activities has an ancient history. Once ubiquitous in almost every Western nation, the infliction of physical pain, such as whipping, branding, and various forms of mutilation, has been largely replaced by imprisonment, community sanctions (e.g., community service and probation), and fines. In short, over the last century and a half, the focus of punishment in the Western world shifted from the body to the mind.

This is not to suggest that incarceration is not inherently physical, but as some have argued,[5] the locus of imprisonment is as much mental as corporeal. While the majority of North American and European countries do not currently employ corporal punishment as a criminal sanction, there are several parts of the world that still rely heavily upon it (i.e., Africa and the Middle East).

The transition from a corporal to a carceral punishment model in Western society has been discussed extensively by scholars such as Georg Rusche and Otto Kirchheimer,[6] Michel Foucault,[7] and Michael Ignatieff,[8] among others. Less commonly does one see comparative analyses of current trends in global corporal

Figure 8.1 Map Showing Distribtion of CP Countries

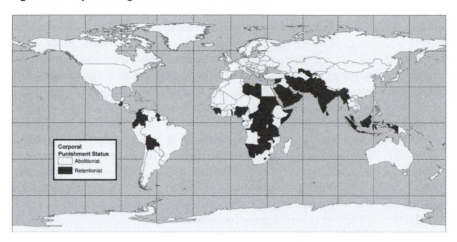

punishment practices. Specifically, the question as to why some countries continue to include corporal punishment as a possible criminal sanction when the majority of the world has turned from it remains understudied. This chapter addresses that void by examining the relationship between social conditions and corporal punishment. If the retention of corporal punishment is to be taken as something other than a randomly occurring phenomenon, it logically follows that a comparison between retentionist and abolitionist countries might reveal the social conditions most likely to promote one modality or the other (see Figure 8.1).

This said, studies in comparative (i.e., cross-national) penology are relatively rare compared to the rest of penological literature, as most penological studies tend to concentrate on the practices of a single nation. While the single-nation approach has many advantages, it fails to provide a sufficiently broad perspective to understand phenomena that bridge cultures and time in the way corporal punishment does. Moreover, it is imperative to understand how and why punishment varies between nations; for without a comparative perspective, it is impossible to make sense of penality in general or to make any meaningful analysis of punishment in one's own culture.[9]

James Lynch provides a useful example of the importance of a comparative approach to penology.[10] He examines the relative length of prison sentences for serious crimes between five industrial democracies. It was long held that the United States was more punitive than other nations because it incarcerates more individuals for longer periods of time. However, when Lynch examined the actual time served by inmates (who committed violent crimes), he found that offenders in the United States serve less time than their counterparts in other nations. While these findings apply only to incarceration length for violent crimes (and not crime in general), they nevertheless demonstrate that examining correctional systems through a comparative lens can challenge conventional wisdom with regard to punishment.

Despite the benefits of comparative penology, cross-national comparisons of criminal justice generally (and correctional systems in particular) present special challenges. For example, data on offenses committed are difficult to compare across a broad range of countries because definitions of offenses may change depending on the jurisdiction or there may be significant levels of underreporting.[11] To complicate matters, comparison of official statistics becomes especially problematic because criminal justice systems are highly decentralized in some countries, which makes data collection on national statistics challenging or nearly impossible.[12]

Although issues such as these must be resolved when comparing countries with vastly different histories and cultures, these criticisms are not intended to imply meaningful comparative research is not possible. Rather, they suggest matters of validity endemic to cross-national research require particular diligence and perspective.[13] The relative opacities and cultural roadblocks to this kind of scholarship, while substantial, are not insurmountable.

As Graeme Newman and Greg Howard maintain, "[A]t the close of the twentieth century, all countries of the world are inextricably tied together by commerce, past colonization and historical circumstance."[14] Building on these commonalities, avenues for otherwise difficult comparisons are expanded.

As above, comparative penology remains an underdeveloped area of scholarship, though significant progress has been made in recent decades. While the categories are by no means mutually exclusive, it is nevertheless useful to frame studies from the comparative literature as either more "theoretical" or "empirical" in nature. Much of the more theoretical literature focuses on the correlation between social relationships and modes of punishment, whereas studies in a more empirical frame tend to focus on comparative examinations of incarceration rates. Because this distinction is not necessarily intuitive to those outside academia, a brief elaboration is warranted.

THEORETICAL LITERATURE

Many characterize the abolition of bodily punishments as an attempt to make the act of punishment more humane and consistent with the ideals of the Enlightenment. David Garland[15] takes a view similar to Norbert Elias[16] in noting that the move away from corporal punishments has occurred because bodily punishments offend modern "repressive" sensibilities. Garland states, "Gross violence, deliberate brutality, the infliction of physical pain and suffering, all these are felt by many people to be intolerably offensive in themselves and to have no legitimate place within the public policy and legal institutions of a civilized nation."[17]

The idea that bodily punishments are associated with uncivilized society or that a reliance on largely carceral punishment is, as some[18] have argued, "a march of progress" fails to fully explain why corporal punishment has waned globally. Furthermore, it does not address an even more basic question: If the march of progress position is correct, why is corporal punishment still used in several countries otherwise characterized as being "civilized" or "modern"?

Another useful juxtaposition of the same kind is found in considering the global distribution of capital punishment. If one holds that capital punishment is more severe than corporal punishment, then it stands to reason that capital punishment should be found only among less-developed nations. This is hardly the case. Just as technologically modern and economically advanced nations like the United States and Japan continue to use capital punishment, nations of low economic development and technological lag such as Haiti and Guinea Bissau do not.[19] Therefore, the bright lines drawn by the "march of progress" paradigm are not especially useful in furthering our understanding of punishment trends.

The notion that corporal punishment is the exclusive purview of barbarian or uncivilized societies also prompts a secondary set of questions. In particular, it begs whether corporal punishment could be imposed in a "civilized" manner. In his extensive treatment of the issue, Graeme Newman[20] observes that corporal punishment offends our current sensibilities because bodily punishments have been linked historically to acts of torture. He concludes corporal punishment need not automatically be considered uncivilized or barbaric, as it can be applied in a numerically based and civilized manner.

Echoing Newman's scholarship, Peter Moskos advances a similar position, contrasting the relative harshness of extended incarceration with the acute pains associated with flogging, "Going to prison means losing your life and everything you care for. Compared to this, flogging is just a few very painful strokes on the behind . . . If you had the choice, you'd probably choose flogging. Wouldn't we all?"[21]

While individual responses will certainly differ, Newman and Moskos raise an important set of points. When the relative perils are posed along the lines of "twenty years or a hundred lashes," many among us would doubtless consider the extent of our pain tolerances. Even simple dichotomies such as this speak to the complexity of corporal punishment as a social phenomenon. How then, does one begin to assail the changes in society that moved the world from a predominance of corporal punishment to a world of incarceration?

Wholesale changes in dominant systems of punishment are likely motivated by forces more tangible than refined sentiments or enlightened ideals. This idea is well supported by the work of Rusche and Kirchheimer.[22] They maintain that shifts in penal practice across Europe in the fifteenth, sixteenth, and nineteenth centuries can be linked to changing labor needs in the capitalist system. As they explain, in fifteenth-century Europe the newly emerging capitalist system produced a labor surplus. This surplus lessened the value of individual human lives. As a result, more severe forms of corporal punishment as well as an increased proliferation of capital punishment took place. However, when labor became scarce, societies developed alternative punishments, such as the galley, transportation, and workhouses (sixteenth century) as well as incarceration (eighteenth and nineteenth centuries). They maintain punishment is inextricably linked to social forces, most determinative among them, the motive for profit.

Nicos Poulantzas helps move the discussion both into the modern era and away from more traditional Marxist interpretations of the role economics plays in the control of society. As he states:

> Every State economic measure therefore has a political content—not only in the general sense that it assists in capital accumulation and exploitation, but also in the sense that it is necessarily adapted to the political strategy of the hegemonic fraction. Not only are the States politico-ideological functions now subordinated to its economic role, but it's economic functions directly involve reproduction of the dominant ideology.[23]

This observation is especially important as it sets all other relations of power as subordinate to economic imperatives. To summarize Poulantzas's position more succinctly, when the State (or a powerful constituency with the backing of the State) exercises control over a segment of society, cultural, religious, ethnic, or even nominally political ends may be presented as the primary motivation, but the ultimate interests served are economic.

Stanley Cohen notes that for Rusche and Kirchheimer, the prison is designed to render "docile the recalcitrant members of the working class, it deters others, it teaches habits of discipline and order, it reproduces the lost hierarchy. It repairs defective humans to compete in the market place."[24] In short, prisons serve as a place in which those who refuse to support the dominant economic model can be retrained and made into obedient workers.

The Rusche–Kirchheimer hypothesis states that punishments will become harsher in times of a labor surplus. Historically, this has meant that punishments will become physically harsher, but the modern interpretation holds that imprisonment rates will be highest in times of increased unemployment.[25] Generally, the Rusche–Kirchheimer hypothesis explains changes in the incarceration rate, a finding with which most studies in this area concur.[26]

However, these findings become less compelling when a cross-national comparative approach is employed.[27] Furthermore, the relationship between unemployment and non-prison sanctions (e.g., corporal punishment) has not been systematically examined. One would also be remiss not to mention an important weakness in the Rusche–Kirchheimer hypothesis, which is the bulk of these studies fail to address the complex issue of punishment severity. Specifically, it is difficult to determine whether imprisonment might be arguably a more severe form of punishment than corporal punishment. Historically, examinations of punishment and employment trends typically sidestep the issue, deferring to incarceration rates as a proxy for severity.

As indicated by Newman and also Moskos, such assumptions may be less self-evident than some corporal punishment opponents might wish to believe. In his analysis of the question, Newman makes a distinction between chronic punishment, in which the pain persists for long periods of time, and acute punishments, characterized by relatively short-lived pain.[28] Imprisonment, in Newman's estimation, fits the description of chronic pain, as its effects last throughout the sentence and beyond. By this reasoning, corporal punishment could be considered either acute or chronic, depending on the length of the effect. Acute corporal punishments might involve short-lived pain and include forms of whipping or paddling, whereas chronic corporal punishments would typically involve lasting disfigurement (i.e., mutilations and limb amputations). Accordingly, corporal punishment could be considered either more or less severe than imprisonment. This issue, though difficult to resolve, does call into question the operationalization of punishment severity in those studies examining the economic link to crime.

Michel Foucault has presented perhaps the most sustained analysis of the shift from corporal punishment to carceral punishment. For Foucault, the move away from bodily punishments was not motivated by benevolence or more progressive thought, but can instead be explained by relations of power. In a now famous quote, he states that punishment reform was prompted largely by a desire "not to punish less, but to punish better; to punish with an attenuated severity perhaps, but in order to punish with more universality and necessity; to insert the power to punish more deeply into the social body."[29]

Following this view, the various modalities of punishment may be regarded as instrumentalities of social power. As such, it is reasonable that one mode of punishment might be better suited than another to exact particular social responses; and that governments may be tailoring the fit to their specific power needs.

As Foucault states, "No-one, strictly speaking, has an official right to power; and yet it is always being exerted in a particular direction, with some people on one side and some on the other. It is often difficult to say who holds power in a precise sense, but it is easy to see who lacks power."[30] Using Foucault's understanding of power as a backdrop, there are several productive ways to analyze social relations. He notes that power can manifest variously in traditions of status or privilege, economic disparities or linguistic and cultural differences.[31] He further states that analyses of power must examine, "the means of bringing power relations into being."[32]

For Foucault, the way power relationships are expressed in society can take myriad forms, "[A]ccording to whether power is exercised by the threat of arms, by the effects of the word, by means of economic disparities, by more or less complex means of control, by systems of surveillance, with or without archives, according to rules which are or are not explicit, fixed or modifiable, with or without the technological means to put all these things into action."[33] This, in many ways, serves as the departure point for the following discussion.

In attempting to understand the mechanisms that prompt changes in punishment, we are largely persuaded by Foucault's observations. Even so, we remain cognizant of the many criticisms of Foucauldian theory. In particular, we are especially mindful of an admonishment provided by Poulantzas. As he states, Foucault's perspective suffers "[from an underestimation] of the role of law in the exercise of power within modern societies . . . also . . . the role of the State itself and [Foucault] fails to understand the function of repressive apparatuses (army, police, judicial system, etc.) as a means of exercising physical violence . . . located at the heart of the modern state."[34]

Aware of this "underestimation," we have attempted to demonstrate the influence that different types of disparity have on the delivery of punishment. In so doing, we are assailing the influences of a number of overlapping and complex social relationships, which is a daunting task at best.

Because the societies of most nations are comprised of multiple groups with conflicting values, interests, and objectives, mechanisms evolve to determine and sustain one group's preferences over another. Theorists such as Richard Quinney contend that any given society's criminal justice processes reflect intergroup conflict and the expression of power interests:

> That criminal definitions are formulated is one of the most obvious manifestations of conflict in society. By formulating criminal law (including legislative statutes, administrative rulings, and judicial decisions), some segments of society protect and perpetuate their own interests . . . It follows that the greater the conflict in interests between the segments of a society, the greater the probability that the power segments will formulate criminal definitions. The interests of the power segments of society are reflected not only in the content of criminal definitions and the kinds of penal sanctions attached to them, but also in the legal policies stipulating how those who come to be defined as 'criminal' are to be handled.[35]

By moving the discussion away from the traditional Marxist focus solely on economic imperatives, a more complex system of social forces emerges. In this ordering, economic motives are still part of the power equation, but they are by no means the only possible axis of determination. Quinney also helps us understand how more powerful groups assert the primacy of their interests by defining which behaviors are crimes and by dictating how criminals will be processed through the prevailing system of formal social reproach. Taken together, these observations suggest that unequal command (or distribution) of societal resources would be reflected in different mechanisms of punishment and control.

Furthermore, Quinney's understanding of socially evolved definitions and responses to crime, when combined with Foucault's explanation of the transition from corporal to carceral punishment suggests a place from which to analyze how a given society determines what mode of punishment is appropriate.

DISPARITY AND SOCIAL CONTROL

The relative distribution of social power varies widely among countries. Just as nations have moved from one economic or political system to another, so, too, have they adopted different modalities of social control. We argue that the distribution of social power and the mechanisms for its exercise are developmentally linked. This position follows directly in line with Foucault's[36] essential thesis that changes in the economic structure of societies necessitate changes in the modalities of punishment. By extension, it may be argued that it is not so much the particular mode of economic production driving punishment as it is the relative economic disparity between strata of society. This is to say, we contend different economic, cultural, ethnic, and political distributions elicit differing mechanisms of social control. Some nations will tend toward incarceration, some toward corporal punishment, and others a mix of the two. To understand how this process operates, a brief review of previous research may be useful.

ECONOMICS OF PUNISHMENT[37]

A number of comparative studies have examined how economic factors may influence correctional systems across a range of countries. Among the specific areas considered, the relationship between unemployment and incarceration rates in capitalist countries has received perhaps the most attention in the literature.[38] Taken together, these studies suggest a large surplus labor pool is associated with high rates of incarceration. That said, there is little consensus about the relationship between unemployment rates and incarceration on a global level.[39] Recently, for example, David Jacobs and Richard Kleban did not find any relationship between unemployment and incarceration in their thirteen-nation study.[40] Explaining penality only in terms of employment measures may lean toward an oversimplification (and ultimately reductionist view) of punishment, as there are likely other social structural factors that influence modes of punishment.

There is a small but growing body of literature that examines economic, social, political, and cultural variables that contribute to punishment. the authors of this volume are the first to focus exclusively on corporal punishment in this light, Martin Killias, Jerome Neapolitan, Terance Miethe, Hong Lu, and Gini Deibert as well as David Greenberg and Valerie West also fill an important empirical void, as they examine socio-political influences in sanctions throughout the world.[41] Overall findings from this literature are mixed, with some studies arguing that economic factors and level of development influence punishment. For example, Killias finds poorer countries are less likely to rely on incarceration as the main form of punishment, mostly due to a lack of resources.[42] Killias also notes a relationship between power concentration and punishment severity, with dictatorships and countries with higher levels of income disparity employing the most severe criminal penalties.

Similarly, Neapolitan examines the relationship between global incarceration rates, capital punishment, civilization, economic inequity, and unemployment.[43] He finds more restrictive countries tend to be more punitive, but less civilized nations are less likely to rely on incarceration. One possible reason cited for the lack of reliance on carceral punishments in developing countries is the use of informal punishments and corporal punishment. Neapolitan notes that the use of these sanctions may well reflect cultural values or a lack of resources for prison construction.

Regarding capital punishment, Neapolitan notes that 17 of 18 Arab countries and 13 of 15 former Soviet republics still retain the death penalty compared to no nations in Western or Eastern Europe.[44] This leads Neapolitan to speculate culture and history are likely important in determining whether a country will include capital punishment in its range of sanctions.

More recent studies call the relationship between the economy and punishment into question. Specifically, Miethe et al. reach somewhat inconclusive findings with regard to economic development and death penalty retention.[45] Specifically, they find the retention of the death penalty is related to economic development as measured by the per capita gross domestic product (GDP), as well as primary religion and political conditions (such as civil liberties, political rights, and stability) and extrajudicial executions.

Despite findings of a positive association between these variables, Miethe et al. note that the relationships to economic development are mixed.[46] As discussed above, countries with lower levels of economic development appear to be more likely to retain the death penalty, whereas some highly developed countries (e.g., the United States and Japan) still employ the death penalty. A number of less-developed countries (e.g., Cape Verde, Guinea-Bissau, and Haiti), however, have abolished it.

Likewise, Greenberg and West find that economic activity does not significantly predict death penalty status.[47] Among those studies finding support for the Rusche–Kirchheimer hypothesis, John Sutton observes these studies often suffer from empirical weaknesses stemming from the reliance on time series data from single jurisdictions, with the United States and the United Kingdom being the most frequently examined.[48] Additional problems stem from a failure to consider alternative explanations.[49] This criticism was answered, in part, by Killias,[50] Neapolitan,[51] Miethe et al.[52] as well as Greenberg and West.[53]

All this said, many important questions in this area have yet to receive satisfactory answers. Critically missing from the empirical literature is an examination of how various social factors influence the types of sanctions imposed. It is commonly held that poorer countries do not rely on imprisonment as much as richer nations, stemming from purely economic factors.[54]

In contrast, we find[55] that economic factors, as well as other indicators of social inequity, play a determinative role as to why some parts of the world still rely on corporal punishment. Following Foucault and Quinney, the distribution of power in society plays an integral role in the inclusion of corporal punishment in the range of available sanctions for many countries.[56] Specifically, we find that countries with greater internal inequalities (along a number of axes, not just economic) are more likely to employ corporal punishment as a possible sanction against offenders. Moreover, we dispute the prevalent assumption that poor nations employ prison less than more wealthy nations strictly as a matter of economic inability.

THE DISCIPLINE OF DIFFERENCE[57]

While the link between economic disparity and social control is well-trodden ground within social science, relative wealth is but one of many axes around which power in society might be distributed. As most nations contain at least a few distinct ethnic, racial, religious or other cultural subpopulations, it is important to understand how different groups in society compete when their central motivations are not necessarily (or centrally) economic.

In developing his "law of ethno-juridical heterogeneity" Pitrim Sorokin theorized more heterogeneous societies tend to use harsher punishments.[58] Although we take no stand on the relative harshness of corporal versus carceral punishment as a generalized matter, Sorokin's observation of differential punishments supports our basic proposition: Just as one sees with economic disparity, we contend that compositional differences in society (particularly those regarding racial, linguistic, and religious characteristics) prompt a qualitative change in the modality of punishment.

To this point, Thorsten Sellin provides a key insight as to how cultural or other inter-ethnic conflicts manifest as both crime and society's response to it. As Sellin argues, cultural conflicts are inevitable and:

> [A] natural outgrowth of processes of social differentiation, which produce an infinity of social groupings, each with its own definitions of life situations, its own interpretations of social relationships, its own ignorance or misunderstanding of the social values of other groups. The transformation of a culture from a homogeneous and well-integrated type to a heterogeneous and disintegrated type is therefore accompanied by an increase of conflict situations.[59]

Mirroring Quinney's observations on the socially evolved meaning of criminality, Sellin contends that cultural conflict contributes heavily to crime, because those who wield power in society and control the political apparatus make and enforce the laws. Liska further clarifies this dynamic with his statement, "Law making is assumed to reflect the interests of the powerful; those activities are criminalized that threaten their interests."[60]

Corollary to these observations, Donald Black provides another bridge between strictly economic explanations and those vested in cultural conflict. He grounds his argument in a quote from Jean-Jacques Rousseau, "The universal spirit of laws, in all countries, is to favor the strong in opposition to the weak, and to assist those who have possessions against those who have none. Thus inconvenience is inevitable, and without exception."

While this speaks directly to stratification via relative wealth, it is also important for present concerns because Black argues that the law will vary according to rank. In particular he states, "all else constant, the lower ranks have less laws than the higher ranks, and the higher or lower they are, the more or less they have."[61]

Extending his theory of law and social control, Black addresses cultural heterogeneity with the argument that the amount of law in a given society varies depending on the level of culture. He contends differential application of laws may occur where there are cultural differences. As he states, "All else being equal, an offense by someone with less culture than his victim is more serious than an offense in the opposite direction ... Correlatively, all else constant – including the offender's characteristics—law varies directly with the culture of the victim."[62]

Lastly, Black posits a curvilinear relationship whereby "law is less likely at the extremes, where there is little or no cultural diversity, and also where there is great."[63] This contention is especially important because it sets up a testable relationship between the amount of cultural heterogeneity and the differential legal treatment of individuals from particular groups. Moreover, it strongly suggests that a qualitative difference may exist in how societies of greater or lesser relative heterogeneity punish their offenders.

In our own study of ethnolinguistic fractionalization[64] we find that nations whose populations are relatively more heterogeneous are also more likely to retain corporal punishment as a judicial sanction.[65] As the scholarly literature reflects, matters of resource division and social power are often decided along racial, ethnic, or religious lines. If one accepts this, then we must ask how corporal punishment retention functions to strengthen these divisions in more heterogeneous societies. In short, what is it about greater heterogeneity that preferences corporal punishment?[66]

In response, one might return to Sorokin's[67] observation that more heterogeneous societies tend to be harsher in their punishments. Given Newman's admonishment that relative "harshness" is a matter for debate, the issue is not easily resolved.[68] Following Newman, we argue corporal punishment is not inherently more severe. Rather, we contend it is retained because it is qualitatively different with respect to the specific social control it reinforces. As discussed above, elements of the racial threat perspective accord well with our interpretation.

This perspective, even as far back as Sellin's culture conflict argument, presents an explanation of punishment vested in perceptions of risk and peril— at the hands of groups dissimilar to one's own.[69] Building fear related to the loss of resources, power, status, wealth, and so on is the necessary predicate to differential punishment. Variants of this dynamic are discussed by Liska with respect to manipulation of the legal system toward preservation of prevailing demographic or cultural ends.[70] Likewise, fear of the "social other" is an implied component of Black's theory of law and social control.[71]

Corollary to these researchers, we argue societies that retain corporal punishment are united by a distribution of social power (reflected in economic disparities) that emanates from a social structure designed to manage the social other. This is accomplished through differential punishment mechanisms that function to marginalize and stigmatize members of the minority (or less powerful) group, a process we term, "subjugative shaming."[72] Through more visible punishment, the social other is economically, culturally, and politically subordinated to the will of the dominant population segment.

PUNISHMENT AS POLITICAL REPRESSION[73]

Even in simple societies, punishment takes on a political dimension. It reflects the will, sensibilities, and goals of those empowered to deliver it. Löic Wacquant goes so far as to characterize criminal justice as "a core political institution."[74] Owing to the fact that nations exist on a continuum from relatively free and open to relatively closed and repressive, it follows that state sanctioned punishment would likewise vary. A substantial body of scholarship suggests that this is indeed the case.[75] Although certainly employed as a mechanism to confront crime, governments have coopted criminal justice functions for many other purposes.[76] As Rick Ruddell and Martin Urbina (2007) note, in states with fragile or repressive regimes, "political leaders may use incarceration as a method of controlling protests, opposition to the regime, or persons who would not ordinarily fit under the definition of a criminal in a nation with a justice system that had high levels of legitimacy and was politically independent."[77]

An expansive cross-national literature substantiates the relationship between various modalities of punishment and style or type of government. David Jacobs and Richard Kleban find that corporatism and federalism are highly correlated with incarceration rates.[78] In their study of death penalty retention Miethe, Lu, and Deibert observe that nations continuing to sanction capital punishment are commonly found in the Middle East, Asia, or Caribbean regions; they have dominant religions other than Christianity; and tend to exhibit lower levels of economic development, lower political "voice," lessened political stability; and have recent histories of extrajudicial killings.[79] Similarly, Ruddell and Urbina find that more repressive states limit freedom of the press and also tend to employ harsher punishments. To this point they state, "Nations where the government cannot provide economic security, control ethnic or religious strife, guarantee basic rights or liberties, or is otherwise fragile, are at higher risk of using criminal justice systems for coercion, control, and repression of dissent."[80]

Despite the broad recognition that physical punishments are linked to governmental repression and unrest, the use of corporal punishment as a sanction against offenders has received only cursory examination within the political repression and punishment literature except for the authors' own recent study.[81] Beyond those studies discussed above, we find that issues of polity are key to understanding why nations punish in the ways they do. In particular, we observe that repressive regimes and failing governments are more likely to use both incarceration and physical punishments (both capital punishment and corporal punishment) than their more open and stable neighbors.

Before moving away from both political and economic motivations, a few observations about the sustained historical intersection of these concerns are warranted. Specifically, it would be incomplete to consider current punishment trends without an inquiry into the effects of postcolonial legacy. In brief, it is worthwhile to ask whether the influence of erstwhile colonial governance might have lingering effects on postcolonial criminal justice. Obviously, the answer is yes.

One only need look anywhere the British flag has ever flown to see that nation's enduring impact. As was discussed previously, British military discipline during the Age of Empire was notoriously strident. Even after the British military had long-since abandoned corporal punishment within its own ranks, the indigenous people of Britain's African colonies (who were supervised by military commanders) were subject to it as late as 1946.

Referring to our previous discussion of criminal justice in Singapore, one sees an interesting meld of British colonial punishments, combined with the importation of Indian penal codes and local values emphasizing communitarian values over individual rights. In the particular example of Singapore, one sees how the imposition of external punishment mechanisms can be modified over time to suit local sensibilities. Given the nation's historic place as a trading crossroads, it is easy to understand the evolved mélange of indigenous culture and alien bureaucracy.

As to the economic component of the equation, conquest and colonization could theoretically be driven by goals of military or political strategy, but ultimately those are second-order causes. Perhaps no thought on the matter sums the dynamic better than that of Cecil Rhodes, the British colonial entrepreneur and founder of Rhodesia, "We must find new lands from which we can easily obtain raw materials and at the same time exploit the cheap slave labor that is available from the natives of the colonies. The colonies would also provide a dumping ground for the surplus goods produced in our factories."[82]

ROLE OF CULTURE

In the face of more complex explanations, some might argue that the primary motivation to retain corporal punishment is less about economic or political arrangements than it is merely a reflection of embedded cultural values, religion in particular. While largely limited to studies of incarceration and the death penalty, researchers have given considerable attention to the influence of religion on state-sanctioned punishment.

In our own studies, we observe that countries with a larger proportion of Catholics in their population are less likely to retain capital punishment.[83] Miethe et al. as well as Greenberg and West conclude that Islamic countries are no more or less likely to retain the death penalty than any other group.[84]

Newman echoes a common explanation for the retention of corporal punishment couched in the predominance of Islam.[85] We concur with Newman on the importance of Islam as a predictor of corporal punishment retention. That said, we observe that the relationship is strongly conditioned by economic inequality.

In specific, when one controls for the influence of Islam as the dominant religion, countries with lower levels of economic disparity have a reduced probability of using corporal punishment. On the other tail of the wealth-distribution continuum, those countries with the highest levels of economic disparity are almost a third more likely to retain corporal punishment. Accordingly, we conclude that, while important, religious predominance as a predictor of corporal punishment retention is trumped by the unequal distribution of wealth. Moreover, we have consistently observed that economic inequality is among the most powerful predictors of corporal punishment retention.[86]

Even so, in nations like Saudi Arabia, where the ultraorthodox Wahhabist movement strongly guides public policy, it would be very difficult to parse out any motives other than religious adherence. That said, in cases like Saudi Arabia it is likely better to conceive of religious directives as furthering and integrating with other goals of state.

To this point, Neapolitan suggests that cultural motives may entwine with economic realities to influence the mode of punishment.[87] He contends the lack of reliance on carceral punishments in developing countries may reflect the use of informal punishments and corporal punishment. Neapolitan also argues that the use of these sanctions may arise either from cultural values or a lack of resources for prison construction.

With regard to Neapolitan's contention that diminished incarceration capacity may drive the retention of corporal punishment, we observe otherwise. In fact, when one looks at the retentionist nations of Sub-Saharan Africa, arguably the cradle of modern corporal punishment, one also sees relatively high rates of incarceration. While Neapolitan may have a point with regard to differential punitiveness, corporal punishment does not appear to supplant incarceration, owing simply to a lack of resources.

SUMMARY

In this chapter a number of social dynamics were presented that each bear on a given nation's likelihood of employing corporal punishment as a criminal sanction. From this discussion, economic motives emerge as the most enduring and strong. That said, they are hardly the only factors that influence modalities of punishment. Of the other sustained predictors, religion, especially the predominance of Islam, is of particular importance. Even so, the influence of Islam is attenuated by the distribution of wealth within society. Similarly, the conjoined influences of political repression, ethnic division, and postcolonial legacy each add a thread to the global tapestry of punishment.

Pulling back from these influences, a single comprehensive thesis becomes clear: Corporal punishment is more likely in those societies with greater than average internal differences. To approach this another way, societies in which there exists a greater concentration of national wealth in fewer hands—leading to the ostensible dichotomy of a wealthy elite and modern peasantry—are far more likely to employ corporal punishment. Another manifestation of heightened internal differences is in terms of ethnolinguistic fractionalization. Along this axis of differentiation, the various ethnic "metals" are poured into the civic melting pot only to remain separate and agitated by the heat. In this construction, the majority or dominant racial group tends to exert hegemony through more visible punishments. The same can be said of the vestigial apparatuses of colonial control. The old order is imposed anew, not by alien invaders, but by native strongmen, unstable regimes, or failing governments. In this, the dominion of combined political and economic agendas is facilitated by positioning the power to punish more visibly.

To quantify this point, in a recently published project we observed that eighteen of the sixty nations currently retaining judicial corporal punishment exhibit both a greater than average level of ethnic fractionalization while simultaneously having higher than average disparity in the distribution of national wealth.[88] Six of these nations exist in Sub-Saharan Africa, a region marked by continued postcolonial violence and instability. Moreover, a majority of retentionist countries have either higher than average levels of ethnic fractionalization or higher than average disparities in the distribution of national wealth. From these observations, one may conclude that nations with greater internal differences (be they ethnoliguistic, economic, or possibly others) have greater than average likelihood of retaining state-sanctioned corporal punishment.

While none of these observations draws a straight line of linear causality, in the words of Morris and Adelman, "[These findings] suggest the existence of a systematic pattern of interaction . . . [which combines to] generate a unified complex of change in the style of life of a community."[89] For present purposes, this distinction is sufficient. Although we do not claim to have fully elucidated the causal mechanisms that push a given society from retention to abolition or, in the rare case, to re-adoption (i.e., The Bahamas), we believe that the constellation of forces presented here sheds important light on the most influential phenomena.

Conclusion

The chains of habit are too weak to be felt until they are too strong to be broken.

—Samuel Johnson

IN ATTEMPTING TO summarize the major points offered in this volume, the words of Graeme Newman in his seminal treatise, *The Punishment Response*, bear repeating, "I have suggested that order was created by a criminal act, that order cannot exist without structured inequality. Order and authority must be maintained by punishment, otherwise there would be even more revolutions and wars than we have had throughout history."[1]

In this passage, Newman outlines in barest terms why we must punish. The endogenous ordering of a society implies the existence of mechanisms to delineate impermeable boundaries. Just as the padded rails and pockets of a billiard table keep balls in play or exclude them, punishment rebounds the social person or removes them from our midst.

To this dynamic, we have added another possibility, one uniquely facilitated by corporal punishment. Specifically, we conclude that corporal punishment is often used to neither fully rebound nor exclude the individual relative to society. Rather, we hold that corporal punishment provides a mechanism by which the criminal (in particular) is permitted to reside within the collective, albeit on the margins. In the billiards analogy, the criminal is the ball pushed against the cushion but removed from advancing play.

While one could argue modern carceral culture functions the same way, we contend there is an important difference. Incarceration removes the offender from our midst as part of the punishment. The removal in many ways *is* the punishment. In contrast, corporal punishment serves primarily to subjugate the offender while nominally keeping them him or her within society. There is no promise of retraining, reform, or penitence, just punishment. Perhaps these processes are assumed to attach as a result of the pain, but the rhetoric of incarceration is far richer with such pledges.

Admittedly, though, the carceral cultures of some nations (e.g., the United States) also employ a subjugative element. This can be seen in the disenfranchisement and permanent labeling of offenders post-release. As was stated early on, physical and psychological punishments seldom occupy exclusive domains.

To be sure, corporal punishment of offenders is but one facet of an expansive phenomenon. As well covered throughout this volume, the administration of corporal punishment is arguably more ubiquitous in other social realms. One of an immense constellation of possible social corrections, corporal punishment occupies an enduring and singular place. It is unique because of the tremendous variability in application and setting. That one social institution could encompass both a mother's swat and the Oprichniki's knout stand as testament to the vastness of its borders. Schoolmarms, sailors, slave masters, and saints have each wielded instruments of physical discipline. Just as the punishing authorities are myriad, so too are their ends: piety; obedience; deference; repentance; docility; confession; rectitude . . . all prompted by pain.

It is easy in the Western world to forget that corporal punishment is not a relegate of history. Almost five dozen countries in the present era permit some form of judicial corporal punishment. Many more permit it in other contexts.

In an effort to understand the forces of abolition and retention, several theories have been offered. The most common denominator between them is simple: power. As Michel Foucault once wrote, "It is often difficult to say who holds power in a precise sense, but it is easy to see who lacks power."[2] History shows this in spades. One need look no further than the waning days of Imperial Russia for proof. Among the central concessions to the nobility, the tsars were obliged to exempt them from the threat of the lash.

This returns us to the point made by Newman: Order cannot exist without structured inequality. A central thesis of this volume has been to elucidate corporal punishment as a mechanism for social ordering. To the extent one may broadly generalize such matters, evidence suggests that corporal punishment as a judicial sanction for criminal offenders is more prone to retention in those nations characterized by high levels of economic disparity, ethnoliguistic fractionalization, and political repression. So, too, is it prevalent in those nations of the developing world still struggling with their postcolonial legacy. Even a short review of many nations in Sub-Saharan Africa reflect a perfect storm of inequality, repression, and intergroup violence—all managed through pain.

Beyond the political and economic, we have noted the influence of religion on the retention of corporal punishment. Certain religious traditions, the predominance of Islam, for example, are more hospitable to retention. Ultimately, the case of Islamic influence yields as many questions as answers. Exactly half of the world's predominantly Islamic nations permit judicial corporal punishment. More allow it in other contexts. That said, a secular criminal justice apparatus and traditional Shari'a justice is a distinction without a difference in many Islamic cultures. Accordingly, we should expect the diffusion of punishments into many spheres of Islamic life.

As discussed, the moralistic distinction made by many Westerners is undercut by our own religious history. Whether the Quaker persecutions of early America or the centuries of Inquisition in Europe, Western cultures have their own heritage of comingled justice, a heritage also managed by physical pain. Here, too, we see our own distinction with not as much difference as some might like to imagine.

This in turn leads us to the nearly canonical explanation of our move from corporal punishment: The March of Progress. Again, clad in the self-righteous veneer of social evolution, proponents of this perspective suggest our sentiments have simply become too refined to tolerate the ethical vicissitude they take corporal punishment to represent. We might be amenable to this perspective save for the fact that the data simply do not support their core argument.

In all of our attempts to match various constructions of "social progress" to a flight from corporal punishment, we find no compelling evidence. Relative development does not have the determinative role many supporters of the so-called "march of progress" paradigm espouse. Simply put, lagging modernity or retarded development are much less consequent as predictors of judicial corporal punishment retention than some scholars contend.

Concomitant to this finding, a given nation's capacity to incarcerate appears unrelated to corporal punishment retention. Again, the data reveal no consistent relationship between levels of incarceration and the retention or abolition of corporal punishment. While they are likely not wholly separable issues, they do not appear to have the strong association often assumed.

Finally, there is the implied subtext of the progress paradigm: If abolition of corporal punishment is an indicator of progress, must we then cede that all retentionist nations are either backward or atavists? Moreover, how are well-developed and indisputably modern countries like the United States and Japan, both death penalty retentionists, to be reconciled? The only plausible retort there is the *reductio ad absurdum* that it's permissible to kill people, just not to cause them pain.

Where, then, does this leave the discussion? Although the ideas summarized above shed light on one aspect of corporal punishment, they leave many more realms in marked shadow. Fully elaborated explanations as to retention in homes, schools, as an element of religious practice, or within certain other social institutions require consideration beyond the confines of this volume.

It is clear, however, that tradition, custom, and relative social transparency all bear on the topic in some profound way. Of these, we suspect that tradition and custom are chief motivations. The thing is done simply because it has always been done. In the case of schools and homes, it represents millennia of precedent.

Be it the Roman *patria potestas*, Vittorino da Feltre's punishment of "last resort," or Scotland's notorious tawse, corporal punishment enjoyed little opposition in most cultures throughout human history. Whether hearthside or in the school hallway, corporal punishment has been long employed as a primary tool for instilling rectitude and respect.

In much this same way, corporal punishment has been widely used among other special populations. Closely allied with its use as a criminal sanction, corporal punishment occupies a central place in the management of correctional populations. Readers will recall Michael Ignatieff's stunning observation that the gaols of England saw a fiftyfold increase in the use of corporal punishment from 1825 to 1835.[3]

More than a century later inmates sentenced to the prison farms of the southern United States provided an economically acceptable substitute for the slave labor they ostensibly replaced. Were one looking for enduring punishment examples apropos of Foucault's *ancient regime*, Arkansas's Tucker or Louisiana's Angola prison farms match very well. Given the protracted legal troubles of Maricopa County, Arizona, Sheriff Joe Arpaio, the self-proclaimed "America's toughest sheriff," it appears that old habits do indeed die hard.

A step away from prisons, the role of corporal punishment in slave-keeping would be difficult to overstate. A tour across the wonders of the ancient world is largely a sojourn through the products of slave labor. Greek and Roman civilizations, held up as pinnacles of art, architecture, philosophy, and justice were both supported by a vast slave-holding economy. The economy was in turn supported by pains of physical compulsion.

Despite Aristotle's pronouncement that slaves were a kind of property that had a soul, they were subjected to different legal treatment (punishment) than free persons. On permission of their master, slaves could be tortured for the purpose of obtaining evidence; and if convicted of a crime, the penalties were often double that of a free person.[4]

While it would be hard to argue otherwise, the move away from slave-holding in the Western world could be held as evidence of a "march of progress." Even so, a few broad (albeit very important) instances do not make the rule. As with the prison farms above, economic systems adapt to the labor available. The fact that the legal status of the peasantry may have been expediently reclassified for purposes of legitimating certain labor and social control arrangements does not change the qualitative aspect of the phenomenon.

Used as a rite of entrance, a tool of discipline, and as a training mechanism, corporal punishment has a similarly ancient pedigree in the military institutions of the world. Writing in the first century BC, the Roman, Sextus Julius Frontinus, observes, "Marcus Cato has handed down the story that, when soldiers were caught in theft, their right hands used to be cut off in the presence of their comrades; or if the authorities wished to impose a lighter sentence, the offender was bled at headquarters."[5]

In October 2011, three U.S. Marines stationed in Afghanistan were subject to an Article 32 disciplinary hearing (the military justice equivalent of a grand jury proceeding) because of their alleged involvement in hazing a fellow Marine. According to prosecutors, the three wanted to punish their fellow Marine for repeatedly falling asleep while on guard duty. Subsequent to the alleged beatings and other physical torments, the subject of the hazing committed suicide rather than face additional reprisals.[6]

Because police agencies often resemble paramilitary organizations, some of the occupational customs of policing are applicable to the military. Following the preceding examples from ancient Rome and modern America, a quote from John Van Maanen's seminal text on the process of becoming a police officer seems appropriate, "The newcomer learns that when the department notices his behavior it is usually to administer a punishment, not a reward."[7]

While certainly appropriate to frame the interactions of individuals with military and paramilitary bureaucracies, Van Maanen's quip may have generalizability beyond those organizational confines. In considering the position of the individual versus the institution (be it a literal bureaucracy or an institution" in the sociological sense), we come full circle to our original point of interrogation: What gives a social authority the right to cause a member of that society to experience physical pain?

Whether this volume has assailed that question directly, it has at least highlighted numerous circumstances in which agents of a social authority have been conferred the power to administer pain. In many instances those agents have asserted that such a "right" exists, but the verification of that right is likely a matter of perspective and position relative to the administration of pain.

A historically important aspect of control through pain is found in ritualized delivery. Foucault's famous narrative of Damines at the scaffold is a testament to the symbolic investiture of and social meaning of ritualized punishment, "It is said that, though he was always a great swearer, no blasphemy escaped his lips; but the excessive pain made him utter horrible cries, and he often repeated: 'My God, have pity on me! Jesus, help me!' The spectators were all edified by the solicitude of the parish priest of St Paul's who despite his great age did not spare himself in offering consolation to the patient."[8]

While the condemned is the direct recipient of the physical ordeal, others have a part to play in the morality tale. The setting is the public square in front of the church. This is the locus of the social body and soul. The executioner and the priest attend the condemned. They are the physical embodiment of state and divine authority. The spectators play the part of conscience, at once egging on the punishment and being reviled by its horrors. As Ted Lewellen observes, "Within the theater of pain, spectators were not mere observers, but were active participants in the re-establishment of order."[9]

This point also brings an element of the discussion full circle. In the introduction to this volume Victor Turner's work on symbol and ritual was referenced briefly. Turner defined ritual as "prescribed formal behavior for occasions not given over to technological routine, having reference to beliefs in mystical beings and powers."[10]

Arguably, the crowd's response to the torture of Damiens is exactly that. Everyone has a role to play. Those roles speak to the transcendence of state, church, and the collective. They represent an assent by the people to being governed and of the state and church to govern them. It is the perfect nexus of power, symbol, and submission.

Stopping short of conclusive pronouncements, the authors hope this volume adds historical and sociological context for this ancient human institution. More than this, it is intended to prompt further inquiry and curiosity about humanity's use of pain as punishment. If these ends are achieved, even in small measure, that will be sufficient.

Notes

Introduction

1. The term "absolve" is used here only as a convention. The infliction of pain could serve many other ends.

2. Turner, Victor. *The forest of symbols: Aspects of Ndembu ritual*. Ithaca: Cornell University Press. 1967, 19.

3. Turner, Victor. *The drums of affliction A study of religious processes among the Ndembu of Zambia*. Oxford: Clarendon Press. 1968, 1–2.

4. Turner. *The forest of symbols*, 19.

5. Turner, Victor. Ritual, tribal and catholic, *Worship* 50, 1977, 504–526.

6. Turner. *The drums*, 2.

7. For additional examples and discussion of cultural universals, see: Steven Pinker. *The blank slate* New York: Viking Press, 2002; Donald Brown. *Human Universals* New York: McGraw-Hill, 1991.

8. Osgood, Charles, William May, and Murray Miron. *Cross-cultural universals of affective meaning* Champaign, IL: University of Illinois Press, 1975, 4.

9. Scott, George. *The History of Corporal Punishment*. London: Senate, 1968, 17–18.

Chapter 1

1. Van Yelyr, Richard G. *The Whip and the Rod: An Account of Corporal Punishment Among All Nations and for All Purposes*. London: Gerald G. Swan, 1941, v.

2. Miethe, Terrence and Hong Lu. *Punishment: A Comparative Historical Perspective*. New York: Cambridge University Press, 2005, xi.

3. Newman, Graeme (1978). *The Punishment Response*. Albany, NY: Harrow and Heston, 1978, 13.

4. Ibid.

5. Scott, George. *The History of Corporal Punishment*. London: Senate, 1968, 17.

6. Ibid.

7. Moskos, Peter. *In Defense of Flogging*. New York: Basic Books, 2011, 1.

8. Foucault, Michel. *Discipline & Punish: The Birth of the Prison*. New York: Vintage, 1977, 7.

9. Peet, T. Eric. *The Great Tomb-Robberies of The Twentieth Egyptian Dynasty: Being A Critical Study, With Translations and Commentaries, of The Papyri in Which These Are Recorded*. Oxford: Clarendon Press. Vol. 1. 1930, 38.

10. Breasted, James H. *Ancient Records of Egypt: Historical Documents from the Earliest Times to the Persian Conquest*, vol. 4. Chicago: University of Chicago Press, 1906, § 551 f.

11. Rosen, Michael. *The Penguin Book of Childhood*. NY: Penguin Putnam. 1974.

12. Tetlow, Elisabeth. *Women, Crime, and Punishment in Ancient Law and Society: The Ancient Near East*. New York: Continuum International Publishing Group, 2004, 73.

13. Ibid.

14. Swift, Fletcher. *Education in ancient Israel, from earliest times to 70 A.D.* Chicago: The Open Court Publishing Company, 1919, pg. 49.

15. Matthews, Victor and Don Benjamin. *Old Testament Parallels: Laws and Stories from the Ancient Near East*. Mahwah, NJ: Paulist Press, 1991, 110.

16. Ibid.

17. Demonsthenes. *Against Androtion and Against Timocrates: With Introductions and English Notes by William Wayte*. Ithaca, NY: Cornell University Libraries, 1893, 178

18. Ibid.

19. Scott, George. *The History of Corporal Punishment*; Parker-Jenkins, Marie. *Sparing the rod: schools, discipline and children's rights*. London: Trentham Books, 1999.

20. Plato. *The Republic*. (trans.) H. D. P. Lee. Baltimore: Penguin Books, 1958, 252.

21. Ibid.

22. Plato. *Protagoras Philebus and Gorgias*. (trans.) Benjamin Jowett. Amherst, NY: Promethius Books, 1996, 18.

23. Plato. *The Laws*. (trans.) Benjamin Jowett. Seattle, WA: Create Space, 2010, 225.

24. Saller, Richard. "Corporal Punishment, Authority and Obedience in the Roman Household." In Beryl Rawson. *Marriage, Divorce and Children in Ancient Rome*. New York: Oxford University Press, 1996, 145.

25. Finley, Moses. *Ancient Slavery and Modern Ideology*. New York: Penguin, 1985.

26. Edwards, Catharine. *The Politics of Immorality in Ancient Rome*. Cambridge University Press, 1993, 124.

27. Baidan, Ernst. "Review of: *Ancient Slavery and Modern Ideology* by Moses Finley." *New York Review of Books*, 1981, 49.

28. Saller. "Corporal Punishment," 156–57.

29. Goffman, Erving. *The Presentation of Self in Everyday Life*. New York: Anchor Books, 1967, 91.

30. Saller. "Corporal Punishment," 153.

31. Quintilian, Marcus. *Institutes of Orator: or, Education of an Orator in Twelve Books Literally Translated with Notes*. John Selby Watson (trans.). Vol. 1. London: George Bell & Sons, 1892, 27.

32. Plutarchus, Lucius. *Plutarch's Lives: The Translation Called Dryden's Corrected from the Greek and Revised in Five Volumes*. John Dryden (trans.). Vol. I. New York: Cosimo, 2008, ix.

33. Woodward, William H. (ed.). *Vittorino da Feltre and Other Humanist Educators*. New York: Teacher's College, Columbia University, 1963, 103.

34. Boyd, William. *The History of Education*. London: Adam and Charles Black, 1952, 164

35. Woodward. *Vittorino da Feltre*, 34.

36. Ibid.

37. Woodward, William. *Studies in Education during the Age of the Renaissance*. New York: Russell and Russell Inc., 1965, 163.

38. Erasmus, Desiderius. "*De pueris statim ac liberaliter instituendis* (On the liberal education of boys from the beginning)." In W. H. Woodward, *Desiderius Erasmus, Concerning the Aim and Method of Education*. New York: Teacher's College, Columbia University. 1964, 205–6.

39. Ibid.

40. Ibid., 206.

41. Montaigne, Michael de. *Montaigne: Essays*. (ed) M. A. Screech. New York: Penguin, 1993, 73.

42. Ibid.

43. Compayré, Gabriel. *The History of Pedagogy*. (trans.) W. H. Payne. Charleston, SC: Nabu Press, 1897, 85.

44. Battersby, William. *De La Salle: A Pioneer of Modern Education*. London: Longman's, Green and Co., 1949, 97.

45. Painter, F. V. N. *Luther on Education*. Philadelphia: Lutheran Publication Society, 1889, 124.

46. Ibid., 125.

47. Ibid., 123.

48. Ibid.

49. Durant, Will. *The Story of Civilization: The Reformation: A History of European Civilization from Wyclif to Calvin: 1300–1564*. New York: MJF Books, 1997, 611.

50. Knox, John. *The Works of John Knox, Vol. 2*. (ed.) David Liang. Charleston, SC: Nabu Press, 2010, 185.

51. Durant. *The Story of Civilization*, 611.

52. Farrell, Colin. "The Cane and the Tawse in Scottish Schools." 2007. Accessed via: http://www.corpun.com/scotland.htm

53. Ibid.

54. Hendrie, Bill. "The Tingle of the Tawse." *Scottish Memories*. 1994. Quoted in Farrell, Colin (2007).

55. Van Yelyr. *The Whip and the Rod*, 177.

56. Farrell. "The Cane and the Tawse."

57. James, William. *Talks to Teachers on Psychology*. New York: Henry Holt and Company, 1899, 182. Accessed online at http://www.des.emory.edu/mfp/ttpreface.html

58. Comenius, John. *The Great Didactic*. (trans. and ed.) M. W. Keatinge. New York: Russell and Russell, 1967, XI, 7.

59. Ibid., XXVI, 4.

60. Ibid., XXVI, 9.

61. Ibid., XXVI, 5.

62. Harrison, Brian. "Torture and Corporal Punishment as a Problem in Catholic Theology." *Living Tradition*. July 2005. Accessed via: http://www.rtforum.org/lt/lt118.html

63. Tanner, Norman. "Inquisition and Holy Office" in *The Oxford Companion to Christian Thought*. (eds.) Hastings, Adrian, Mason, Alistar and Hugh Pyper. New York: Oxford University Press U.S., 2007.

64. Ibid.

65. *King James Bible*. Romans 13:1–2.

66. Farrell, Allan. *The Jesuit Ratio Studiorum of 1599*. Washington, DC: Conference Of Major Superiors Of Jesuits, 1970. Accessed via: http://bc.edu/sites/libraries/ratio/ratio1599.pdf

67. Holder, R. Ward. *Crisis and Renewal: The Era of the Reformations*. Louisville, KY: Westminster John Knox Press, 2009, 200–201.

68. McGucken, William. *The Jesuits and Education: The Society's Teaching Principles and Practice, especially in Secondary Education in the United States*. Eugene, OR: Wipf & Stock Publishers, 2008, 143.

69. Battersby, William. *De La Salle: A Pioneer of Modern Education*. London: Longman's, Green and Co., 1949, 97.

70. Blötzer, Joseph. "Inquisition." *The Catholic Encyclopedia*. New York: Robert Appleton Company, 1910. Accessed via: http://www.newadvent.org/cathen/08026a.htm

71. Johnson, Thomas. *Life's Greatest Questions*. Springville, UT: Bonneville Books, 2004, 123.

72. Foxe, John. *Fox's Book of Martyrs—Or A History of the Lives, Sufferings, and Triumphant—Deaths of the Primitive Protestant Martyrs*. Minneapolis, MN: Fili-Quarian Classics, 2010, 37.

73. Ibid.

74. Vacandard, Elphège. *The Inquisition: A Critical and Historical Study of the Coercive Power of the Church*. (trans.) Bertrand Conway. New York: Longman, Green & Company, 1915, 46.

75. Gaddis, Michael. *There Is No Crime for Those Who Have Christ: Religious Violence in the Christian Roman Empire*. Berkeley, CA: University of California Press. 2005, 131.

76. Ibid., 141.

77. Ibid.

78. Blötzer. "Inquisition."

79. Peters, Edward. *Heresy and Authority in Medieval Europe*. Philadelphia: University of Pennsylvania Press, 1980.

80. Foxe. *Fox's Book of Martyrs*, 60.

81. Vose, Robin. "Introduction to inquisition policies and proceedings documents." Hesburgh Libraries of Notre Dame, Department of Rare Books and Special Collections. Notre Dame, IN: University of Notre Dame, 2010. Accessed via: http://www.library.nd.edu/rarebooks/digital_projects/inquisition/collections/RBSC-INQ:COLLECTION/essays/RBSC-INQ:ESSAY_PoliciesAndProceedings

82. Vidmar, John. *The Catholic Church through the ages: a history*. Mahwah, NJ: Paulist Press, 2005, 149.

83. Durant. *The Story of Civilization*, 209.

84. Foxe. *Fox's Book of Martyrs*, 62.

85. Parker, Geoffrey. *The Dutch Revolt*. Baltimore: Penguin, 1990.

86. Lea, Henry. "Persecution." *The Inquisition of the Middle Ages*, 2010. Accessed via: http://www.third-millennium-library.com/MedievalHistory/Inquisition-in-the-Middle-Ages/C5-PERSECUTION.html

87. Vose. "Introduction."

88. Ibid.

89. Durant. *The Story of Civilization*.

90. Durant. *The Story of Civilization*, 211.

91. Ibid.

92. Ibid.

93. Peters. *Heresy and Authority*; Kelly, Henry. *Inquisitions and Other Trial Procedures in the Medieval West*. London: Ashgate Publishing, 2001.

94. Ibid.

95. Lea. "Persecution."

96. Plaidy, Jean. *The Spanish Inquisition*. New York: The Citadel Press, 1967, 86.

97. Roth, Cecil. *The Spanish Inquisition*. New York: W. W. Norton & Company, 1964.

98. Castro, Americo. *The Structure of Spanish History*. (trans.) E. L. King. Princeton, NJ: Princeton Univ. Press, 1954, 525, 531.

99. White, Heather. "Between the Devil and the Inquisition: African Slaves and the Witchcraft Trials in Cartagena de Indies." *The North Star: A Journal of African American Religious History*, Vol. 8 (2), Spring 2005, 2.

100. Battersby. *De La Salle*, 97.

101. Meithe and Lu. *Punishment*, 34.

102. Durant. *The Story of Civilization*.

103. Rummell, R. J. *Death By Government*. Piscataway, NJ: Transaction Press, 1997.

104. Johnson, Paul. *A History of the Jews*. London: Harper Perennial, 1987, 226.

105. Ibid., 227.

106. Trueblood, Elton. *The People Called Quakers*. Richmond, IN: Friends United Press, 1985.

107. Sewel, William. *The history of the rise, increase, and progress of the Christian people called Quakers. Intermixed with several remarkable occurrences. Written Originally in Low Dutch, and also translated into English*. Farmington Hills, MI: Gale ECCO, 2010, 194.

108. Falk, Herbert. *Corporal Punishment: A social interpretation of its theory and practice in the schools of the United States*. New York: Columbia University, 1941.

109. Ibid.

110. Piehl, Anne. "Neither Corporal Punishment Cruel nor Due Process Due: The United States Supreme Court's Decision in *Ingraham v. Wright*." *Corporal punishment in American education: Readings in history, practice, and alternatives*. (eds.) Irwin Hyman & James Wise. Philadelphia, PA: Temple University Press, 1979.

111. Williams, Gertrude. "Social Sanctions for Violence Against Children: Historical Perspectives." *Corporal punishment in American education: Readings in history,*

practice, and alternatives. (eds.) Irwin Hyman & James Wise. Philadelphia, PA: Temple University Press, 1979.

112. Madison, James. *The Papers of James Madison.* (ed.) William T. Hutchinson et al. Chicago and London: University of Chicago Press, 1962.

113. Sage, Jud. "Virginia Slave Laws." *Academic American History: Colonial America 1607–1767,* 2010. Accessed via: http://www.academicamerican.com/colonial/docs/vaslavestatutes.html

114. Ibid.

115. Van Yelyr. *The Whip and the Rod,* 146.

116. Ibid.

117. Friedman, Lawrence. *Crime and Punishment in American History.* New York: Basic Books, 1994, 37.

118. Ibid.

119. Friedman, Lawrence. *History of American Law.* New York: Simon & Schuster, 1986, 69.

120. Van Yelyr. *The Whip and the Rod,* 154.

121. Ibid., 18–20, 42–45.

122. Earle, Alice. *Curious Punishments of Bygone Days.* Rutland, VT: Charles E. Tuttle, 1983, 147–48.

123. Middleton, Richard. *Colonial America: A History 1565–1776.* Hoboken, NJ: Wiley-Blackwell, 2002, 204.

124. Friedman. *History of American Law,* 70.

125. Sage. "Virginia Slave Laws."

126. Earle. *Curious Punishments,* 144–45.

127. Friedman, *History of American Law,* 600.

128. Ibid., 600, 602.

129. Van Yelyr. *The Whip and the Rod,* 110–11.

130. Ibid., 110.

131. *Brown v. State of Mississippi,* 297 U.S. 278 (1936).

132. Ibid.

133. Ibid.

134. Clark, Robin and Judith Clark. *The Encyclopedia of Child Abuse.* New York: Facts on File, 2007, 89.

135. *Ingraham v. Wright.* 430 U.S. 651 (1977).

136. *Baker v. Owen.* 423 U.S. 907 (1975).

137. See for instance Newman, Graeme. *Just and Painful: A Case for the Corporal Punishment of Criminals.* London: Harrow and Heston, 1983; or Moskos. *In Defense of Flogging.*

138. Meithe and Lu. *Punishment,* 119.

139. Möllendorf, Paul. *The Family Law of the Chinese.* Shanghai, China: Kelly & Walsh, 1896.

140. Faber, Ernst. *China in the Light of History.* Shanghai, China: General Evangelical Protestant Missionary Society of Germany, 1897, 18.

141. Faber, Ernst. *Chronological Handbook of the History of China.* (ed.) P. Krantz. Shanghai, China: General Evangelical Protestant Missionary Society of Germany, 1902, 3.

142. Werner, Edward. *China of the Chinese.* New York: Charles Scribner's Sons, 1919, 141.

143. Head, John and Yanping Wang. *Law codes in dynastic China: a synopsis of Chinese legal history in the thirty centuries from Zhou to Qing*. Durham, NC: Carolina Academic Press, 2005.

144. Bodde, Derek and Clarence Morris. *Traditional Chinese Penal Law*. Edinburgh, England: Endinburgh, University Press, 1973.

145. Gernet, Jacques. *A History of Chinese Civilization*. Cambridge: Cambridge University Press, 1996.

146. Ibid.

147. Ibid.

148. Meithe and Lu. *Punishment*, 129.

149. Dikotter, Frank. *Crime, Punishment, and the Prison in Modern China, 1895–1949*. New York: Columbia University Press, 2002.

150. Kahan, Arcadius. *The Plow, the Hammer, and the Knout: An Economic History of Eighteenth-Century Russia*. Chicago: University of Chicago Press, 1985, 5.

151. Schrader, Abby. "Branding the Exile as 'Other': Corporal Punishment and the Construction of Boundaries in Mid-Nineteenth Century Russia." in *Russian Modernity: Politics, Knowledge, Practices*. (eds.) David Hoffmann and Yanni Kotsonis. New York: Palgrave Macmillan Press, 2002, 21.

152. Reyfman, Irina. "The Emergence of the Duel in Russia: Corporal Punishment and the Honor Code." The *Russian Review*, vol. 54, January 1995, 28.

153. See Griffiths, David and George E. Munro (ed. and trans). *Catherine II's Charters of 1785 to the Nobility and the Towns*. Bakersfield, CA: Charles Schlacks Jr., 1991., p. 6; as well as Jones, Robert. *The Emancipation of the Russian Nobility. 1762–1785*. Princeton, NJ: Princeton University Press, 1973, 33, 114, 278, 279.

154. Reyfman. "The Emergence of the Duel in Russia," 39–40.

155. Kuromiya, Hiroaki. *Freedom and Terror in the Donbas: A Ukrainian-Russian Borderland, 1870s–1990s*. Cambridge: Cambridge University Press, 1998, 55.

156. Ibid., 101.

157. Schrader, Abby. *Languages of the Lash: Corporal Punishment and Identity in Imperial Russia*. DeKalb, IL: Northern Illinois University Press, 2002.

158. Engelstein, Laura. *The Keys to Happiness: Sex and the Search for Modernity in Fin-de-Siecle Russia*. Ithaca: Cornell University Press, 1992, 74.

159. Ibid., 94–95.

160. Ibid., 95.

161. Teitelbaum, Salomon. "Parental Authority in the Soviet Union," *American Slavic and East European Review*, Vol. 4, (3/4), December 1945, 65.

162. Ibid.

163. Ibid.

164. McNeilly, Mark. *Sun Tzu and the Art of Modern Warfare*. Oxford: Oxford University Press, 2001.

165. Cowley, Robert and Geoffrey Parker. The Reader's Companion to Military History. Chicago, IL: Houghton Mifflin Harcourt, 2001.

166. Sun Bin. *Sun Bin: The Art of Warfare: A Translation of the Classic Chinese Work of Philosophy and Strategy*. (trans.) D. C. Lau and Roger T. Ames. Albany, NY: State University of New York Press, 2003.

167. Ward, Harry. *George Washington's Enforcers: Policing the Continental Army*. Carbondale, IL: Southern Illinois University Press, 2009, 3.

168. Earle. *Curious Punishments*, 119.

169. Ibid., 119–37.

170. Ward. *George Washington's Enforcers*, 5.

171. Glenn, Myra. *Campaigns Against Corporal Punishment*. Albany, NY: State University of New York Press, 1984, 9.

172. Ibid.

173. "Sepoy" comes from the Persian term for "soldier." Contextually it denoted an indigenous member of the British colonial military, in this case an Indian member of the British army.

174. Peers, Douglas (1995). "Sepoys, soldiers and the Lash: Race, Caste and Army Discipline in India, 1820–50." *The Journal of Imperial and Commonwealth History*. 23(2), 1995, 211.

175. Ibid.

176. Killingray, David. "The 'Rod of Empire': The Debate over Corporal Punishment in the British African Colonial Forces, 1888–1946." *The Journal of African History*, 35 (2), 1994, 202.

177. Tasaki, Hanama (1950). *Long the Imperial Way*. Chicago, IL: Houghton Mifflin Company, 1950, 38–39.

178. Keep, John. "No Gauntlet for Gentlemen: Officers' Privileges in Russian Military Law, 1716–1855." *Cahiers du Monde russe et soviétique. (Noblesse, état et société en russie XVIe: Début du XIXe siècle)*. 34 (1/2). 1993, 172.

179. Ibid.

180. Puleo, Louis. "Fraternization." *Proceedings Magazine: United States Naval Institute*. June 1992, 40.

181. Ibid.

182. James Gilligan. Quoted in Mackey, Robert. "The Way We Live Now: 3-19-00: Expert Opinion: Hazing; Join the Club" *The New York Times*. March 13, 2000. Accessed via: http://www.nytimes.com/2000/03/19/magazine/the-way-we-live-now-3-19-00 -expert-opinion-hazing-join-the-club.html

183. Moskos, Charles. Quoted in Mackey, Robert. "The Way We Live Now: 3-19 -00: Expert Opinion: Hazing; Join the Club" *The New York Times*. March 13, 2000. Accessed via: http://www.nytimes.com/2000/03/19/magazine/the-way-we-live-now-3 -19-00-expert-opinion-hazing-join-the-club.html

184. Tiger, Lionel. Quoted in Mackey, Robert. "The Way We Live Now: 3-19-00: Expert Opinion: Hazing; Join the Club" *The New York Times*. March 13, 2000. Accessed via: http://www.nytimes.com/2000/03/19/magazine/the-way-we-live-now-3-19-00 -expert-opinion-hazing-join-the-club.html

185. See for instance: Andrews, William. *Old Time Punishments*. New York: Dorset. 1991; Earle. *Curious Punishments*; Scott. *History of Corporal Punishment*; Rühling. Rühling, Erik. *Infernal Device: Machinery of Torture and Execution*. New York: Disinformation Inc., 2007.

186. Foucault. *Discipline & Punish*, 8–9.

187. Hocking, William. *The Coming World Civilization*. Crows Nest: Australia: George Allen & Unwin Ltd., 1958, 7.

188. Scott. *History of Corporal Punishment*

189. Andrews. *Old Time Punishments*, 147.

190. Morgan, Michael. *Pirates & Patriots: Tales of the Delaware Coast*. New York: Algora, 2004, 172.

191. Ibid.

192. Ibid.

193. Andrews. *Old Time Punishments*, 130.

194. Ibid., 121–30 in particular, but throughout as well.

195. Earle. *Curious Punishments*, 96.

196. Ibid., 98.

197. Ibid., 4. Earle likens the shape of the machine to a trebuchet.

198. Andrews. *Old Time Punishments*, 5.

199. Rühling. *Infernal Device*, 76.

200. Ibid., 80.

Chapter 2

1. Scott, George Ryley. *The History of Corporal Punishment*. London: Random House, 1938, 116.

2. Maugham, Somerset. *A Writer's Notebook (1874–1965)*. New York: Vintage, 2009, 67.

3. Adams, Robert. *The Abuses of Punishment*. London: Palgrave Macmillan, 1998; Van Yelyr, R. G. *The Whip and Rod: An Account Of Corporal Punishment Among All Nations And For All Purposes*. London: Gerald G. Swain, 1942; Scott. *The History of Corporal Punishment*.

4. This construction of punishment stands in contrast to one offered by Newman, Graeme (1978). *The Punishment Response*. Albany, NY: Harrow and Heston, 1978, 9. "[Punishment] must be administered by human beings other than the offender." This said, Newman's qualification that another person administer the punishment does not fully accord with the long history of self-punishment, reflecting an individual's religious piety. Indeed, Newman himself states (p.13), "But we should not assume that because of this universality punishment originated with society or that it is entirely social in nature." On this point, we concur. Punishment in the traditions of religious asceticism may reflect certain social values, but it is not necessarily a social event. Indeed, it may be a very atomized and personal event.

5. Foucault, Michel. *Discipline and Punish*. New York: Vintage Books, 1979, 201.

6. Nietzsche, Frederick. *On the Genealogy of Morals*. In Kauffman (ed.) *Basic Writings of Nietzsche*. New York: The Modern Library, 1968, 480–482.

7. Beloe, William. *Herodotus: Translated from the Greek with Notes. Vol. 2. Euterpe*. 2nd Ed. London: Leigh and Sotheby, 1803, 360–361.

8. Fowler, William Warde. *The Roman Festivals of the Period of the Republic*. London: Kennikat Publishing, 1969; Rose, Herbert Jennings. *Ancient Roman Religion*. London: Hutchinson's University Library, 1948.

9. Dryden, John. 2005. *Plutarch: Lives*. Mineola: New York.

10. Van Yelyr, R. G. *The Whip and Rod: An Account of Corporal Punishment Among All Nations and for All Purposes*. London: Gerald G. Swain, 1942, 18.

11. In this verse, the "cup" is a reference to God's wrath as exemplified by Isaiah 51:17, "Awake, awake! Stand up, O Jerusalem, You who have drunk at the hand of the LORD The cup of His fury; You have drunk the dregs of the cup of trembling, *and* drained *it* out.

12. Tanner, Norman "Inquisition and Holy Office" in *The Oxford Companion to Christian Thought*. (eds.) Hastings, Adrian, Mason, Alistar and Hugh Pyper. New York: Oxford University Press US, 2000, 327.

13. Hofstetter, Edwin. "Christianity," in *Encyclopedia of Crime and Punishment*. (ed.) David Levinson. New York: Sage, 2002, 216.

14. Leeson, Peter T. *Ordeals* (January 10, 2010). SSRN: http://ssrn.com/abstract=1530944

15. Tanner. "Inquisition and Holy Office," 327.

16. Scott. *The History of Corporal Punishment*, 100.

17. Ibid., 108.

18. Barrett, Michael. "*Opus Dei* and Corporal Mortification," July 11, 2006, http://www.opusdei.us/art.php?p=16367

19. Ibid.

20. Scott. *The History of Corporal Punishment*, 96–97.

21. Kimbrough (2002) provides an extensive treatment of the legal challenges faced by the snake handlers of rural Kentucky.

22. Fox News. "Foster Parents Who Refused to Stop Attending Snake-Handling Services Sue After Losing License," Nov. 30, 2007, http://www.foxnews.com/story/0,2933,314128,00.html

23. Gascoigne, Bamber. "History of Arabia" *HistoryWorld*, 2001, ongoing, http://www.historyworld.net/wrldhis/PlainTextHistories.asp?groupid=54&HistoryID=aa06&gtrack=pthc

24. Ibid.

25. Meithe, Terrence and Lu, Hong. *Punishment A Comparative Historical Perspective*. New York: Cambridge University Press, 2005, 158.

26. Gascoigne. "History of Arabia"; Meithe and Lu. *Punishment*; Lippman, Mathew; Sean McConville and Mordechai Yerushalmi. *Islamic Criminal Law and Procedure*. New York: Praeger Publishers. 1988.

27. Ibid.

28. Ibid.

29. Meithe and Lu. *Punishment*, 159.

30. An-na'im, Abdullahi Ahmed. *Toward an Islamic Reformation: Civil Liberties, Human Rights, and International Law*. Syracuse, NY: Syracuse University Press, 1990.

31. The *Sunnah* is also known as the also known as *Sahih Bukhari* in reference to the early Muslim scholar, Abu Abdullah Muhammad bin Ismail bin Ibrahim bin al-Mughira al-Ja'fa (a.k.a. Bukhari). Bukhari lived approximately two centuries after Muhammad's death. His collection of Muhammad's sayings or *ahadith* is accepted by the majority of Muslim scholars as the authoritative collection of Muhammad's sayings.

32. Meithe and Lu. *Punishment*.

33. Lippman, McConville, and Yerushalmi. *Islamic Criminal Law and Procedure*.

34. Meithe and Lu. *Punishment*, 159–60.

35. Ibid., 160.

36. Drapkin, Israel. *Crime and Punishment in the Ancient World*. New York: Lexington Books, 1986.

37. Meithe and Lu. *Punishment*, 156.

38. Ibid.

39. Lippman, McConville, and Yerushalmi. *Islamic Criminal Law and Procedure*.

40. Hasan, Ahmad. *The Doctrine of Ijma': A Study of the Juridical Principle of Consensus*. New Delhi, India: Kitab Bhaban, 2003.

41. Ibid.

42. Kamali, Mohammad Hashim. *Principles of Islamic Jurisprudence*. Cambridge, UK: Islamic Texts Society, 2003, 229–230.

43. Ibid., 232.

44. Lippman, McConville, and Yerushalmi. *Islamic Criminal Law and Procedure*.

45. Nader, M. M. J. *Aspects of Saudi Arabi Law*. Riyadh, Saudi Arabia: Nader, 1990; Meithe and Lu. *Punishment*.

46. Amin, Hussein Abdulwaheed. 2010. "The Origins of the *Sunni*/Shia split in Islam." *Islam for Today*, 2010, http://www.islamfortoday.com/shia.htm

47. Lippman, McConville, and Yerushalmi. *Islamic Criminal Law and Procedure*; An-na'im. *Toward an Islamic Reformation*.

48. Lippman, McConville, and Yerushalmi. *Islamic Criminal Law and Procedure*.

49. Meithe and Lu. *Punishment*, 165.

50. Ibid., 167.

51. Dhahabi, Shamsu ed-Deen. *Major Sins*. Translated by Mustafa M. Dhahabi, 2001, http://www.islamtomorrow.com/books/major_sins/majorSins.pdf

52. Meithe and Lu. *Punishment*, 167.

53. Madkoar, Mohammed Salam. "Human Rights from an Islamic Worldview: An outline of *Hudud*, Ta'zir & *Qisas*," Accessed March 30, 2011, http://www.muhajabah.com/docstorage/*hudud*.htm

54. Bin Mohamed, Mahfodz. "The Concept of Ta'zir in The Islamic Criminal Law." *Sunni Forum*, 2005, http://www.*sunni*forum.com/forum/showthread.php?6205-The-Concept-of-Ta%92zir-in-Islamic-Criminal-Law

55. Ibid.

56. Ibid.

57. 'Audah,'Abdul Qadir. n.d. *Al-Tashri al-Jina'I al-Islami*, Beirut. vol. I; Bin Mohamed. "The Concept of Ta'zir in The Islamic Criminal Law."

58. Ibn Hazm, n.d. *al-Ihkam fi Usul al-Ahkam*. vol. I. Lebanon: Dar al-Kutub al-Ilmeyah.

59. Al-Kasani, Mas'ud. n.d. *Badai' al-Sana'i' fi Tartib al-Syarai'*. vol. 7. Beirut: Dar al-Kutub al-'Ilmiyyah.

60. Bin Mohamed. "The Concept of Ta'zir in The Islamic Criminal Law."

61. Sahih Bukhari. "English Translation of Sahih Bukhari." Accessed March 25, 2011, http://www.sahih-bukhari.com/

62. It bears noting that different Sunni schools have prescribed varying lower proportional assessments of value for individuals of religions other than Christianity and Judaism (e.g., Hindus, Zoroastrians, Mandaens, Buddhists, etc). For additional information see: Fyzee, Asaf Ali Asghar. *Outlines of Muhammadan Law*. 3d ed. London: Oxford University Press, 1964.

63. A *dhimmi* is a class of protected non-Muslim residents in an Islamic state. They typically have reduced rights or live under certain restrictions, but this is a highly variable construct, and one that has been judicially and legislatively evolved over time. For more information see: Lewis, Bernard. 2002. *The Arabs in History*. Oxford: Oxford University Press.

64. Islamweb. "Fatwa No: 85544," 2003, http://www.islamweb.net/emainpage/index.php?page=showfatwa&Option=FatwaId&Id=85544

65. Sahih Bukhari. 9.83.19.

66. Fadlallah, Sayyed Muhammed Hussein. "Kaffarahs." Bayynat, 2011, http://english.bayynat.org.lb/fatawa/s6ch.htm

67. Ibid.

68. Ibid.

69. Greenberg, Yudit Kornberg. *Encyclopedia of love in world religions.* Vol. 1. Santa Barbara, CA: ABC-CLIO, 2008, 62–63.

70. Ibid., 63.

71. This commemoration is also known as the *Remembrance of Muharram.*

72. Sahih Bukhari. 2:23:382.

73. Teachings of Islam. "Tatbir Fatawa" 2008, http://imamshirazi.com/tatbir%20fatawa.html

74. Mazrui, Ali. "Sari'a Law" Voice of America, 2003, http://www.globalsecurity.org/military/library/news/2000/03/000314-nigeria1.htm

75. Meithe and Lu. *Punishment*, 180–181.

76. Mazrui, Ali. 2003. "Sari'a Law" Voice of America. Accessed via: http://www.globalsecurity.org/military/library/news/2000/03/000314-nigeria1.htm

77. Refer back to the section on Antiquity in this chapter for an additional discussion on the agent/subject relationship in punishment.

78. Foucault, Michel. *Discipline & Punish: The Birth of the Prison.* New York: Vintage, 1977.

79. Center for Applied Research in the Apostolate. "Frequently requested church statistics" Washington, DC: Georgetown University, 2011, http://cara.georgetown.edu/CARAServices/requestedchurchstats.html

80. Nietzsche, Frederick. *On the Genealogy of Morals/Ecce Homo.* trans. by Walter Kaufman. New York: Vintage, 1989 [1887].

81. Ibid., 118.

82. Miladinov, Marina. *Margins of Solitude: Eremitism In Central Europe Between East and West.* Zagreb: Leykam International, 2008.

83. United States Catholic Church. (1995). *Catechism of the Catholic Church.* New York: Image Press. Can. 603 §1: footnote.

84. Bacchus, F. J. "St. Pachomius." *The Catholic Encyclopedia.* New York: Robert Appleton Company, 1911, http://www.newadvent.org/cathen/11381a.htm

85. Zimmerman, John and R. Avery (trans.). *Life and Miracles of St. Benedict Book II, Dialogues.* Westport, CT: Greenwood Press, 1980.

86. Adherents to Sufism are sometimes also referred to as a Dervish or Darvish.

87. Mahmud, 'Abd al-Halim. *Fatawa on Sufism.* trans by A. Godlas, 1998, http://www.uga.edu/islam/abdalhalim.html

88. Keller, Nuh Ha Mim. "How would you respond to the Claim that Sufism is bid'a?", 1995, http://www.masud.co.uk/ISLAM/nuh/sufism.htm

89. Al-Ghazali, Abu Hamid Muhammad. *Al-Ghazali on Disciplining the Soul and on Breaking the Two Desires: Books XXII and XXIII of the Revival of the Religious Sciences.* trans. by T. J. Winter. Cambridge: Islamic Texts Society, 1997.

90. The term "fakir" (or "faqr") is also used to describe Dervishes, but the usage is more commonly limited to wandering mendicants. Fakir has also been adopted by numerous other cultures as a synonym for beggars. The term has a broad currency in describing

Islamic holy men. That said, it has also been adopted to describe certain Buddhist and Hindu ascetics.

91. Gülen, M. Fethullah. "Sufism and Its Origins," *The Whirling Dervishes of Rumi*, 2011, http://www.whirlingdervishes.org/sufizm.htm

92. Azeemi, Khwaja Shamsuddin. *Muraqaba: Art and Science of Sufi Meditation*. Houston, TX: Plato Publishing, 2005.

93. Parker, Richard. *A Practical Guide to Islamic Monuments in Morocco*. Charlottesville: Baraka Press, 1981.

94. Ansari, Sarah. *Sufi Saints and State Power: The Pirs of Sind, 1843–1947*. Cambridge: Cambridge University Press, 2003.

95. Kloppenborg, Ria. *The Paccekabuddha: A Buddhist Ascetic, A Study of the Concept of the Paccekabuddha in Pali Canonical and Commentarial Literature*. Sri Lanka: Buddhist Publication Society Kandy, 1993.

96. Hartsuiker, Dolf. *Sadhus: India's Mystic Holy Men*. Rochester, Vermont: Inner Traditions, 1993.

97. Ibid.

98. Veda. "Yamas and Niyamas." *Vedic Knowledge Online*, 2011, http://veda .wikidot.com/yama-niyama#toc23

99. Hartsuiker. *Sadhus: India's Mystic Holy Men*.

100. Streeter, Burnett Hillman and A. J. Appasamy. *The Sadhu: A Study In Mysticism And Practical Religion*. Whitefish, MT: Kessinger Publishing, 2008 [1921].

101. Oldmeadow, Harry. 2007. *Light from the East: Eastern Wisdom for the Modern West*. Bloomington, IN: World Wisdom, 2007, 118.

102. BBC News. "Jainism at a Glance." *Religions*, 2009, http://www.bbc.co.uk/ religion/religions/jainism/ataglance/glance.shtml

103. Oldmeadow. *Light from the East: Eastern Wisdom for the Modern West*.

104. Ibid.

105. Jainworld.com. (n.d.), http://jainworld.com/GJE.asp?id=42

106. Shah, Natubhai. *Jainism: The World of Conquerors*. New Delhi: Motilal Banarsidass, 2003.

107. Jainworld.com.

108. Shah. *Jainism: The World of Conquerors*.

109. Buddha Dharma Education Association. 2011. "Lay Guide to the Monk's Rules." *Buddhist Studies*, 2011, http://www.buddhanet.net/e-learning/buddhistworld/ layguide.htm

110. Ibid.

Chapter 3

1. Bitensky, Susan. *Corporal punishment of children: A human rights violation*. New York: Transnational, 2006.

2. Straus, Murray and Denise Donnelly. *Beating the devil out of them: Corporal Punishment in American Families*. Lexington Books, 1994), 420.

3. Ibid., 5

4. Gershoff, Elizabeth. "Corporal Punishment by Parents and Associated Child Behaviors and Experiences: A Meta-Analytic and Theoretical Review." *Psychological Bulletin* 128 (2002): 539–579.

5. Gershoff. "Corporal Punishment by Parents," 540.

6. Gershoff. "Corporal Punishment by Parents."

7. Heymann, Tom. *The unofficial U.S. census*. New York: Fawcett Columbine, 1991.

8. World Health Organization. Preventing child maltreatment: a guide to taking action and generating evidence (2006).

9. Gershoff. "Corporal Punishment by Parents," 550.

10. World Health Organization. Preventing child maltreatment.

11. Edwards, Leonard. "Corporal punishment and the legal system." *Santa Clara Law Review* 36 (1996).

12. Ibid.

13. Straus and Donnelly. *Beating the devil out of them.*

14. Edwards. "Corporal punishment and the legal system."

15. Gershoff. "Corporal Punishment by Parents."

16. Straus and Donnelly. *Beating the devil out of them.*

17. Ibid.

18. Ibid., 51

19. Schoolland, Ken. *Shogun's ghost: The dark side of Japanese Education*. Bergin and Garvey, 1990.

20. Chang, I. J., Rebecca Pettit, and Emiko Katsurada. "Where and When to Spank: A Comparison Between U.S. and Japanese College Students." *Journal of Family Violence* 21 (2006): 281–286.

21. Ibid.

22. Alyahria, Abdullah and Robert Goodman. "Harsh corporal punishment of Yemeni children: Occurrence, type, and associations." *Child abuse and Neglect*, 32 (2008): 766–773.

23. Ibid., 769.

24. Ibid.

25. United Nations Convention on the Rights of the Child (Article 19).

26. Freeman, Michael. "Children are Unbeatable." *Children & Society* 13 (1999):130–141.

27. Ibid.

28. Global Initiative to End the Corporal Punishment of Children. "States with full abolition." Accessed July 20, 2010. http://www.endcorporalpunishment.org/pages/frame.html

29. World Health Organization. Preventing child maltreatment.

30. Durrant, Joan. "The Swedish Ban on Corporal Punishment: Its History and Effects," In *Family Violence Against Children: A Challenge for Society*, ed. Detlev Frehsee, Wiebke Horn, and Kai-D Bussmann, 19–25. Walter de Gruyter & Co., Berlin, New York, 1996.

31. Ombudsman for Children in Sweden. "The Swedish Corporal Punishment Ban." Accessed July 30, 2010. http://www.barnombudsmannen.se/Adfinity.aspx?pageid=90

32. Durrant. Swedish Ban.

33. Ibid.

34. Children's Ombudsman. Swedish Corporal Punishment Ban.

35. Durrant. Swedish Ban.

36. Children's Ombudsman. Swedish Corporal Punishment Ban.

37. Durrant. Swedish Ban.

38. Ibid., 2.

39. Children's Ombudsman. Swedish Corporal Punishment Ban.

40. Freeman. Unbeatable.

41. Global Initiative to End the Corporal Punishment of Children. "Full abolition."

42. Freeman. Unbeatable.

43. Ibid.

44. Government of South Sudan. "Laws, Legislation, and Policies." Accessed June 1, 2010. http://www.goss-online.org/magnoliaPublic/en/Laws—Legislation—Policies/

45. Freeman. Unbeatable, 133.

46. Freeman. Unbeatable.

47. Durrant. Swedish Ban; Children's Ombudsman. Swedish Corporal Punishment Ban.

48. Children's Ombudsman. Swedish Corporal Punishment Ban

49. Statistics Sweden. "Spanking and other forms of physical punishment: A study of adults' and middle school students' opinions, experience, and knowledge," Demographic Report No. 1.2 (Demography, the Family, and Children 1996:1.2). Stockholm, Sweden.

50. Durrant. Swedish Ban, 23.

51. Global Initiative to End the Corporal Punishment of Children. "Full abolition."

52. CBC News. "To spank or not to spank." Accessed June 3, 2010 from: http://www.cbc.ca/canada/story/2009/07/31/f-spanking-discipline-debate.html#ixzz0orxhn8oP

53. Global Initiative to End the Corporal Punishment of Children. "State Reports: Canada." Accessed June 2, 2010 from http://www.endcorporalpunishment.org/

54. CBC News. To spank.

55. Global Initiative to End the Corporal Punishment of Children. Canada.

56. Ibid.

57. Straus and Donnelly. *Beating the devil out of them.*

58. Gershoff. "Corporal Punishment by Parents."

59. Ibid.

60. Straus, Murray and Glenda Kantor. "Corporal punishment of adolescents by parents: A risk factor in the epidemiology of depression, suicide, alcohol abuse, child abuse, and wife beating." *Adolescence*, 29 (1994): 543–561.

61. Straus and Donnelly. *Beating the devil out of them.*

62. Straus, Murray and Julie Stewart. "Corporal punishment by American parents: National data on prevalence, chronicity, severity, and duration, in relation to child and family characteristics." *Clinical Child and Family Psychology Review* 2 (1999): 55–70.

63. Straus and Stewart. American parents; Gershoff. "Corporal Punishment by Parents."

64. O'Brian, Charles and Laurel Lau. "Defining child abuse in Hong Kong." *Child Abuse Review*, 4 (1995): 38–46.

65. Segal, Uma. "Children are abused in eastern countries: A look at India." *International Social Work* 42 (1999): 39–52.

66. Chang et al. "Where and When."

67. Buldukoglu, Kadriye and Kamile Kukulu. "Maternal punishment practices in a rural area of Turkey." *Child care, health, and development* 34 (2007): 180–184.

68. Brown, Janet and Sharon Johnson. "Childrearing and child participation in Jamaican families." *International Journal of Early Years Education* 16 (2008): 31–40, PG 34

69. Segal. Children are abused.

70. Youseff, Randa, Medhat Attia, and Mohamed Kamel. "Children experiencing violence I: Parental use of corporal punishment." *Child Abuse and Neglect* 22 (1998): 959–973.

71. Hicks-Pass, Stephanie. "Corporal Punishment in America Today: Spare the Rod, Spoil the Child? A Systematic Review of the Literature." *Best Practices in Mental Health* 5 (2009): 71–88.

72. Knox, Michele and Jason Brouwer. "Early Childhood Professionals' Recommendations for Spanking Young Children." *Journal of Child & Adolescent Trauma* 1 (2008): 341–348.

73. American Academy of Pediatrics. "Policy Statement: Guidance for Effective Discipline. Committee on Psychosocial Aspects of Child and Family Health." *Pediatrics* 101 (1998): 723–728.

74. Gershoff. "Corporal Punishment by Parents."

75. Straus and Donnelly. *Beating the devil out of them.*

76. Lopez, N., J. Bonenberger, and H. Schneider. "Parental disciplinary history, current levels of empathy, and moral reasoning in young adults." *North American Journal of Psychology* 3 (2001): 193–204.

77. Ibid., 200.

78. Lansford, Jennifer, Kenneth Dodge, Gregory Pettit, Michael Criss, Daniel Shaw, John Bates. "Trajectories of physical discipline: Early childhood antecedents and developmental outcomes." *Child Development* 80 (2009): 1385–1402.

79. Straus, Murray and Carrie Yodanis. "Corporal punishment in adolescence and physical assaults on spouses later in life: What accounts for the link?" *Journal of Marriage and Family* 58 (1996): 825–841.

80. Piper, Heather. "The Linkage of Animal Abuse with Interpersonal Violence: A Sheep in Wolf's Clothing?" *Journal of social work* 3 (2003):161–177.

81. Wareham, Jennifer, Denise Boots, and Jorge Chavez. "A test of social learning and intergenerational transmission among batterers." *Journal of Criminal Justice* 37 (2009): 163–173.

82. Ibid.

83. Bandura, Albert. *Psychological modeling: Conflicting Theories.* New Jersey: Transaction Publishers, 2006.

84. Flynn, Clifton. "Exploring the link between corporal punishment and children's cruelty to animals." *Journal of Marriage and Family* 61 (1999): 971–981. PG 971.

85. Flynn. "Corporal punishment and children's cruelty to animals"; Piper. "Linkage of Animal Abuse."

86. Carroll, Joseph. "The intergenerational transmission of family violence: The long term effects of aggressive behavior." *Aggressive Behavior* 3 (1977): 289–299; Straus and Yodanis. "Corporal punishment in adolescence."

87. Carroll, Joseph. "The intergenerational transmission of family violence."

88. Ibid.

89. Straus and Yodanis. "Corporal punishment in adolescence."

90. Wareham et al. "Social Learning."

91. Ibid.

92. Straus and Donnelly. *Beating the devil out of them*, 71.

93. Straus and Donnelly. *Beating the devil out of them.*

94. Greven, Philip. *Spare the child: The religious roots of physical punishments and the psychological impact of physical abuse*. New York: Knopf, 1991, 129. As cited in: Strauss and Donnelly. *Beating the devil out of them*.

95. Straus and Kantor. "Corporal punishment of adolescents."

96. Baumrind, Diana and Allen Black. "Socialization practices associated with dimensions of competence in preschool boys and girls." *Child Development* 3 (1967): 291–327; Lasky, Melvin. "Family genesis of aggression." *Psychiatric Annals 23* (1993): 494–499.

97. Tomoda, Akemi, Hanako Suzuki, Keren Rabi, Yi-Shin Sheu, Ann Polcari, and Martin Teicher. "Reduced prefrontal cortical gray matter volume in young adults exposed to harsh corporal punishment." *NeuroImage* 47 (2009): T66–T71.

98. Ibid.

Chapter 4

1. Straus, Murray and Denise Donnelly. *Beating the devil out of them: Corporal Punishment in American Families*. Lexington Books, 1994, 42.

2. American Civil Liberties Union and Human Rights Watch. "A violent Education: Corporal Punishment of children in US public schools." Accessed June 1, 2010. www .hwr.org

3. Humphreys, Sara. "Gendering corporal punishment: beyond the discourse of human rights," *Gender and Education* 20 (2008): 527–540.

4. Ibid.

5. *State of Indiana v. Paula J. Fettig*, No. 49A02-0709-CR-807. www.in.gov/judiciary/opinions/pdf/04150805par.pdf

6. Ibid.

7. Ibid.

8. The American Civil Liberties Union and Human Rights Watch. "A violent Education," 4.

9. Ibid.

10. Parker-Jenkins, Marie. *Sparing the rod: School discipline and children's rights*. Staffordshire, England: Trentham Books Limited, 1999.

11. *Ingraham v. Wright*. 430 U.S. 651 (1977).

12. Middleton, Jacob. "The Experience of Corporal Punishment in Schools, 1890–1940." *History of Education* 37 (2008): 253–275, 253.

13. Middleton. "Corporal Punishment in Schools," 254.

14. Axelrod, Paul. "No Longer a 'Last Resort' The End of Corporal Punishment in the Schools of Toronto." *The Canadian Historical Review* 91(2010): 261–285.

15. *Gardner v. Bygrave* (1889) 53 J.P. 743.

16. Middleton. "Corporal Punishment in Schools," 255.

17. Grasmick, Harold, Carolyn Morgan, and Mary Kennedy. "Support for corporal punishment in the schools: A comparison of the effects of socioeconomic status and religion." *Social Science Quarterly* 73 (1992): 177–187.

18. Global Initiative to End the Corporal Punishment of Children. "State Reports: Malaysia." Accessed July 14, 2010. http://www.endcorporalpunishment.org/

19. Ibid.

20. Humphreys. "Gendering corporal punishment."

21. Ibid.

22. *Ingraham v. Wright,* 430 U.S. 651 (1977).

23. Ibid.

24. Ibid.

25. Farmer, Alice and Kate Stinson. "Failing the Grade: How the Use of Corporal Punishment in U.S. Public Schools Demonstrates the Need for U.S. Ratification of the Children's Rights Convention and the Convention on the Rights of Persons with Disabilities," *New York Law School Law Review* (2009): 1035-1069.

26. Ferraro, Paul and Joan Weinreich. "Unprotected in the classroom," *American School Board Journal* (2006): 40–43.

27. The American Civil Liberties Union and Human Rights Watch. "A violent Education."

28. Ibid.

29. Ibid.

30. Ibid.

31. Farmer and Stinson. "Failing the Grade."

32. American Civil Liberties Union and Human Rights Watch. "Impairing Education: Corporal Punishment of Students with Disabilities in US Public Schools."Accessed March 2, 2010. www.hrw.org

33. Farmer and Stinson. "Failing the Grade"; The American Civil Liberties Union and Human Rights Watch. "A violent Education."

34. Farmer and Stinson. "Failing the Grade."

35. American Civil Liberties Union. Statement Before the House Education and Labor Subcommittee on Healthy Families and Communities Hearing on "Corporal Punishment in Schools and Its Effect on Academic Success, 2010." Accessed April 2, 2010. www.hrw.org

36. Axelrod. "No Longer a 'Last Resort' "

37. *The Canadian Foundation for Children, Youth and the Law v. The Attorney General of Canada,* [2004] 1 S.C.R. 76, 2004 SCC 4.

38. Canadian Children's Rights Council. "Supreme Court takes strap out of teachers' hands." Accessed June 3, 2010. http://www.canadiancrc.com/Newspaper_Articles/Edmonton_Journal_Supreme_Court_Schools_strap_31JAN04.aspx

39. BBC News. "The loophole that allows smacking in some schools." Accessed June 1, 2010. http://news.bbc.co.uk/2/hi/uk_news/education/8468918.stm

40. *Case of Campbell and Cosans v. The United Kingdom* (1976) 4 EHRR 293. European Court of Human Rights.

41. Ibid.

42. "European Convention for the Protection of Human Rights and Fundamental Freedoms." Accessed August 16, 2010. http://conventions.coe.int/treaty/en/treaties/html/005.htm

43. *Case of Campbell and Cosans v. The United Kingdom.*

44. Ibid.

45. Ibid.

46. Global Initiative to End the Corporal Punishment of Children. "State Reports: England and Wales." Accessed July 14, 2010. www.endcorporalpunishment.org

47. BBC News. "Smacking pupils in part-time schools could be banned." Accessed July 13, 2010. http://news.bbc.co.uk/2/hi/uk_news/education/8466801.stm

48. BBC News. "The loophole that allows smacking in some schools."

49. Yoneyama, Shoko and Asao Naito. "Problems with the paradigm: The school as a factor in understanding bullying." *British Journal of Sociology of Education* 24 (2003): 315–330, 322.

50. Schoolland, Ken. *Shogun's ghost: The dark side of Japanese Education* (New York, NY: Bergin and Garvey, 1990).

51. Global Initiative to End the Corporal Punishment of Children. "State Reports: Japan." Accessed July 28, 2010. http://www.endcorporalpunishment.org

52. Sugimoto, Yoshio. *An Introduction to Japanese Society*. Cambridge: Cambridge University Press, 2003.

53. Schoolland. *Shogun's ghost*, 2.

54. Ibid.

55. Miller, Aaron. "*Taibatsu*: 'Corporal punishment' in Japanese socio-cultural context." *Japan Forum* 21 (2009): 233–254.

56. Ibid.

57. Archambault, Caroline. "Pain with punishment and the negotiation of childhood: An ethnographic analysis of children's rights processes in Maasailand." *Africa* 79 (2009): 282–302.

58. Human Rights Watch. "Spare the Child: Corporal Punishment in Kenyan Schools." Accessed July 14, 2011. http://www.unhcr.org/refworld/docid/45d1adbc2.html

59. UNICEF Bangladesh. "Opinions of children of Bangladesh on corporal punishment." Accessed July 21, 2011. www.unicef.org/bangladesh/Opinion_Poll_2009.pdf

60. Ibid.

61. Ibid.

62. BBC News. "Bangladesh orders corporal punishment to be stopped." Accessed August 1, 2011. http://www.bbc.co.uk/news/world-south-asia-10687875

63. Ibid.

64. UNICEF India. "Progress on Banning Corporal Punishment in India." Accessed August 2, 2011. www.unicef.org/india/banningcorporalpunishment.pdf

65. Global Initiative to End the Corporal Punishment of Children. "State Reports: India." Accessed June 10, 2011. http://www.endcorporalpunishment.org

66. Ibid.

67. NDTV. "Indian government bans corporal punishment in schools." Accessed June 10, 2011. http://www.ndtv.com/article/india/indian-government-bans-corporal -punishment-in-schools-38661&cp

68. Ibid.

69. Adegbehingbe, Bernice and Ajite Kayode. "Corporal punishment-related ocular injuries in Nigerian Children," *Journal of the Indian Association of Pediatric Surgery* 12 (2007): 76–79.

70. Ibid.

71. Ibid.

72. Adegbehingbe and Ajite. Corporal punishment-related ocular injuries, 78.

73. Cameron, Mark. "Managing School Discipline and Implications for School Social Workers: A Review of the Literature." *Children and Schools* 28 (2006): 219–227.

74. Arcus, Doreen. "School Shooting Fatalities and School Corporal Punishment: A Look at the States," *Aggressive Behavior* 28 (2002): 173–183.

75. Ibid.

76. Ibid., 182.

77. The American Civil Liberties Union and Human Rights Watch, "Impairing Education," 57.

78. Integrated Regional Information Networks (IRIN). "Pakistan: Corporal punishment key reason for school dropouts." Accessed July 14, 2011. http://www.unhcr.org/refworld/docid/4832c17f1e.html

79. Ibid.

80. Ibid.

81. UNICEF Regional Office for South Asia. (2001). Corporal punishment in schools in South Asia. Committee on the Rights of the Child. Accessed May 3, 2010. ...www .childtrafficking.com/.../unicef_2001_corporal_punishment_in_south_asia_1.pdf

82. Plan International. "School violence costs billions, reveals report." Accessed June 1, 2010. http://www.planusa.org/contentmgr/showdetails.php/id/1540357

83. Ibid.

84. Grasmick. et al. "Support for corporal punishment in the schools."

85. Noonan, David. "A Catholic-School Veteran Tells All," Newsweek, 153(2009), 44.

86. O'Donoghue, Tom. "Teachers and the child abuse in catholic schools." Editoris Potts, Anthony and Tom O'Donoghue. *Schools and dangerous places: A historical perspective*, 145–166 (New York: Cambria Press, 2007).

87. Ibid.

88. O'Donoghue. "Teachers and the child abuse," 161.

89. Vaaler, Margaret, Christopher Ellison, Karissa Horton, and John Marcum. "Spare the Rod? Ideology, Experience, and Attitudes Toward Child Discipline Among Presbyterian Clergy." *Pastoral Psychology* 56 (2008): 533–546.

90. Ibid., 543.

91. Benavot, Aaron and Braslavsky, Cecilia. *School knowledge in comparative and historical perspective: changing curricula in primary and secondary education*. Springer Publishing.

92. Daun, Holger and Walford, Geoffrey. *Educational strategies among Muslims in the context of globalization: Some national case studies*. Koninkijke Brill, NV, Leiden, The Netherlands.

93. Ibid.

94. Hartung, Jan-Peter and Reifeld, Helmut. Islamic education, diversity and national identity: dīnī madāris in India post 9/11, 2006. Sage Publications.

95. Ibid.

96. Humphreys. "Gendering corporal punishment."

97. Ibid.

98. The American Civil Liberties Union and Human Rights Watch. "A violent Education."

99. Ibid.

100. Ibid., 31

101. Harver, Clive. Schooling as violence: how schools harm pupils and societies. New York: Routledge Falmer.

102. Ibid., 74.

Chapter 5

1. Igantieff, Michael. *A just measure of pain: The penitentiary in the industrial revolution 1750–1850*. New York: Random House, 1978.

2. Ibid., 178.

3. Great Britain Parliament, House of Commons. *Reports from Committees: Gaols and Houses of Correction, vol. 4.* (Session 5 February–28 July 1863), 148.

4. Ibid., 148.

5. Ibid., 322.

6. *Public Opinion: A comprehensive summary of the press throughout the world on all important current topics, vol. 25.* New York: The public opinion company, 1898.

7. Ibid.

8. Salt, Henry,. *The Humane Review, vol. 7–8.* York House: Earnest Bell, 1907.

9. Ibid., 89.

10. Criminal Justice Act (1967). Office of Public Sector Information. http://www.opsi.gov.uk/RevisedStatutes/Acts/ukpga/1967/cukpga_19670080_en_5

11. Banks, Cindi. *Punishment in America: A reference handbook.* Santa Barbara: ABC-CLIO, 2005.

12. Glenn, Myra. *Campaigns against corporal punishment: Prisoners, sailors, women, and children, and antebellum America.* Albany: State University of New York Press, 1984.

13. Ibid.

14. Ibid., 34.

15. Ibid.

16. Glenn. *Campaigns against corporal punishment.*

17. Ibid., 35.

18. Ibid.

19. Klein, Philip. "*Prison methods in New York state: A contribution to the study of theory and practice of correctional institutions in New York state.*" PhD diss, Columbia University, 1920, 228.

20. Gillin, John. *Criminology and Penology, v. 2.* The Century Company, 1926.

21. Ibid., 614.

22. McShane, Marilyn and Frank Williams. *Encyclopedia of American Prisons.* Taylor and Francis, 1996.

23. Newman, Graeme. *Just and painful: A case for the corporal punishment of criminals, 2nd edition.* Criminal Justice Pr, 1995.

24. Ibid.

25. Ibid.

26. Ibid.

27. Finkelman, Paul. *Encyclopedia of American civil liberties, Volume 1.* Routledge Taylor and Francis Group, 2006.

28. *Jackson v. Bishop, 404 F.2d 971.*

29. Ibid.

30. McShane and Williams. *Encyclopedia of American Prisons.*

31. The Encyclopedia of Arkansas History and Culture. "Tucker Telephone." Accessed April 19, 2012. http://www.encyclopediaofarkansas.net/encyclopedia/entry-detail.aspx?entryID=4923

32. *Jackson v. Bishop, 404 F.2d 971.*

33. Wooden, Kenneth. *Weeping in the playtime of others*. Columbus, Ohio: Ohio State University Press, 2000.

34. Ibid.

35. Ibid., 7.

36. Ibid.

37. Ibid., 8.

38. The handbook of Texas online. "Gatesvile school for boys." Accessed February 3, 2011. http://www.tshaonline.org/handbook/online/articles/jjg02

39. Global Initiative to End the Corporal Punishment of Children. "Country Reports: The United States, 2011." Accessed July 15, 2010. http://www.endcorporalpunishment.org/

40. McShane and Williams. *Encyclopedia of American Prisons*.

41. *Graves v. Arpaio* (2010) No. 08-17601. Accessed August 16, 2011. http://caselaw.findlaw.com/us-9th-circuit/1540979.html

42. Ibid.

43. Kadish, Doris. *Slavery in the Caribbean Francophone world: distant voices, forgotten acts, forged identities*. Athens, GA: University of Georgia Press, 2000.

44. Office of the United Nations High Commissioner for Human Rights, 1955. Accessed July 10, 2010. http://www2.ohchr.org/english/law/treatmentprisoners.htm

45. Nowak, Manfred. "Report of the Special Rapporteur on torture and other cruel, inhuman or degrading treatment or punishment. Study on the phenomena of torture, cruel, inhuman or degrading treatment or punishment in the world, including an assessment of conditions of detention." Human Rights Council, Thirteenth session, 2010. Accessed June 1, 2010. . . .www2.ohchr.org/english/bodies/hrcouncil/. . ./A.HRC.13.39.Add.5_en.pdf

46. Nowak. "Report of the Special Rapporteur on torture," 58–59.

47. Ibid.

48. BBC News. "Egypt moves to ban jail flogging, 2000." Accessed June 10, 2010. http://news.bbc.co.uk/2/hi/middle_east/926572.stm; Middle East Watch, *Prison Conditions in Egypt: A filthy system* (New York: Human Rights Watch, 1993).

49. Middle East Watch. *Prison Conditions*.

50. Ibid., 88.

51. Ibid.

52. Ibid., 90.

53. Amnesty International. "Egypt:Torture remains rife as cries for justice go unheeded, 2001."Accessed June 1, 2010. http://www.amnesty.org/en/library/info/MDE12/001/2001/en; BBC News. "Widespread torture in Egypt, 2001." Accessed June 10, 2010. http://news.bbc.co.uk/2/hi/middle_east/1194697.stm

54. Amnesty International. "Torture remains rife."

55. BBC News. "Widespread torture in Egypt."

56. Rejali, Darius. *Torture and Democracy*. New Jersey: Princeton University Press, 2007.

57. Ibid., 53.

58. Amnesty International. "Singapore: Cruel Punishment, 1991." Accessed June 1, 2010. http://www.amnesty.org/en/library/info/ASA36/003/1991/en

59. Singapore Statutes. "Prisons Act, Chapter 247." Accessed August 1, 2010. http://statutes.agc.gov.sg

60. Ibid.

61. Ibid.

62. Ibid.

63. Amnesty International. "Singapore: Cruel Punishment."

64. United States Department of State. "Human rights reports: North Korea." Accessed June 1, 2010. http://www.state.gov/g/drl/rls/hrrpt/2010/eap/154388.htm

65. Amnesty International. "North Korea: Torture, death penalty and abductions—Information sheet." Accessed June 1, 2010. http://www.amnesty.org/en/library/info/ASA24/003/2009/ja

66. Ibid.

67. Ibid., 1.

68. Chol-hwan Kang and Pierre Rigoulot. *The Aquariums of Pyongyang: Ten Years in the North Korean Gulag*. New York, NY: Basic Books, 2005.

69. Kim, Mike. *Escaping North Korea: defiance and hope in the world's most repressive country*. Lanham, Maryland: Rowman & Littlefield Publishers, Inc, 2008, 110.

70. Ibid.

71. Human Rights Information Center. "Political prisoner Hada suffers torture in prison." Accessed May 30, 2010. http://www.smhric.org/news_69.htm

72. Williams, Philip and Yenna Wu., *The great wall of confinement: The Chinese prison camp through contemporary fiction and reportage*. Berkeley and Los Angeles, CA: University of California Press, 2004.

73. BBC News. "China's "reforming" work programme, 2005." Accessed June 5, 2010. http://news.bbc.co.uk/2/hi/asia-pacific/4515197.stm

74. Laws of Bangladesh. "The prisons act, 1894." Accessed May 30, 2010. http://bdlaws.com/prisons-act-1894/

75. Glenn. *Campaigns against corporal punishment*, 41.

76. Amnesty International. "Photographic evidence shows the cruelty of caning in Malaysia, 2009." Accessed June 1, 2010. http://www.amnesty.org/en/news-and-updates/news/photographic

77. Jaranson, James and Michael Popkin. *Caring for victims of torture*. Washington, D.C.: American Psychiatric Press, 1998.

78. Ibid.

79. Rintamaki, Lance, Francis Weaver, Philip Elbaum, Edward Klama, and Scott Miskevics. "Persistence of Traumatic Memories in World War II Prisoners of War." *Journal of the American Geriatrics Society*, 57 (2009): 2257–2262.

80. Gerrity, Ellen, Terence Keane, and Farris Tuma. *The mental health consequences of torture* (New York, NY: Springer Publishers, 2001).

81. Ibid., 115.

82. Goldfeld, Anne, Richard Mollica, Barbara Pesavento and Stephen Faraone. "The physical and psychological sequelae of torture: Symptomatology and diagnosis." *Journal of the American Medical Association*, 259 (1988): 2725–2729.

83. Rintamaki. et al., "Persistence of Traumatic Memories"; Gerrity et al., *The mental health consequences of torture*.

84. Newman, Graeme. *Just and painful*, 27.

Chapter 6

1. Central Intelligence Agency. "The World Factbook." Accessed March 1, 2011. https://www.cia.gov/library/publications/the-world-factbook/

2. Ibid.

3. Anyanwu, Ogechi. "Crime and Justice in postcolonial Nigeria: The justifications and challenges of Islamic law of Shari'a," *Journal of Law and Religion*, 22 (2006): 315–347. Central Intelligence Agency. "The World Factbook."

4. United Nations. "Country profile of human development indicators." Accessed May 10, 2011. http://hdr.undp.org/en/data/profiles/

5. Ibid.

6. Ibid.

7. Ibid.

8. Ibid.

9. Abia, Adamawa, Akwa Ibom, Anambra, Bauchi, Bayelsa, Benue, Borno, Cross River, Delta, Ebonyi, Edo, Ekiti, Enugu, Federal Capital Territory, Gombe, Imo, Jigawa, Kaduna, Kano, Katsina, Kebbi, Kogi, Kwara, Lagos, Nassarawa, Niger, Ogun, Ondo, Osun, Oyo, Plateau, Rivers, Sokoto, Taraba, Yobe, Zamfara.

10. Human Rights Watch. "Political Shari'a? Human Rights and Islamic Law in Northern Nigeria," Human Rights Watch, 16 (2004).

11. Ibid., 9.

12. Central Intelligence Agency. "The World Factbook."

13. Metz, Helen. "Nigeria: A Country Study" (Washington: GPO for the Library of Congress). Accessed March 10, 2011. http://lcweb2.loc.gov/frd/cs/cshome.html

14. Ibid.

15. Sodiq, Yushau. "Can Muslims and Christians Live Together Peacefully in Nigeria?" *The Muslim World*, 99 (2009): 646–688. Motin, A. Rashad. "Political Dynamism of Islam in Nigeria." *Islamic Studies*, 26 (1987): 179–189.

16. Anyanwu. "Crime and Justice in postcolonial Nigeria."

17. Smith, M. G. "The jihad of Shehu dan Fodio: some problems." In *Islam in Tropical Africa*, (ed.) I. M. Lewis, 408–424. London: Oxford University Press, 1966, 408.

18. Jihad is a term that can be described as making "the word of Allah [God] supreme; to bring unbelief, corruption and tyranny to naught; to bring dignity and honour to Muslims [Moslems] and save them from the humiliation of having to live under an un-Islamic power" (Suleiman, 1987 as cited in Anyanwu, 2006:316).

19. Metz. "Nigeria: A Country Study."

20. Ibid.

21. Anyanwu. "Crime and Justice in postcolonial Nigeria," 332.

22. Ibid.

23. Human Rights Watch. "Political Shari'a? ", 14.

24. Metz. "Nigeria: A Country Study."

25. Lovejoy, Paul. "The impact of the Atlantic slave trade on Africa: A review of the literature," *Journal of African History*, 30 (1989): 365–394.

26. BBC News. "Focus on the slave trade." Accessed March 10, 2011. http://news.bbc.co.uk/2/hi/africa/1523100.stm

27. Metz. "Nigeria: A Country Study."

28. Ibid.

29. Ifedi, J. P. Afam and Anyu, J. Ndumbe. "Blood Oil, Ethnicity, and Conflict in the Niger Delta Region of Nigeria," *Mediterranean Quarterly*, 22 (2011): 74–92.

30. Ibid., 77.

31. Akinwumi, Olayemi. *The colonial contest for the Nigerian region, 1884–1900: A history of the German participation*. LIT Verlag Münster, 2002.

32. Ibid., 16.

33. Pakenham, Thomas. *The Scramble for Africa: White Man's Conquest of the Dark Continent from 1876–1912*. New York: Avon Books, 1992.

34. Saleh-Hanna, Viviane. "Nigerian penal interactions." In *Colonial systems of control: Criminal justice in Nigeria*. (eds.) Viviane Saleh-Hanna and Chris Affor, 173–222. University of Ottowa Press, 2008, 22.

35. Ifedi, et al. "Blood Oil, Ethnicity."

36. Saleh-Hanna, Viviane. "Nigerian penal interactions," 21.

37. Metz. *"Nigeria: A Country Study."*

38. Falola, Troy and Heaton, Matthew. *A history of Nigeria* (Cambridge University Press, 2008).

39. Ibid., 136.

40. Anyanwu. "Crime and Justice in postcolonial Nigeria."

41. Ibid., 316.

42. Okereafoezeke, Nonso. *Law and justice in post-British Nigeria: Conflicts and interactions between native and foreign systems of social control in Igbo*. Westport, Conn., Greenwood Press, 2002, 164.

43. Taiwo, E. Adewale. "Justifications, challenges, and constitutionality of the penal aspects of Shari'ah law in Nigeria." *Griffith Law Review*, 17 (2008): 183–202.

44. Ogbu, Osita. "Punishments in Islamic criminal law as antithetical to human dignity: The Nigerian experience." *International Journal of Human Rights*, 9 (2005): 165–182.

45. Ibid.

46. Human Rights Watch. "Political Shari'a?"

47. Ogbu. "Punishments in Islamic criminal law."

48. Ibid., 168.

49. Ibid.

50. Human Rights Watch. "Political Shari'a?"

51. Ogbu, Osita. "Punishments in Islamic criminal law."

52. Ibid.

53. Ibid.

54. Ibid.

55. Ibid., 179.

56. Human Rights Watch. "Political Shari'a?"

57. Ibid., 38.

58. Human Rights Watch. "Political Shari'a?"

59. Ibid.

60. BBC News. "Nigeria stoning verdict quashed." Accessed March 30, 2011. http://news.bbc.co.uk/2/hi/africa/3164303.stm

61. Human Rights Watch. "Political Shari'a?"

62. Amnesty International. "Amnesty International Report 2004—Nigeria." Accessed August 16, 2011. http://www.unhcr.org/refworld/docid/40b5a1fdc.html

63. Ibid.

64. Ibid.

65. Stacy, Helen. *Human rights for the 21st century: Sovereignty, civil society, culture.* Stanford University Press, 2009.

66. Ibid.

67. Human Rights Watch. "Political Shari'a?"

68. Nathan, Clemens. *The changing face of religion and human rights: A personal reflection.* Martinus Nijhoff Publishers, 2009.

69. Stacy. *Human rights for the 21st century.*

70. Human Rights Watch. "Political Shari'a?"

71. Nathan. *The changing face of religion.*

72. Human Rights Watch. "Political Shari'a?"; Nathan. *The changing face of religion.*; Stacy. *Human rights for the 21st century.*

73. Nathan. *The changing face of religion.*

74. Stacy. *Human rights for the 21st century,* 141.

75. Taiwo. "Justifications, challenges, and constitutionality."

76. Ibid.,193.

77. Ogbu, "Punishments in Islamic criminal law," 169.

78. Alemika, E.E.O., Chukwuma, Innocent, Lafratta, Donika, Messerli, Daniel, and Souckova, Jarmila. "Rights of the Child in Nigeria." A report prepared for the Committee on the Rights of the Child 38th Session, Geneva, 2005, 17. Accessed May 2, 2011. www.cleen.org/nigeria_ngo_report_OMCT.pdf

79. Global Initiative to End the Corporal Punishment of Children. "Country Reports: Nigeria." Accessed March 1, 2011. http://www.endcorporalpunishment.org/

80. Alemika. et al., "Rights of the Child in Nigeria," 20.

81. Alemika. E. E. O. and Chukwuma, I .C. Innocent. Juvenile justice administration in Nigeria: Philosophy and Practice. Centre for Law Enforcement Education, 2001.

82. Ibid., 61.

83. Global Initiative to End the Corporal Punishment of Children. "Country Reports: Nigeria."

84. Alemika et al., "Rights of the Child in Nigeria," 18.

85. Ibid.,18–19.

86. Chianu, Emeka."Two deaths, one blind eye, one imprisonment: Child abuse in the guise of corporal punishment in Nigerian schools," *Child Abuse & Neglect,* 24 (2000), 1005–1009, 1006.

87. Ibid.

88. Ibid., 1008.

89. Central Intelligence Agency. "The World Factbook."

90. Lepoer, Barbara."Singapore: A country study." Washington: GPO for the Library of Congress. Accessed March 30, 201. http://lcweb2.loc.gov/frd/cs/cshome.html

91. Swee-Hock, S. *The population of Singapore, 2nd edition.* ISEAS Publishing, 2007.

92. Ibid.

93. Central Intelligence Agency. "The World Factbook."

94. United Nations. "Country profile of human development indicators."

95. Ibid.

96. Ibid.

97. Lepoer. "Singapore: A country study."

98. Lee, E., Cheng, S., Lee, E. *Singapore: The unexpected nation.* Singapore: ISEAS Publishing, 2008.

99. Lepoer. "Singapore: A country study."

100. Ibid.

101. Ibid.

102. Ibid.

103. Page, Melvin. *Colonialism: An international social, cultural, and political encyclopedia*. Santa Barbara: ABC-CLIO, 2003.

104. Ibid.

105. Warren, Alan. *Britain's Greatest Defeat* (Cornwall: MPG Books, 2007).

106. Ibid.

107. Ibid.

108. Ibid.

109. Yao, Souchou. *Singapore: The state and culture of excess*. New York: Routledge, 2007.

110. Ibid.

111. Ibid., 75.

112. Harwood, John. *The acts and ordinances of the legislative council of the Straits Settlements, from the 1st April 1867 to the 1st June 1886*. London: Eyre and Spottiswoode, 1886, 351–352.

113. Yao. *Singapore*.

114. Singapore Statutes. "Penal Code: Chapter 224." Accessed August 1, 2010. http://statutes.agc.gov.sg/

115. Yao. *Singapore*.

116. Peerenboom, Randal, Peterson, Carole, and Chen, Hongyi. *Human rights in Asia: A comparative legal study of twelve Asian jurisdictions, France, and USA*. New York: Routledge, 2006.

117. Tan, Eugene, *Singapore shared values*. National Library Board Singapore, 2001.

118. Peerenboom et al., *Human rights in Asia*.

119. Ibid.

120. Amnesty International. "Singapore: Cruel Punishment, 1991." Accessed May 1, 2011. http://www.amnesty.org/en/library/asset/ASA36/003/1991/en/9913b9e1 -ee3f-11dd-99b6-630c5239b672/asa360031991en.html

121. Ibid.

122. Asia One News. "Man caned 48 strokes-twice the legal limit-sues government, 2007." Accessed May 1, 2011. http://news.asiaone.com/a1news/20070701_story5_1.html

123. Ibid.

124. Channel News Asia. "American who overstayed in S'pore under investigation for cheating, 2010." Accessed May 3, 2011. http://www.channelnewsasia.com/stories/ singaporelocalnews/view/1088689/1/.html

125. Ibid.

126. Channel News Asia. "American Kamari Charlton pleads guilty to phone scams, 2011." Accessed May 3, 2011. http://www.channelnewsasia.com/stories/singapore localnews/view/1111295/1/.html

127. BBC News. "Swiss graffiti man faces Singapore caning, 2010." Accessed May 5, 2011. http://www.bbc.co.uk/news/10417167

128. Channel News Asia. "Swiss vandal Fricker's jail term extended to 7 months, 2011." Accessed May 5, 2011. http://www.channelnewsasia.com/stories/singaporelocal news/view/1075780/1/.html

129. Global Initiative to End the Corporal Punishment of Children. "Country Reports: Singapore." Accessed May 6, 2011. http://www.endcorporalpunishment.org/

130. Epstein, Irving. *The Greenwood Encyclopedia of Children's Issues Worldwide, Asia and Oceana*. Westport, Connecticut: Greenwood Press, 2008, 385.

131. Global Initiative to End the Corporal Punishment of Children. "Country Reports: Singapore." Epstein. *Children's Issues Worldwide*.

132. Global Initiative to End the Corporal Punishment of Children. "Country Reports: Singapore."

133. Central Intelligence Agency. World Factbook, 2011. Accessed September 28, 2011. https://www.cia.gov/library/publications/the-world-factbook/geos/sa.html

134. Foreign and Commonwealth Office. Saudi Arabia, 2011. Accessed September 28, 2011. http://www.fco.gov.uk/en/travel-and-living-abroad/travel-advice-by -country/country-profile/middle-east-north-africa/saudi-arabia

135. Ibid.

136. United Nations. Human Development Index, 2010. Accessed September 28, 2011. http://hdrstats.undp.org/en/countries/profiles/SAU.html

137. Ibid.

138. Wynbrandt, James and Gerges, Fawaz. *A Brief History of Saudi Arabia*, 2nd edition, 2010. Factsonfile.

139. Ibid.

140. Ibid.

141. Metz, Helen. Saudi Arabia: A country study. Washington D.C.: Library of Congress.

142. Ibid.

143. Please refer to Chapter 3 for a detailed exposition of the development of Islam.

144. Metz. Saudi Arabia.

145. Ibid.

146. Ibid.

147. Blanchard, Christopher. The Islamic Traditions of Wahhabism and Salafiyya, 2008. CRS Report for Congress.

148. Fattah, Hala. 'Wahhabi' Influences, Salafi Responses: Shaikh Mahmud Shukri and the Iraqi Salafi Movement, 1745–1930. *Journal of Islamic Studies* 14:2 (2003), 127–148.

149. Miethe, Terance and Lu, Hong. Punishment: a comparative historical perspective, 2005. Cambridge University Press.

150. Ibid.

151. Ibid.

152. Ibid., 181.

153. Amnesty International. Saudi Arabia: Puthen Veetil Abdul Latheef Noushad. Accessed September 30, 2011, from http://www.amnestyinternational.be/doc/actions-en -cours/Les-actions-urgentes/Les-actions-urgentes-en-anglais/article/saudi-arabia-puthen -veetil-abdul

154. Human Rights Watch. Saudi Arabia: Court Orders Eye to Be Gouged Out. Accessed September 30, 2011, from http://www.hrw.org/news/2005/12/08/saudi-arabia -court-orders-eye-be-gouged-out

155. Ibid.

156. Ibid.

157. *Human Rights Watch*. Eye to Be Gouged Out.

158. Ibid.

159. Ibid.

160. MSNBC. Saudi judge considers punishment by paralysis. Accessed September 30, 2011 from http://www.msnbc.msn.com/id/38799106/ns/world_news-mideast_n _africa/t/saudi-judge-considers-punishment-paralysis/#.ToXVck8hI68

161. Ibid.

162. Ibid.

163. Voice of America News. Saudi Court Rejects Paralysis as Punishment. Accessed September 30, 2011 from http://www.voanews.com/english/news/middle-east/ Saudi-Court-Rejects-Paralysis-as-Punishment-101315989.html

164. ABC News. Exclusive: Saudi Rape Victim Tells Her Story. Accessed September 30, 2011 from http://abcnews.go.com/International/story?id=3899920&page=2

165. Ibid.

166. Ibid.

167. Ibid.

168. BBC. Saudi king 'pardons rape victim.' Accessed September 30, 2011 fromhttp://news.bbc.co.uk/2/hi/7147632.stm

169. Amnesty International. Saudi Arabia: Flogging: Mohammed 'Ali al-Sayyid, Egyptian national. Accessed October 3, 2011 from http://www.amnesty.org/en/library/ info/MDE23/004/1995/en

170. Ibid.

171. The Guardian. "Saudi lawbreakers face rough justice." Accessed October 3, 2011 from http://www.guardian.co.uk/world/2001/jun/01/saudiarabia

172. Amnesty International. "Saudi Arabia: A secret state of suffering, 2000." http:// www.amnesty.org/en/library/info/MDE23/001/2000/cn

Chapter 8

1. Global Initiative to End the Corporal Punishment of Children. "Country Report: Bolivia, 2011," accessed June 15, 2001. http://www.endcorporalpunishment.org

2. Central Intelligence Agency. "The World Factbook," accessed April 1, 2011. https://www.cia.gov/library/publications/the-world-factbook/

3. Morales, Waltraud. *A Brief History of Bolivia*. New York: Lexington Associates, 2010.

4. Galvan, Javier. *Culture and Customs of Bolivia*. Santa Barbara, CA: ABC-CLIO, 2011.

5. Central Intelligence Agency. *The World Factbook*.

6. Waltraud. *A Brief History of Bolivia*, xxxix.

7. Galvan. *Culture and customs of Bolivia*.

8. Central Intelligence Agency. *The World Factbook*.

9. United Nations. "Country profile of human development indicators," accessed May 10, 2011. http://hdr.undp.org/en/data/profiles/

10. Ibid.

11. Ibid.

12. Ibid.

13. Morales. *A Brief History of Bolivia*.

14. Rex A. Hudson and Dennis M. Hanratty. "Library of congress country studies: Bolivia, 1989," accessed June 15, 2011. http://lcweb2.loc.gov/frd/cs/cshome.html

15. Ibid.

16. Morales. *A Brief History of Bolivia*.

17. Hudson and Hanratty. "Library of congress country studies: Bolivia."

18. Ibid.

19. Morales. *A Brief History of Bolivia*.

20. Ibid.

21. Ibid.

22. Hudson and Hanratty. "Library of congress country studies: Bolivia."

23. Morales. *A Brief History of Bolivia*.

24. Hudson and Hanratty. "Library of congress country studies: Bolivia."

25. Morales. *A Brief History of Bolivia*, 5.

26. Hudson and Hanratty. "Library of congress country studies: Bolivia."

27. Ibid.

28. Ibid.

29. Ibid.

30. Morales. *A Brief History of Bolivia*.

31. Klein, Herbert. *A Concise History of Bolivia, 2nd ed.* Cambridge University Press, 2011.

32. Ibid., 29.

33. Ibid.

34. Ibid.

35. This area is now part of modern day Bolivia.

36. Ibid., 31.

37. For a more thorough exposition of the Spanish conquest and the resulting colonial period in Bolivia see Klein, 2011.

38. Canessa, Andrew, "The Past is Not Another Country: Exploring Indigenous Histories in Bolivia." *History and Anthropology*, 19 (2008): 353–369.

39. Ibid.

40. Ibid.

41. Kronik, Jakob and Verner, Dorte. *Indigenous Peoples and Climate Change in Latin America and the Caribbean*. Washington, D.C.: The World Bank, 2010.

42. Fretes-Cibils, Vicente, Guigale, Marcelo, Luff, Connie. *Bolivia: Public Policy Options for the Well-being of All*. Washington, D.C.: The World Bank, 2006.

43. Ibid.

44. BBC News. "Bolivia's new leader vows change." Accessed June 1, 2011. http://news.bbc.co.uk/2/hi/americas/4636190.stm

45. *New York Times*. "Bolivia, 2011." Accessed July 3, 2011. http://topics.nytimes.com/top/news/international/countriesandterritories/bolivia/index.html

46. Faundez, Julio. "Legal Pluralism and International Development Agencies: State Building or Legal Reform?" *Hague Journal on the Rule of Law*, 3 (2011): 18–38.

47. Ibid.

48. Ibid.

49. Ibid., 28.

50. Ibid., 28.

51. Human Rights Foundation. "Country Report: Bolivia 2007." Accessed July 10, 2011. www.humanrightsfoundation.org/reports/Bolivia_Communal_Justice_Report_01 -15-2008.pdf

52. *Washington Post.* "Bolivia's Burning Question: Who May Dispense Justice?" Accessed June 15, 2011. http://www.washingtonpost.com/wp-dyn/content/article/2008/ 02/01/AR2008020103426.html

53. Ibid.

54. Galvan, Javier. *Culture and customs of Bolivia.* Santa Barbara, CA: ABC-CLIO, 2011.

55. Ibid., 35.

56. Human Rights Foundation. "Country Report: Bolivia 2007."

57. Ibid., 2.

58. Ibid., 3.

59. United States Department of State. "Human rights reports: Bolivia." Accessed June 1, 2010. http://www.state.gov/g/drl/rls/hrrpt/2010/wha/154495.htm

60. Human Rights Watch. "Enshrining Mob Rule in Bolivia: Communal Justice and the New Constitution." Accessed August 15, 2011. http://www.thehrf.org/media/ BolReportJan08.html

61. Van Der Velden, Maurice. "Access to justice: perspectives for indigenous communities in Ecuador and Bolivia." *Effectius Newsletter*, 8 (2010). Accessed August 15, 2011. http://www.effectius.com/yahoo_site_admin/assets/docs/Access_to_justice_perspectives _for_indigenous_communities_in_Ecuador_and_Bolivia_MVDV_Newsletter8 .27185913.pdf

62. "Constitution of the Republic of Bolivia." Accessed June 1, 2011. http://pdba .georgetown.edu/constitutions/bolivia/bolivia.html

63. Ibid.

64. United Nations Office at Geneva. "Committee on rights of child examines report of Bolivia, 2009." Accessed June 1, 2011. http://www.hrea.org/lists2/display.php ?language_id=1&id=14438

65. Ibid.

66. Global Initiative to End the Corporal Punishment of Children. "Country Report: Bolivia, 2011." Accessed May 15, 2011. http://www.endcorporalpunishment.org

67. Global Initiative to End the Corporal Punishment of Children. "Country Report: Bolivia."

68. UNICEF Bolivia. "The situation of children in Bolivia, 2003." Accessed June 1, 2011. http://www.unicef.org/bolivia/children_1540.htm

69. Ibid.

70. United States Department of State. "Human rights reports: Bolivia." Accessed June 1, 2010. http://www.state.gov/g/drl/rls/hrrpt/2010/wha/154495.htm

71. Harvey, Holly. "Of flogging and electric shock: A comparative tale of colonialism, commonwealth, and the cat-o'-nine-tales." *The University of Miami Inter-American Law Review*, 24(1992): 87–119.

72. Central Intelligence Agency. "*The World Factbook.*"

73. Ibid; the Bahamas ranks #177 out of 237 countries in population density (CIA, 2011).

74. Ibid.

75. Ibid.

76. United Nations. "Country profile of human development indicators."

77. Ibid.

78. Ibid.

79. Hassam, John. *The Bahama Islands: Notes on an early attempt at colonization.* Cambridge: John Wilson and Son, 1899; Meditz, Sandra and Dennis M. Hanratty. "Islands of the Commonwealth Caribbean: A regional study." Washington: GPO for the Library of Congress. Accessed March 10, 2011. http://lcweb2.loc.gov/frd/cs/cshome.html

80. Meditz and Hanratty. "Islands of the Commonwealth Caribbean."

81. Hassam. *The Bahama Islands.*

82. Meditz and Hanratty. "Islands of the Commonwealth Caribbean."

83. Ibid.

84. Ibid.

85. Hassam. *The Bahama Islands.*

86. Ibid.

87. Meditz and Hanratty. "Islands of the Commonwealth Caribbean."

88. Hassam. *The Bahama Islands*, 3.

89. Harvey. "Of flogging and electric shock."

90. Ibid.

91. Ibid.

92. Ibid., 92.

93. Ibid.

94. Ibid.

95. Ibid.

96. Statute of the law of The Bahamas. "Criminal Law (Measures) Act, 1991." Accessed June 3, 2011. http://laws.bahamas.gov.bs/cms/

97. Ibid.

98. Ibid.

99. Ibid.

100. Ibid.

101. Amnesty International. "Bahamas: medical concern: corporal punishment, 1995." Accessed June 15, 2011. http://www.amnesty.org/en/library/info/AMR14/010/1995/en

102. Ibid.

103. Ibid.

104. Ibid.

105. Amnesty International. "Bahamas Flogging: Alutus Newbold, 2006." Accessed June 15, 2011. http://www.amnesty.org/en/library/asset/AMR14/005/2006/en/120ac49d -d3e5-11dd-8743-d305bea2b2c7/amr140052006en.html

106. Ibid.

107. *Andrew Bridgewater v. Regina.* Commonwealth of The Bahamas in the Court of Appeal. SCCrApp. No 8 of 2007.

108. Ibid.

109. Ibid.

110. Ibid.

111. Ibid.

112. Global Initiative to End the Corporal Punishment of Children. "Country Report: Bahamas, 2011." Accessed June 1, 2011. http://www.endcorporalpunishment.org

113. Commonwealth Secretariat. "Bahamas to ratify key UN human rights covenants by year's end, 2008." Accessed June 1, 2011. http://www.thecommonwealth.org/news/34581/185605/031208bahmas.htm

114. Global Initiative to End the Corporal Punishment of Children. "Country Report: Bahamas."

115. Universal Periodic Review Monitor. "Universal Periodic Review, 3rd Session The Bahamas, 2008." Accessed July 5, 2011. www.ishr.ch/component/docman/doc.../165-upr-of-bahamas-3rd-session

116. Commonwealth Secretariat. Bahamas to ratify key UN human rights.

117. Brennan, Shane, Fielding, William, Carroll, Marie, Miller, Janice, Adderlay, Latanya, Thompson, Mary Ann, A, "Preliminary Investigation of the Prevalence of Corporal Punishment of Children and Selected Co-occurring Behaviours in Households on New Providence, The Bahamas." *The International Journal of Bahamian Studies*, 16 (2010):1–18.

118. Ibid., 1.

119. Ibid.

120. Global Initiative to End the Corporal Punishment of Children. "Country Report: Bahamas."

121. Committee on the Rights of the Child. "CRC Concluding Observations: Bahamas, 2005." Accessed June 1, 2011. http://sim.law.uu.nl/SIM/CaseLaw/uncom.nsf/fe005fcb50d8277cc12569d5003e4aaa/5e76eb3f62b1118dc1256fa80049e02d?OpenDocument

122. Statute Law of The Bahamas. "Prisons Act." Accessed June 1, 2011. http://laws.bahamas.gov.bs/cms/

123. Ibid.

124. Ibid.

Chapter 8

1. Readers should note that a substantial portion of this chapter reflects a series of studies previously published elsewhere by the authors: Gould, Laurie and Matthew Pate. "Discipline, docility and disparity: A study of inequality and corporal punishment." *British Journal of Criminology*, 50 (2010), 185–205; Gould, Laurie and Matthew Pate. "Penality, Power and Polity: Exploring the Relationship Between Political Repression and Corporal Punishment." *International Criminal Justice Review*, 21,4 (2011): 443–461; Pate, Matthew and Laurie Gould. "The Discipline of Difference: Ethnolinguistic Heterogeneity and Corporal Punishment." *International Journal of Comparative and Applied Criminal Justice*. Forthcoming 2012. The source material remains copyright of the respective publications/owners.

2. Liska, Alan. "A Critical Examination of Macro Perspectives on Crime Control." *Annual Review of Sociology*, 13 (1987):67–88.

3. Ibid.

4. Adelman, Irma and Cynthia Morris. "A factor analysis of the interrelationship between social and political variables and per capita gross national product." *The Quarterly Journal of Economics*, 4 (1965): 556.

5. See for example: Newman, Graeme. *Just and Painful: A Case for Corporal Punishment of Criminals*, 2nd ed. New York: Criminal Justice Press, 1995; Moskos, Peter. *In Defense of Flogging*. New York: Basic Books, 2011.

6. Rusche, Georg and Otto Kirchheimer. *Punishment and Social Structure*. New York: Russell and Russell, 1968.

7. Foucault, Michel. *Discipline and Punish*. (trans. A. Sheridan). London: Peregrine Books, 1977.

8. Ignatieff, Michael. *A Just Measure of Pain: The Penitentiary in the Industrial Revolution, 1750–1850*. New York: Pantheon, 1978.

9. Cavadino, Mick and James Dignan. *Penal Systems: A Comparative Approach*. Thousand Oaks, CA: Sage, 2006.

10. Lynch, James. "A Cross-National Comparison of the Length for Serious Crimes." *Justice Quarterly*, 10 (1993): 639–659.

11. Barclay, Gordon. "The Comparability of Data on Convictions and Sanctions: Are International Comparisons Possible?" *European Journal on Criminal Policy and Research*, 8 (2000): 13–26.

12. Newman, Graeme and Greg Howard. "Data Sources and Their Use." *Global Report on Crime and Justice*. United Nations, Office for Drug Control and Crime Prevention, 1990, 2.

13. See for example: Bennett, Richard and James Lynch. "Does a Difference Make a Difference: Comparing Cross-National Crime Indicators." *Criminology*, 28 (1990): 153–181; Cavadino and Dignan. *Penal Systems*; Gertz, Michael and Laura Myers. "Impediments to Cross-National Research: Problems of Reliability and Validity." *International Journal of Comparative and Applied Criminal Justice*, 16 (1992): 57–65; Lynch. "A Cross-National Comparison"; Mauer, Mark. "The International Use of Incarceration." *The Prison Journal*, 75 (1995): 113–23; Weiss, Robert and Nigel South. *Comparing Prison Systems: Toward a Comparative and International Penology*. Amsterdam: Gordon and Breach, 1998.

14. Newman and Howard. "Data Sources and their Use."

15. Garland, David. *Punishment and Modern Society*. Chicago: University of Chicago Press, 1990.

16. Elias, Norbert. *The Civilizing Process, Volume 2: Power and Civility*. Malden, MA: Blackwell, 2000.

17. Garland. *Punishment and Modern Society*, 242.

18. Ibid.

19. Miethe, Terrence, Hong Lu and Gini Deibert. "Cross-National Variability in Capital Punishment: Exploring the Sociopolitical Sources of its Differential Legal Status." *International Criminal Justice Review*, 15 (2005): 115–130.

20. Newman. *Just and Painful*.

21. Moskos. *In Defense of Flogging*, 2.

22. Rusche and Kirchheimer. *Punishment and Social Structure*.

23. Poulantzas, Nicos. *State, Power Socialism*. (trans.) Patrick Camiller. London: Verso, 2000, 169.

24. Cohen, Stanley. *Visions of Social Control: Crime, Punishment, and Classification*. Cambridge: Polity Press, 1985, 23.

25. Chiricos, Theodore and Miriam Delone. "Labor Surplus and Punishment: A Review and Assessment of Theory and Evidence." *Social Problems*, 39 (1992): 421–446.

26. Ibid.

27. Melossi, Dario. "Forward," in *Punishment and Social Structure*, edited by G. Rusche, O. Kirchheimer and D. Melossi. New York: Transaction Publishers, 2003.

28. Newman. *Just and Painful*.

29. Foucault. *Discipline and Punish*, 82.

30. Ibid., 213.

31. Foucault, Michel. "The Subject and Power." *Critical Inquiry*, 8 (1982): 777–795.

32. Ibid., 792.

33. Ibid.

34. Poulantzas. *State, Power Socialism*, 77.

35. Quinney, Richard. *Bearing Witness to Crime and Social Justice*. SUNY Press: Albany, 2001, 76.

36. See: Foucault. *Discipline and Punish*; and Foucault, Michel. *Language, Counter-Memory, Practice: Selected Essays and Interviews*. (trans. D. Bouchard) (edited by D. Bouchard and S. Simon). New York: Prentice Hall, 1980.

37. Readers seeking greater detail may wish to see our analysis of the relationship between economic disparity and corporal punishment: Gould, Laurie and Matthew Pate. Discipline, docility and disparity: A study of inequality and corporal punishment. *British Journal of Criminology*, 50 (2010), 185–205.

38. Box, Steven and Chris Hale. "Unemployment, Crime and Imprisonment, and the Enduring Problem of Prison Overcrowding," in R. Matthews and J. Young (eds.), *Confronting Crime*, 72–99. London: Sage, 1986; Greenberg, David. "The Dynamics of Oscillatory Punishment Processes." *Journal of Criminal Law and Criminology*, 68 (1977): 643–651; Hale, Chris. "Unemployment, Imprisonment, and the Stability of Punishment Hypothesis: Some Results Using Cointegration and Error Corrections Models." *Journal of Quantitative Criminology*, 5(1989): 169–186; Jankovic, Ivan. "Labor Market and Imprisonment." *Crime and Social Justice*, 8 (1977): 17–31.

39. Melossi, "Forward."

40. Jacobs, David and Richard Kleban. "Political Institutions, Minorities, and Punishment: A Pooled Cross-National Analysis of Imprisonment Rates." *Social Forces*, 80 (2003): 725–755.

41. Greenberg, David and Valerie West. "Siting the Death Penalty Internationally." *Law & Social Inquiry*, 33 (2008): 295–343; Killias, Martin, "Power Concentration, Legitimation Crisis and Penal Severity: A Comparative Perspective," in W. B. Groves and G. Newman (eds.), *Punishment and Privilege*, 95–117. New York: Harrow and Heston, 1986; Miethe, Lu and Deibert. "Cross-National Variability in Capital Punishment"; Neapolitan, Jerome. "An Examination of Cross-National Variation in Punitiveness." *International Journal of Offender Rehabilitation and Comparative Criminology*, 45 (2001): 691–710.

42. Killias. "Power Concentration, Legitimation Crisis and Penal Severity."

43. Neapolitan. "An Examination of Cross-National Variation in Punitiveness."

44. Ibid.

45. Miethe, Lu and Deibert. "Cross-National Variability in Capital Punishment."

46. Ibid.

47. Greenberg and West. "Siting the Death Penalty Internationally."

48. Sutton, John. "Imprisonment and Social Classification in Five Common-Law Democracies, 1955–1985." *American Journal of Sociology*, 106 (2000): 350–386.

49. Ibid.

50. Killias. "Power Concentration, Legitimation Crisis and Penal Severity."

51. Neapolitan. "An Examination of Cross-National Variation in Punitiveness."

52. Miethe, Lu and Deibert. "Cross-National Variability in Capital Punishment."

53. Greenberg and West. "Siting the Death Penalty Internationally."

54. Durkheim, Emile. "The Evolution of Punishment" edited by Steven Lukes and Andrew Scull. *Durkheim and the Law*, 25–77. New York: St Martin's Press, 1986; Killias. "Power Concentration, Legitimation Crisis and Penal Severity"; Neapolitan. "An Examination of Cross-National Variation in Punitiveness."

55. Gould and Pate. "Discipline, Docility and Disparity."

56. Foucault. *Discipline and Punish*.

57. For an expanded treatment of this topic, see: Pate, Matthew and Laurie Gould. "The Discipline of Difference: Ethnolinguistic Heterogeneity and Corporal Punishment." *International Journal of Comparative and Applied Criminal Justice* (forthcoming 2012).

58. Sorokin, Pitrim. *Social and Cultural Dynamics: A Study of Change in Major Systems of Art, Truth, Ethics, Law, and Social Relationships*. 4 Vols. (New York: Bedminster), 1962.

59. Sellin, Thorsten. Culture Conflict and Crime, in Williams, Frank and Marilyn McShane, *Criminological Theory: Selected Classic Readings*. Cincinnati, OH: Anderson Publishing Company, 1998, 73.

60. Liska. A Critical Examination, 78.

61. Black, Donald. *Behavior of Law*. Bingley, UK: Emerald Publishing Group, 2010, 17.

62. Ibid., 65–66.

63. Ibid., 74.

64. The term, "ethnolinguistic fractionalization," provides a succinct way to describe a complex set of internal population differences. Dissecting it a bit, "ethnolinguistic" simply means the ethnic, racial, religious, linguistic or other cultural groups to which an individual may belong or have an affinity. "Fractionalization" is used to describe the degree of difference between groups in society. In other words, fractionalization is a way to quantify a given society's relative heterogeneity. In more technical (sic. statistical) parlance, "fractionalization" is may be operationalized as an index of dispersion. This is to say, a measure of fractionalization provides a quantified statement of how a given resource or attribute is dispersed across a population. Taken together, these terms provide a standardized mechanism by which to assess whether a given society is more or less heterogeneous than another. For a more detailed explanation, see: Pate and Gould. "The Discipline of Difference."

65. Pate and Gould. "The Discipline of Difference."

66. Ibid.

67. Sorokin. *Social and Cultural Dynamics*.

68. Newman. *Just and Painful*.

69. Sellin. "Culture Conflict and Crime."

70. Liska. "A Critical Examination."

71. Black. *Behavior of Law*.

72. Pate and Gould. "The Discipline of Difference."

73. For an expanded treatment of this topic, see: Gould, Laurie and Matthew Pate. "Penality, Power and Polity: Exploring the Relationship Between Political Repression and Modalities of Punishment." *International Criminal Justice Review* 21, 4 (2011): 443–461.

74. Wacquant, Loic. *Punishing the poor: The neoliberal government of social insecurity*. Durham, NC: Duke University Press, 2009: xviii.

75. Jacobs, David and Richard Kleban. "Political institutions, minorities, and punishment: A pooled cross-national analysis of imprisonment rates." *Social Forces*, 80 (2003):725–755. Killias, M. Power concentration, legitimation crisis and penal severity: A comparative perspective. In W. B. Groves & G. Newman (eds.), *Punishment and privilege*. New York, NY: Harrow and Heston, 1986, 95–117; Miethe, Terrence, Hung Lu & G. Deibert. "Cross-national variability in capital punishment: Exploring the socio-political sources of its differential legal status." *International Criminal Justice Review*, 15 (2003):115–130; Neapolitan. "An Examination of Cross-National Variation in Punitiveness"; Ruddell, Rick and Martin Urbina. "Weak nations, political repression, and punishment." *International Criminal Justice Review*, 17 (2007):84–107.

76. Ruddell and Urbina. "Weak nations."

77. Ibid., 87.

78. Jacobs and Kleban. "Political institutions."

79. Miethe, Lu and Deibert. "Cross-national variability in capital punishment," 122.

80. Ruddell and Urbina. "Weak nations,"101.

81. Gould, Laurie and Matthew Pate. "Penality, Power and Polity: Exploring the Relationship Between Political Repression and Corporal Punishment." *International Criminal Justice Review*, 21, 4 (2011): 443–461.

82. Wiley, David. *South Africa: Overcoming Apartheid Building Democracy*. Accessed at: http://overcomingapartheid.msu.edu/unit.php?id=12

83. Gould and Pate. "Discipline, Docility and Disparity."

84. Miethe, Lu and Deibert. "Cross-national variability in capital punishment"; Greenberg and West, "Siting the Death Penalty Internationally."

85. Newman. "Just and Painful."

86. Gould and Pate. "Discipline, Docility and Disparity."

87. Neapolitan. "An examination of cross-national variation in punitiveness."

88. Pate and Gould. "The Discipline of Difference."

89. Adelman and Morris. "A factor analysis of the interrelationship," 556.

Conclusion

1. Newman, Graeme. *The Punishment Response*. Albany, NY: Harrow and Heston, 1978, 273.

2. Foucault, Michel. *Language, Counter-Memory, Practice: Selected Essays and Interviews*. New York: Cornell University Press, 1977, 7.

3. Igantieff, Michael. A *just measure of pain: The penitentiary in the industrial revolution 1750–1850*. New York: Random House, 1978.

4. Westermann, William. *Slave Systems of Greek and Roman Antiquity*. Philadelphia, PA: American Philosophical Society, 1955, 273.

5. Frontinus, Sextus Julius. *The Stratagems and the Aqueducts of Rome*. (trans. Charles E. Bennett). Cambridge: Harvard University Press, 1950, 17.

6. Associated Press. "Three face hazing charges after Marine commits suicide." September 8, 2011. Accessed via: http://www.foxnews.com/us/2011/09/08/3-face-hazing-charges-after-marine-commits-suicide/

7. Van Maanen, John. "Working the Street: A Developmental View of Police Behavior." *Annals of Criminal Justice*, Vol. III. Ed. Herbert Jacobs. Beverly Hills, CA: Sage Publishing, 1973, 90.

8. Foucault, Michel. *Discipline and Punish: The Birth of the Prison*. (trans. Alan Sheridan). New York: Vintage, 1977, 3.

9. Lewellen, Ted. *Political Anthropology: An Introduction*. Santa Barbara, CA: ABC-CLIO, 189.

10. Turner, Victor. *The forest of symbols: Aspects of Ndembu ritual*. Ithaca: Cornell University Press. 1967, 19.

Index

About the Authors

MATTHEW PATE is a senior research fellow and lecturer with the Violence Research Group in the School of Criminal Justice at the State University of New York, University at Albany. In addition to a doctorate in criminal justice, Pate also holds an undergraduate degree in history as well as advanced degrees in sociology and environmental design. Pate's research centers on comparative criminal justice and the history of crime. He has published extensively on matters of race, inequality, and disparity. Pate is a former law enforcement executive and has served as a consultant to police agencies across the United States. Apart from academic pursuits, Pate writes a nationally syndicated column for the Stephens Media Group. Along with his wife, Kathleen, and their dogs, Trooper and Tilly, Pate resides in his hometown, Pine Bluff, AR. While on furlough from the computer keyboard, he spends his time renovating the family's century-old craftsman style home.

LAURIE A. GOULD is an assistant professor of Criminal Justice and Criminology at Georgia Southern University in Statesboro, Georgia. Previously, she was an assistant professor of Criminology and Criminal Justice at the University of Texas at Arlington in Arlington, Texas. Gould has spent the past five years researching comparative penology and her work has been published in numerous national and international journals. She maintains an active research agenda that includes comparative penology, as well as gender issues in punishment. She currently divides her time between Statesboro, GA and Charleston, SC where she lives with her husband, Vern, their five cats (Hannah, Gracie, Isabelle, Bobby, and Katie), and dog, Abby. When she's not writing, she can usually be found at the beach or outside taking pictures.